ABOUT THIS PUBLICATION

FOR SERVICE ASSISTANCE

Customer Service Department
704.898.0770

North Carolina General Statues is published by The Muliti-Media Group of Greater Charlotte in Charlotte, North Carolina. Copyright 2015 by the Multi-Media Group of Greater Charlotte. This book or parts thereof may not be reproduced in any form, stored in a retrieval system, or transmitted in any form by any means—electronic, mechanical, photocopy, recording or otherwise—without prior written permission of the publisher, except as provided by United States of America copyright law.

The records required by U.S. Code 2257(a) through (c) and the pertinent regulations 28 C.F.R. Cli. 1, Part 75 with respect to this publication and all materials associated with such records are maintained by The Multi-Media Group of Greater Charlotte, Publisher and available for review by Attorney General.

www.visionbooks.org

Copyright © 2015 by MMGGC
All rights reserved!

TID: 5037828
ISBN (10) digit: 1502745046
ISBN (13) digit: 978-1502745040

123-4-56789-01239-Paperback
123-4-56789-01239-Hardback

First Edition

090520140547

Printed in the United States of America

2015 EDITION

North Carolina Criminal Law And Procedure-Pamphlet # 25

Printed In conjunction with the Administration of the Courts

North Carolina Criminal Law and Procedure
Pamphlet Reference Guide

Chapters	Pamphlet
Chapter 1 Civil Procedure	1
Chapter 1 Civil Procedure (Continue)	2
Chapter 1A Rules of Civil Procedure	2
Chapter 1B Contribution.	2
Chapter 1C Enforcement of Judgments.	2
Chapter 1D Punitive Damages.	2
Chapter 1E Eastern Band of Cherokee Indians.	2
Chapter 1F North Carolina Uniform Interstate Depositions and Discovery Act.	2
Chapter 2 - Clerk of Superior Court [Repealed and Transferred.]	3
Chapter 3 - Commissioners of Affidavits and Deeds [Repealed.]	3
Chapter 4 - Common Law	3
Chapter 5 - Contempt [Repealed.]	3
Chapter 5A - Contempt	3
Chapter 6 - Liability for Court Costs	3
Chapter 7 - Courts [Repealed and Transferred.]	3
Chapter 7A – Judicial Department	3
Chapter 7A – Continuation (Judicial Department)	4
Chapter 7A – Continuation (Judicial Department)	5
Chapter 7B - Juvenile Code	5
Chapter 8 - Evidence	6
Chapter 8A - Interpreters for Deaf Persons [Recodified.]	6
Chapter 8B - Interpreters for Deaf Persons	6
Chapter 8C - Evidence Code	6
Chapter 9 - Jurors	6
Chapter 10 - Notaries [Repealed.]	6
Chapter 10A - Notaries [Recodified.]	6
Chapter 10B - Notaries	6
Chapter 11 - Oaths	6
Chapter 12 - Statutory Construction	6
Chapter 13 - Citizenship Restored	6
Chapter 14 - Criminal Law	7
Chapter 14 –Criminal Law (Continuation)	8
Chapter 15 - Criminal Procedure	9
Chapter 15A - Criminal Procedure Act (Continuation)	10
Chapter 15A - Criminal Procedure Act (Continuation)	11
Chapter 15B - Victims Compensation	11
Chapter 15C - Address Confidentiality Program	11
Chapter 16 - Gaming Contracts and Futures	11
Chapter 17 - Habeas Corpus	11

Chapter 17A - Law-Enforcement Officers [Recodified.]	11
Chapter 17B - North Carolina Criminal Justice Education and Training System [Recodified.] Chapter 17C - North Carolina Criminal Justice Education and Training Standards Commission	11
	11
Chapter 17D - North Carolina Justice Academy	11
Chapter 17E - North Carolina Sheriffs' Education and Training Standards Commission	11
Chapter 18 - Regulation of Intoxicating Liquors [Repealed.]	12
Chapter 18A - Regulation of Intoxicating Liquors [Repealed.]	12
Chapter 18B - Regulation of Alcoholic Beverages	12
Chapter 18C - North Carolina State Lottery	12
Chapter 19 - Offenses against Public Morals	12
Chapter 19A - Protection of Animals	12
Chapter 20 - Motor Vehicles	13
Chapter 20 - Motor Vehicles (Continuation)	14
Chapter 20 - Motor Vehicles (Continuation)	15
Chapter 20 - Motor Vehicles (Continuation)	16
Chapter 21 - Bills of Lading	17
Chapter 22 - Contracts Requiring Writing	17
Chapter 22A - Signatures	17
Chapter 22B - Contracts Against Public Policy	17
Chapter 22C - Payments to Subcontractors	17
Chapter 23 - Debtor and Creditor	17
Chapter 24 – Interest	17
Chapter 25 – Uniform Commercial Code	18
Chapter 25 – Uniform Commercial Code (Continuation)	19
Chapter 25A – Retail Installment Sales Act	20
Chapter 25B - Credit	20
Chapter 25C - Sales of Artwork	20
Chapter 26 - Suretyship	20
Chapter 27 - Warehouse Receipts [Repealed.]	20
Chapter 28 - Administration [Repealed.]	20
Chapter 28A - Administration of Decedents' Estates	20
Chapter 28B - Estates of Absentees in Military Service	20
Chapter 28C - Estates of Missing Persons	20
Chapter 29 - Intestate Succession	21
Chapter 30 - Surviving Spouses	21
Chapter 31 - Wills	21
Chapter 31A - Acts Barring Property Rights	21
Chapter 31B - Renunciation of Property and Renunciation of Fiduciary Powers Act	21
Chapter 31C - Uniform Disposition of Community Property Rights at Death Act	21
Chapter 32 - Fiduciaries	21
Chapter 32A - Powers of Attorney	21
Chapter 33 - Guardian and Ward [Repealed and Recodified.]	21

Chapter 33A - North Carolina Uniform Transfers to Minors Act	21
Chapter 33B - North Carolina Uniform Custodial Trust Act	21
Chapter 34 - Veterans' Guardianship Act	22
Chapter 35 - Sterilization Procedures	22
Chapter 35A - Incompetency and Guardianship	22
Chapter 36 - Trusts and Trustees [Repealed.]	22
Chapter 36A - Trusts and Trustees	22
Chapter 36B - Uniform Management of Institutional Funds Act [Repealed.]	22
Chapter 36C - North Carolina Uniform Trust Code	22
Chapter 36D - North Carolina Community Third Party Trusts, Pooled Trusts	23
Chapter 36E - Uniform Prudent Management of Institutional Funds Act	23
Chapter 37 - Allocation of Principal and Income [Repealed.]	23
Chapter 37A - Uniform Principal and Income Act	23
Chapter 38 - Boundaries	23
Chapter 38A - Landowner Liability	23
Chapter 38B - Trespasser Responsibility	23
Chapter 39 - Conveyances	23
Chapter 39A - Transfer Fee Covenants Prohibited	23
Chapter 40 - Eminent Domain [Repealed.]	23
Chapter 40A - Eminent Domain	23
Chapter 41 - Estates	23
Chapter 41A - State Fair Housing Act	23
Chapter 42 - Landlord and Tenant	23
Chapter 42A - Vacation Rental Act	23
Chapter 43 - Land Registration	23
Chapter 44 - Liens	24
Chapter 44A - Statutory Liens and Charges	24
Chapter 45 - Mortgages and Deeds of Trust	24
Chapter 45A - Good Funds Settlement Act	24
Chapter 46 - Partition	24
Chapter 47 - Probate and Registration	25
Chapter 47A - Unit Ownership	25
Chapter 47B - Real Property Marketable Title Act	25
Chapter 47C - North Carolina Condominium Act	25
Chapter 47D - Notice of Settlement Act [Expired.]	25
Chapter 47E - Residential Property Disclosure Act	25
Chapter 47F - North Carolina Planned Community Act	25
Chapter 47G - Option to Purchase Contracts	25
Chapter 47H - Contracts for Deed	25
Chapter 48 - Adoptions +	26
Chapter 48A - Minors	26
Chapter 49 - Bastardy	26
Chapter 49A - Rights of Children	26
Chapter 50 - Divorce and Alimony	26

Chapter 50A - Uniform Child-Custody Jurisdiction and Enforcement Act	26
Chapter 50B - Domestic Violence	26
Chapter 50C - Civil No-Contact Orders	26
Chapter 51 - Marriage	26
Chapter 52 - Powers and Liabilities of Married Persons	27
Chapter 52A - Uniform Reciprocal Enforcement of Support Act [Repealed.]	27
Chapter 52B - Uniform Premarital Agreement Act	27
Chapter 52C - Uniform Interstate Family Support Act	27
Chapter 53 - Banks	27
Chapter 53A - Business Development Corporations and North Carolina Capital Resource Corporations	28
Chapter 53B - Financial Privacy Act	28
Chapter 54 - Cooperative Organizations	28
Chapter 54A - Capital Stock Savings and Loan Associations [Repealed.]	28
Chapter 54B - Savings and Loan Associations	29
Chapter 54C - Savings Banks	29
Chapter 55 - North Carolina Business Corporation Act	30
Chapter 55A - North Carolina Nonprofit Corporation Act	31
Chapter 55B - Professional Corporation Act	31
Chapter 55C - Foreign Trade Zones	31
Chapter 55D - Filings, Names, and Registered Agents for Corporations, Nonprofit Corporations, and Partnerships	31
Chapter 56 - Electric, Telegraph and Power Companies [Repealed.]	31
Chapter 57 - Hospital, Medical and Dental Service Corporations [Recodified.]	31
Chapter 57A - Health Maintenance Organization Act [Recodified.]	31
Chapter 57B - Health Maintenance Organization Act [Recodified.]	31
Chapter 57C - North Carolina Limited Liability Company Act.	31
Chapter 58 - Insurance.	32
Chapter 58 - Insurance (Continuation)	33
Chapter 58 - Insurance (Continuation)	34
Chapter 58 - Insurance (Continuation)	35
Chapter 58 - Insurance (Continuation)	36
Chapter 58 - Insurance (Continuation)	37
Chapter 58 - Insurance (Continuation)	38
Chapter 58A - North Carolina Health Insurance Trust Commission [Recodified.]	38
Chapter 59 - Partnership.	39
Chapter 59B - Uniform Unincorporated Nonprofit Association Act.	39
Chapter 60 - Railroads and Other Carriers [Repealed and Transferred.]	39
Chapter 61 - Religious Societies	39
Chapter 62 - Public Utilities	39

Chapter 62 - Public Utilities (Continuation)	40
Chapter 62A - Public Safety Telephone Service And Wireless Telephone Service	40
Chapter 63 - Aeronautics	40
Chapter 63A - North Carolina Global TransPark Authority	40
Chapter 64 - Aliens	40
Chapter 65 – Cemeteries	40
Chapter 66 - Commerce and Business	41
Chapter 67 - Dogs	41
Chapter 68 - Fences and Stock Law	41
Chapter 69 - Fire Protection	41
Chapter 70 - Indian Antiquities, Archaeological Resources and Unmarked Human Skeletal Remains Protection	42
Chapter 71 - Indians [Repealed]	42
Chapter 71A - Indians	42
Chapter 72 - Inns, Hotels and Restaurants	42
Chapter 73 - Mills	42
Chapter 74 - Mines and Quarries	42
Chapter 74A - Company Police [Repealed]	42
Chapter 74B - Private Protective Services Act [Repealed.]	42
Chapter 74C - Private Protective Services	42
Chapter 74D - Alarm Systems	42
Chapter 74E - Company Police Act	42
Chapter 74F - Locksmith Licensing Act	42
Chapter 74G - Campus Police Act	42
Chapter 75 - Monopolies, Trusts and Consumer Protection	42
Chapter 75A - Boating and Water Safety	43
Chapter 75B - Discrimination in Business	43
Chapter 75C - Motion Picture Fair Competition Act	43
Chapter 75D - Racketeer Influenced and Corrupt Organizations	43
Chapter 75E - Unlawful Activities in Connection With Certain Corporate Transactions	43
Chapter 76 - Navigation	43
Chapter 76A - Navigation and Pilotage Commissions	43
Chapter 77 - Rivers, Creeks, and Coastal Waters	43
Chapter 78 - Securities Law [Repealed]	43
Chapter 78A - North Carolina Securities Act	43
Chapter 78B - Tender Offer Disclosure Act [Repealed.]	43
Chapter 78C - Investment Advisers	43
Chapter 78D - Commodities Act	43
Chapter 79 - Strays [Repealed]	43
Chapter 80 - Trademarks, Brands, etc.	44
Chapter 81 - Weights and Measures [Recodified.]	44
Chapter 81A - Weights and Measures Act of 1975.	44
Chapter 82 - Wrecks [Repealed.]	44
Chapter 83 - Architects [Recodified.]	44

Chapter 83A - Architects	44
Chapter 84 - Attorneys-at-Law	44
Chapter 84A - Foreign Legal Consultants	44
Chapter 85 - Auctions and Auctioneers [Repealed.]	44
Chapter 85A - Bail Bondsmen and Runners [Recodified.]	44
Chapter 85B - Auctions and Auctioneers	44
Chapter 85C - Bail Bondsmen and Runners [Recodified.]	44
Chapter 86 - Barbers [Recodified.]	44
Chapter 86A - Barbers	44
Chapter 87 - Contractors	44
Chapter 88 - Cosmetic Art [Repealed.]	44
Chapter 88A - Electrolysis Practice Act	44
Chapter 88B - Cosmetic Art	45
Chapter 89 - Engineering and Land Surveying [Recodified.]	45
Chapter 89A - Landscape Architects	45
Chapter 89B - Foresters	45
Chapter 89C - Engineering and Land Surveying	45
Chapter 89D - Landscape Contractors	45
Chapter 89E - Geologists Licensing Act	45
Chapter 89F - North Carolina Soil Scientist Licensing Act	45
Chapter 89G - Irrigation Contractors	45
Chapter 90 - Medicine and Allied Occupations	45
Chapter 90 - Medicine and Allied Occupations (Continuation)	46
Chapter 90 - Medicine and Allied Occupations (Continuation)	47
Chapter 90 - Medicine and Allied Occupations (Continuation)	48
Chapter 90A - Sanitarians and Water and Wastewater Treatment Facility Operators	48
Chapter 90B - Social Worker Certification and Licensure Act	48
Chapter 90C - North Carolina Recreational Therapy Licensure Act	48
Chapter 90D - Interpreters and Transliterators	48
Chapter 91 - Pawnbrokers [Repealed.]	48
Chapter 91A - Pawnbrokers Modernization Act of 1989	48
Chapter 92 - Photographers [Deleted.]	48
Chapter 93 - Certified Public Accountants	48
Chapter 93A - Real Estate License Law	49
Chapter 93B - Occupational Licensing Boards	49
Chapter 93C - Watchmakers [Repealed.]	49
Chapter 93D - North Carolina State Hearing Aid Dealers and Fitters Board.	49
Chapter 93E - North Carolina Appraisers Act	49
Chapter 94 - Apprenticeship	49
Chapter 95 - Department of Labor and Labor Regulations	49
Chapter 95 - Department of Labor and Labor Regulations (Continuation)	50
Chapter 96 - Employment Security	50
Chapter 97 - Workers' Compensation Act	50
Chapter 97 - Workers' Compensation Act (Continuation)	51

Chapter 98 - Burnt and Lost Records	51
Chapter 99 - Libel and Slander	51
Chapter 99A - Civil Remedies for Criminal Actions	51
Chapter 99B - Products Liability	51
Chapter 99C - Actions Relating to Winter Sports Safety and Accidents	51
Chapter 99D - Civil Rights	51
Chapter 99E - Special Liability Provisions	51
Chapter 100 - Monuments, Memorials and Parks	51
Chapter 101 - Names of Persons	51
Chapter 102 - Official Survey Base	51
Chapter 103 - Sundays, Holidays and Special Days	51
Chapter 104 - United States Lands	51
Chapter 104A - Degrees of Kinship	51
Chapter 104B - Hurricanes or Other Acts of Nature	51
Chapter 104C - Atomic Energy, Radioactivity and Ionizing Radiation [Repealed and Recodified.]	51
Chapter 104D - Southern States Energy Compact	51
Chapter 104E - North Carolina Radiation Protection Act	51
Chapter 104F - Southeast Interstate Low-Level Radioactive Waste Management Compact [Repealed]	51
Chapter 104G - North Carolina Low-Level Radioactive Waste Management Authority Act of 1987 [Repealed]	51
Chapter 105 - Taxation	51
Chapter 105 - Taxation (Continuation)	52
Chapter 105 - Taxation (Continuation)	53
Chapter 105 - Taxation (Continuation)	54
Chapter 105A - Setoff Debt Collection Act	55
Chapter 105B - Defaulted Student Loan Recovery Act	55
Chapter 106 - Agriculture	55
Chapter 106 - Agriculture (Continue)	56
Chapter 106 - Agriculture (Continue)	57
Chapter 107 - Agricultural Development Districts [Repealed.]	57
Chapter 108 - Social Services [Repealed and Recodified.]	57
Chapter 108A - Social Services	57
Chapter 108B - Community Action Programs	58
Chapter 108C Medicaid and Health Choice Provider Requirements.	58
Chapter 108D Medicaid Managed Care for Behavioral Health Services.	58
Chapter 109 - Bonds [Recodified.]	58
Chapter 110 - Child Welfare	58
Chapter 111 - Aid to the Blind	58
Chapter 112 - Confederate Homes and Pensions [Repealed.]	58
Chapter 113 - Conservation and Development	58
Chapter 113 - Conservation and Development (Continuation)	59

Chapter 113A - Pollution Control and Environment	59
Chapter 113A - Pollution Control and Environment (Continuation)	60
Chapter 113B - North Carolina Energy Policy Act of 1975	60
Chapter 114 - Department of Justice	60
Chapter 115 - Elementary and Secondary Education [Repealed.]	60
Chapter 115A - Community Colleges, Technical Institutes, and Industrial Education Centers [Repealed.]	60
Chapter 115B - Tuition and Fee Waivers	60
Chapter 115C - Elementary and Secondary Education	60
Chapter 115C - Elementary and Secondary Education (Continuation)	61
Chapter 115C - Elementary and Secondary Education (Continuation)	62
Chapter 115C - Elementary and Secondary Education (Continuation)	63
Chapter 115D - Community Colleges	63
Chapter 115E - Private Educational Facilities Finance Act [Recodified]	63
Chapter 116 - Higher Education	63
Chapter 116 - Higher Education (Continuation)	63
Chapter 116A - Escheats and Abandoned Property [Repealed.]	64
Chapter 116B - Escheats and Abandoned Property	64
Chapter 116C - Continuum of Education Programs	64
Chapter 116D - Higher Education Bonds	64
Chapter 117 - Electrification	64
Chapter 118 - Firemen's and Rescue Squad Workers' Relief and Pension Funds [Recodified.]	64
Chapter 118A - Firemen's Death Benefit Act [Repealed.]	64
Chapter 118B - Members of a Rescue Squad Death Benefit Act [Repealed.]	64
Chapter 119 - Gasoline and Oil Inspection and Regulation	64
Chapter 120 - General Assembly	65
Chapter 120 - General Assembly (Continuation)	66
Chapter 120 - General Assembly (Continuation)	67
Chapter 120C - Lobbying	67
Chapter 121 - Archives and History	67
Chapter 122 - Hospitals for the Mentally Disordered [Repealed.]	67
Chapter 122A - North Carolina Housing Finance Agency	67
Chapter 122B - North Carolina Agricultural Facilities Finance Act [Repealed.]	67
Chapter 122C - Mental Health, Developmental Disabilities, and Substance Abuse Act of 1985	67
Chapter 122C - Mental Health, Developmental Disabilities, and Substance Abuse Act of 1985 (Continuation)	68
Chapter 122D - North Carolina Agricultural Finance Act	68

Chapter 122E - North Carolina Housing Trust and Oil Overcharge Act	68
Chapter 123 - Impeachment	69
Chapter 123A - Industrial Development [Repealed.]	69
Chapter 124 - Internal Improvements	69
Chapter 125 - Libraries	69
Chapter 126 - State Personnel System	69
Chapter 127 - Militia [Repealed.]	69
Chapter 127A - Militia	69
Chapter 127B - Military Affairs	69
Chapter 127C - Advisory Commission on Military Affairs	69
Chapter 128 - Offices and Public Officers	69
Chapter 128 - Offices and Public Officers (Continuation)	70
Chapter 129 - Public Buildings and Grounds	70
Chapter 130 - Public Health [Repealed.]	70
Chapter 130A - Public Health	70
Chapter 130A - Public Health (Continuation)	71
Chapter 130A - Public Health (Continuation)	72
Chapter 130B - Hazardous Waste Management Commission [Repealed.]	72
Chapter 131 - Public Hospitals [Repealed.]	72
Chapter 131A - Health Care Facilities Finance Act	72
Chapter 131B - Licensing of Ambulatory Surgical Facilities [Repealed.]	72
Chapter 131C - Charitable Solicitation Licensure Act [Repealed.]	72
Chapter 131D - Inspection and Licensing of Facilities	72
Chapter 131E - Health Care Facilities and Services	72
Chapter 131E - Health Care Facilities and Services (Continuation)	73
Chapter 131F - Solicitation of Contributions	73
Chapter 132 - Public Records	73
Chapter 133 - Public Works	74
Chapter 134 - Youth Development [Recodified.]	74
Chapter 134A - Youth Services [Repealed.]	74
Chapter 135 - Retirement System for Teachers and State Employees; Social Security; Health Insurance Program for Children	74
Chapter 135 - Retirement System for Teachers and State Employees; Social Security; Health Insurance Program for Children	75
Chapter 136 - Transportation	75
Chapter 136 - Transportation (Continuation)	76
Chapter 137 - Rural Rehabilitation [Repealed.]	76
Chapter 138 - Salaries, Fees and Allowances	76
Chapter 138A - State Government Ethics Act	76
Chapter 139 - Soil and Water Conservation Districts	76

Chapter 140 - State Art Museum; Symphony and Art Societies	76
Chapter 140A - State Awards System	76
Chapter 141 - State Boundaries	76
Chapter 142 - State Debt	76
Chapter 143 - State Departments, Institutions, and Commissions	77
Chapter 143 - State Departments, Institutions, and Commissions (Continuation)	78
Chapter 143 - State Departments, Institutions, and Commissions (Continuation)	79
Chapter 143 - State Departments, Institutions, and Commissions (Continuation)	80
Chapter 143A - State Government Reorganization	80
Chapter 143B - Executive Organization Act of 1973	80
Chapter 143B - Executive Organization Act of 1973 (Continuation)	81
Chapter 143B - Executive Organization Act of 1973 (Continuation)	82
Chapter 143C - State Budget Act	83
Chapter 143D - The State Governmental Accountability and Internal Control Act	83
Chapter 144 - State Flag, Official Governmental Flags, Motto, and Colors	83
Chapter 145 - State Symbols and Other Official Adoptions.	83
Chapter 146 - State Lands	83
Chapter 147 - State Officers	83
Chapter 148 - State Prison System	84
Chapter 149 - State Song and Toast	84
Chapter 150 - Uniform Revocation of Licenses [Repealed.]	84
Chapter 150A - Administrative Procedure Act [Recodified.]	84
Chapter 150B - Administrative Procedure Act	84
Chapter 151 - Constables [Repealed.]	84
Chapter 152 - Coroners	84
Chapter 152A - County Medical Examiner [Repealed.]	84
Chapter 152A - County Medical Examiner [Repealed.] (Continuation)	85
Chapter 153 - Counties and County Commissioners [Repealed.]	85
Chapter 153A - Counties	85
Chapter 153B - Mountain Resources Planning Act	85
Chapter 153C - Uwharrie Regional Resources Act	85
Chapter 154 - County Surveyor [Repealed.]	85
Chapter 155 - County Treasurer [Repealed.]	85
Chapter 156 - Drainage	85
Chapter 156 – Drainage (Continuation)	86

Chapter 157 - Housing Authorities and Projects	86
Chapter 157A - Historic Properties Commissions [Transferred.]	86
Chapter 158 - Local Development	86
Chapter 159 - Local Government Finance	86
Chapter 159 - Local Government Finance (Continuation)	87
Chapter 159A - Pollution Abatement and Industrial Facilities Financing Act [Unconstitutional.]	87
Chapter 159B - Joint Municipal Electric Power and Energy Act	87
Chapter 159C - Industrial and Pollution Control Facilities Financing Act	87
Chapter 159D - The North Carolina Capital Facilities Financing Act	87
Chapter 159E - Registered Public Obligations Act	87
Chapter 159F - North Carolina Energy Development Authority [Repealed.]	87
Chapter 159G - Water Infrastructure	87
Chapter 159H - [Reserved.]	87
Chapter 159I - Solid Waste Management Loan Program and Local Government Special Obligation Bonds	87
Chapter 160 - Municipal Corporations [Repealed And Transferred.]	87
Chapter 160A - Cities and Towns	88
Chapter 160A - Cities and Towns (Continuation)	89
Chapter 160B - Consolidated City-County Act	89
Chapter 160C - Baseball Park Districts [Repealed.]	90
Chapter 161 - Register of Deeds	90
Chapter 162 - Sheriff	90
Chapter 162A - Water and Sewer Systems	90
Chapter 162B Continuity of Local Government in Emergency.	90
Chapter 163 Elections and Election Laws.	90
Chapter 163 Elections and Election Laws. (Continuation)	91
Chapter 164 Concerning the General Statutes of North Carolina.	92
Chapter 165 Veterans.	92
Chapter 166 Civil Preparedness Agencies [Repealed.]	92
Chapter 166A North Carolina Emergency Management Act.	92
Chapter 167 State Civil Air Patrol [Repealed.]	92
Chapter 168 Persons with Disabilities.	92
Chapter 168A Persons With Disabilities Protection Act.	92

Chapter 47

Probate and Registration.

Article 1.

Probate.

§ 47-1. Officials of State authorized to take probate.

The execution of all deeds of conveyance, contracts to buy, sell or convey lands, mortgages, deeds of trust, instruments modifying or extending the terms of mortgages or deeds of trust, assignments, powers of attorney, covenants to stand seized to the use of another, leases for more than three years, releases, affidavits concerning land titles or family history, any instruments pertaining to real property, and any and all instruments and writings of whatever nature and kind which are required or allowed by law to be registered in the office of the register of deeds or which may hereafter be required or allowed by law to be so registered, may be proved or acknowledged before any one of the following officials of this State: The justices, judges, magistrates, clerks, assistant clerks, and deputy clerks of the General Court of Justice, and notaries public. (Code, s. 1246; 1895, c. 161, ss. 1, 3; 1897, c. 87; 1899, c. 235; Rev., s. 989; C.S., s. 3293; 1951, c. 772; 1969, c. 44, s. 52; 1971, c. 1185, s. 9.)

§ 47-2. Officials of the United States, foreign countries, and sister states.

The execution of all such instruments and writings as are permitted or required by law to be registered may be proved or acknowledged before any one of the following officials of the United States, of the District of Columbia, of the several states and territories of the United States, of countries under the dominion of the United States and of foreign countries: Any judge of a court of record, any clerk of a court of record, any notary public, any commissioner of deeds, any commissioner of oaths, any mayor or chief magistrate of an incorporated town or city, any ambassador, minister, consul, vice-consul, consul general, vice-consul general, associate consul, or any other person authorized by federal law to acknowledge documents as consular officers, or commercial agent of the United States, any justice of the peace of any state or territory of the United States, any officer of the United States Army or Air Force or United States Marine Corps having the rank of warrant officer or higher, any officer of the

United States Navy or Coast Guard having the rank of warrant officer, or higher, or any officer of the United States Merchant Marine having the rank of warrant officer, or higher. No official seal shall be required of a military or merchant marine officer, but the officer shall sign the officer's name, designate the officer's rank, and give the name of the officer's ship or military organization and the date, and for the purpose of certifying the acknowledgment, the officer shall use a form in substance as follows:

On this the ____ day of ____, ____, before me ____, the undersigned officer, personally appeared _____, known to me (or satisfactorily proven) to be accompanying or serving in or with the Armed Forces of the United States (or to be the spouse of a person accompanying or serving in or with the Armed Forces of the United States) and to be the person whose name is subscribed to the within instruments and acknowledged that ____ the person ____ executed the same for the purposes therein contained. And the undersigned does further certify that the undersigned is at the date of this certificate a commissioned officer of the rank stated below and is in the active service of the Armed Forces of the United States.

Signature of Officer

Rank of Officer and command to which attached.

If the proof or acknowledgment of the execution of an instrument is had before a justice of the peace of any state of the United States other than this State or of any territory of the United States, the certificate of the justice of the peace shall be accompanied by a certificate of the clerk of some court of record of the county in which the justice of the peace resides, which certificate of the clerk shall be under the clerk's hand and official seal, to the effect that the justice of the peace was at the time the certificate of the justice bears date an acting justice of the peace of the county and state or territory and that the genuine signature of the justice of the peace is set to the certificate. (1899, c. 235, s. 5; 1905, c. 451; Rev., s. 990; 1913, c. 39, s. 1; Ex. Sess. 1913, c. 72, s. 1; C.S., s. 3294; 1943, c. 159, s. 1; c. 471, s. 1; 1945, c. 6, s. 1; 1955, c. 658, s. 1; 1957, c. 1084, s. 1; 1967, c. 949; 1999-456, s. 59; 2004-199, s. 16; 2011-183, s. 30.)

§ 47-2.1. Validation of instruments proved before officers of certain ranks.

Any instrument or writing, required by law to be proved or acknowledged before an officer, which prior to the ratification of this section was proved or acknowledged before an officer of the United States Army or Marine Corps having the rank of second lieutenant or higher, or any officer of the United States Navy, or United States Coast Guard, or United States Merchant Marine, having the rank of ensign or higher, is hereby validated and declared sufficient for all purposes. (1945, c. 6, s. 2; 2011-183, s. 31.)

§ 47-2.2. Notary public of sister state; lack of seal or stamp or expiration date of commission.

(a)   If the proof or acknowledgment of any instrument is had before a notary public of any state other than North Carolina and the instrument does not (i) show the seal or stamp of the notary public, (ii) provide evidence pursuant to subsection (b) of this section that a seal or stamp is not required and the expiration date of the commission of the notary public, or (iii) state that the notary's commission does not expire or is a lifetime appointment, the certificate of proof or acknowledgment made by such notary public shall be accompanied by the certificate of the county official before whom the notary qualifies for office or of a state officer authorized to issue certificates regarding notary commission status, stating that such notary public was at the time his certificate bears date an acting notary public of such state, and that such notary's genuine signature is set to his certificate. The certificate of the official herein provided for shall be under his hand and official seal.

(b)   A proof or acknowledgement which does not require a seal or stamp of the notary to be effective in the jurisdiction issuing the notary's commission shall include either (i) a statement by the notary within the proof or acknowledgement area of the instrument that the notary is not required to utilize a seal or stamp or (ii) a reference that purports to be the statute of the commissioning state which provides that no seal or stamp is required together with a statement that the notary is not required to utilize a seal or stamp. The register of deeds may rely upon this statement and is not responsible for confirming its validity or the authority of the person making it. A register of deeds may not refuse to accept a record for registration because a notarial seal or stamp is omitted from the proof or acknowledgement if the provisions of this subsection have been complied with in the proof or acknowledgement. The acceptance of a record for registration under this subsection shall give rise to a presumption that the seal or stamp was not required to be affixed by the notary. This presumption is rebuttable and shall apply to all instruments whenever recorded. However, a court order finding the lack of a valid seal shall not affect the rights of a person who (i) records an interest in the real property described in the instrument before the finding of a lack of a valid seal and (ii) would otherwise have an enforceable interest in the real property. (1973, c. 1016; 2013-204, s. 1.12.)

§ 47-3: Repealed by Session Laws 1987, c. 620, s. 3.

§ 47-4. Repealed by Session Laws 1971, c. 1185, s. 10.

§ 47-5. When seal of officer necessary to probate.

When proof or acknowledgment of the execution of any instrument by any maker of such instrument, whether a person or corporation, is had before any official authorized by law to take such proof and acknowledgment, and such official has an official seal, he shall set his official seal to his certificate. If the official before whom the instrument is proved or acknowledged has no official seal he shall certify under his hand, and his private seal shall not be essential. When the instrument is proved or acknowledged before the register of deeds of the county in which the instrument is to be registered, the official seal shall not be necessary. (1899, c. 235, s. 8; Rev., s. 993; C.S., s. 3297; 1969, c. 664, s. 3; 1977, c. 375, s. 12.)

§ 47-6. Officials may act although land or maker's residence elsewhere.

The execution of all instruments required or permitted by law to be registered may be proved or acknowledged before any of the officials authorized by law to take probates, regardless of the county in this State in which the subject matter of the instrument may be situated and regardless of the domicile, residence or citizenship of the person who executes such instrument, or of the domicile, residence or citizenship of the person to whom or for whose benefit such instrument may be made. (1899, c. 235, s. 13; Rev., s. 994; C.S., s. 3298.)

§ 47-7: Repealed by Session Laws 1987, c. 620, s. 3.

§ 47-8: Repealed by Session Laws 1991, c. 543, s. 1.

§ 47-8.1. Certain documents verified by attorneys validated.

Final judgments otherwise proper, entered in actions or proceedings in which the complaints or any other documents were verified in violation of G.S. 47-8 prior to its repeal shall not be void or voidable. (1991, c. 543, s. 2.)

§ 47-9. Probates before stockholders in building and loan associations.

No acknowledgment or proof of execution of any mortgage or deed of trust executed to secure the payment of any indebtedness to any building and loan association shall hereafter be held invalid by reason of the fact that the officer taking such acknowledgment or proof is a stockholder in said building and loan association. This section does not authorize any officer or director of a building and loan association to take acknowledgments or proofs. The provisions of this section shall apply to federal savings and loan associations having their principal offices in this State. Acknowledgments and proofs of execution, including private examinations of any married woman taken before March 20, 1939, by an officer who is or was a stockholder in any federal savings and loan association, are hereby validated. (1913, c. 110, ss. 1, 3; C.S., s. 3301; 1939, c. 136; 1977, c. 375, s. 12.)

§ 47-10. Probate before stockholders or directors in banking corporations.

No acknowledgment or proof of execution, including privy examination of married women, of any mortgage, or deed of trust executed to secure the payment of any indebtedness to any banking corporation, taken prior to the first day of January, 1929, shall be held invalid by reason of the fact that the officer taking such acknowledgment, proof or privy examination, was a stockholder or director in such banking corporation. (1929, c. 302, s. 1.)

§ 47-11. Subpoenas to maker and subscribing witnesses.

The grantee or other party to an instrument required or allowed by law to be registered may at his own expense obtain from the clerk of the superior court of the county in which the instrument is required to be registered a subpoena for any or all of the makers of or subscribing witnesses to such instrument, commanding such maker or subscribing witness to appear before such clerk at his office at a certain time to give evidence concerning the execution of the instrument. The subpoena shall be directed to the sheriff of the county in which the person upon whom it is to be served resides. If any person refuses to obey such subpoena he is liable to a fine of forty dollars ($40.00) or to be attached for contempt by the clerk, upon its being made to appear to the satisfaction of the clerk that such disobedience was intentional, under the same rules of law as are prescribed in the cases of other defaulting witnesses. (Code, s. 1268; 1897, c. 28; 1899, c. 235, s. 16; Rev., s. 996; C.S., s. 3302.)

§ 47-12. Proof of attested instrument by subscribing witness.

Except as provided by G.S. 47-12.2, the execution of any instrument required or permitted by law to be registered, which has been witnessed by one or more subscribing witnesses, may be proved for registration before any official authorized by law to take proof of such an instrument, by a statement under oath of any such subscribing witness that the maker either signed the instrument in his presence or acknowledged to him the execution thereof. Nothing in this section in anywise affects any of the requirements set out in G.S. 52-10 or 52-10.1. (1899, c. 235, s. 12; Rev., s. 997; C.S., s. 3303; 1935, c. 168; 1937, c. 7; 1945, c. 73, s. 11; 1947, c. 991, s. 1; 1949, c. 815, ss. 1, 2; 1951, c. 379, s. 1; 1953, c. 1078, s. 1; 1977, c. 375, s. 12.)

§ 47-12.1. Proof of attested instrument by proof of handwriting.

(a) If all subscribing witnesses have died or have left the State or have become of unsound mind or otherwise incompetent or unavailable, the execution of such instrument, except as provided by G.S. 47-12.2, may be proved for registration, before any official authorized by law to take proof of such an instrument, by a statement under oath that the affiant knows the handwriting of the maker and that the purported signature of the maker is in the handwriting of the maker, or by a statement under oath that the affiant knows the handwriting of a particular subscribing witness and that the purported signature of such subscribing witness is in the handwriting of such subscribing witness.

(b) Nothing in this section in anywise affects any of the requirements set out in G.S. 52-10 or 52-10.1. (1899, c. 235, s. 12; Rev., s. 997; C.S., s. 3303; 1935, c. 168; 1937, c. 7; 1945, c. 73, s. 11; 1947, c. 991, s. 1; 1949, c. 815, ss. 1, 2; 1951, c. 379, s. 1; 1977, c. 375, s. 12.)

§ 47-12.2. Subscribing witness incompetent when grantee or beneficiary.

The execution of an instrument may not be proved for registration by a subscribing witness who, at the time of the execution of the instrument by the subscribing witness, is the grantee or beneficiary therein nor by proof of his signature as such subscribing witness. Nothing in this section invalidates the registration of any instrument registered prior to April 9, 1935. (1899, c. 235, s. 12; Rev., s. 997; C.S., s. 3303; 1935, c. 168; 1937, c. 7; 1945, c. 73, s. 11; 1947, c. 991, s. 1; 1949, c. 815, ss. 1, 2; 1951, c. 379, s. 1; 2013-204, s. 1.13.)

§ 47-13. Proof of unattested writing.

If an instrument required or permitted by law to be registered has no subscribing witness, the execution of the same may be proven before any official authorized to take the proof and acknowledgment of such instrument by proof of the handwriting of the maker and this shall likewise apply to proof of execution of instruments by married persons. (1899, c. 235, s. 11; Rev., s. 998; C.S., s. 3304; 1945, c. 73, s. 12; 1977, c. 375, s. 12.)

§ 47-13.1. Certificate of officer taking proof of instrument.

The person taking proof of an instrument pursuant to G.S. 47-12, 47-12.1 or 47-13 shall execute a certificate on or attached to the instrument being proved, certifying to the fact of proof substantially as provided in the certificate forms set out in G.S. 47-43.2, 47-43.3 and 47-43.4, and such certificate shall be prima facie evidence of the facts therein certified. (1951, c. 379, s. 2; 1953, c. 1078, s. 2.)

§ 47-14. Register of deeds to verify the presence of proof or acknowledgement and register instruments and electronic documents; order by judge; instruments to which register of deeds is a party.

(a) Verification of Instruments. - The register of deeds shall not accept for registration any instrument that requires proof or acknowledgement unless the execution of the instrument by one or more signers appears to have been proved or acknowledged before an officer with the apparent authority to take proofs or acknowledgements, and the proof or acknowledgement includes the officer's signature, commission expiration date, and official seal, if required. The register of deeds shall accept an instrument for registration that does not require proof or acknowledgement if the instrument otherwise satisfies the requirements of G.S. 161-14. Any instrument previously recorded or any certified copy of any instrument previously recorded may be rerecorded provided the instrument is conspicuously marked on the first page as a rerecording. The register of deeds may rely on the marking and the appearance of the original recording office's recording information to determine that an instrument is being presented as it was previously recorded. The register of deeds is not required to further verify the proof or acknowledgement of or determine whether any changes or alterations have been made after the original recording to an instrument presented for rerecording. The register of deeds is not required to verify or make inquiry concerning any of the following:

(1) The legal sufficiency of any proof or acknowledgement.

(2) The authority of any officer who took a proof or acknowledgement.

(3) The legal sufficiency of any document presented for registration.

(a1) Verification of Electronic Documents. - The requirements of subsection (a) of this section for verification of the execution of an instrument are satisfied with respect to an electronic document if all of the conditions in this subsection are met. For purposes of this subsection, the term "electronic document" is as defined in G.S. 47-16.2(3). The conditions are:

(1) The register of deeds has authorized the submitter to electronically register the electronic document.

(2) The document is submitted by a United States federal or state governmental unit or instrumentality or a trusted submitter. For purposes of this subsection, "a trusted submitter" means a person or entity that has entered into a memorandum of understanding regarding electronic recording with the register of deeds in the county in which the electronic document is to be submitted.

(3) The execution of the instrument by one or more signers appears to have been proved or acknowledged before an officer with the apparent authority to take proofs or acknowledgements, and the proof or acknowledgment includes the officer's signature, commission expiration date, and official seal, if required, based on the appearance of these elements on the digitized image of the document as it will appear on the public record.

(4) Evidence of other required governmental certification or annotation appears on the digitized image of the document as it will appear on the public record.

(5) With respect to a document submitted by a trusted submitter, the digitized image of the document as it will appear on the public record contains the submitter's name in the following completed statement on the first page of the document image: "Submitted electronically by ___ (submitter's name) in compliance with North Carolina statutes governing recordable documents and the terms of the submitter agreement with the ___ (insert county name) County Register of Deeds."

(6) Except as otherwise provided in this subsection, the digitized image of the electronic document conforms to all other applicable laws and rules that prescribe recordation.

(a2)   Verification of Officer's Signature. - Submission to a register of deeds of an electronic document requiring proof or acknowledgement is a representation by the submitter that, prior to submission, the submitter verified the officer's signature required under subdivision (a1)(3) of this section to be one of the types of signatures listed in this subsection. The register of deeds may rely on this representation for purposes of determining compliance with the signature requirements of this section. The electronic registration of a document with a register of deeds prior to the effective date of this statute is not invalid based on whether the register verified the officer's signature in accordance with this subsection. The types of signatures are:

(1)   A signature in ink by hand.

(2)   An electronic signature as defined in G.S. 10B-101(7).

(b)   Order by Judge. - If a register of deeds denies registration pursuant to subsection (a), the person offering the instrument for registration may apply to any judge of the district court in the district, including the county in which the instrument is to be registered, for an order for registration. Upon finding all of the requirements in this subsection, the judge shall order the instrument to be registered, together with the certificates, and the register of deeds shall register them accordingly. The requirements are:

(1)   If the instrument requires proof or acknowledgement, that the signature of one or more signers has been proved or acknowledged before an officer authorized to take proofs and acknowledgements.

(2)   That the proof or acknowledgement includes the officer's signature and commission expiration date and official seal, if required.

(c)   Repealed by Session Laws 2008-194, s. 7(a), effective October 1, 2008.

(d)   Scope. - Registration of an instrument pursuant to this section is not effective with regard to parties who have not executed the instrument or whose execution thereof has not been duly proved or acknowledged.

(e)   Register of Deeds as Party. - Any instrument required or permitted by law to be registered in which the register of deeds of the county of registration is a party may be proved or acknowledged before any magistrate or any notary public.

(f) Presumption of Notarial Seal. - The acceptance of a record for registration by the register of deeds shall give rise to a presumption that, at the time the record was presented for registration, a clear and legible image of the notary's official seal was affixed or embossed on the record near the notary's official signature. This presumption applies regardless of whether the image is legible or photographically reproduced in the records maintained by the register of deeds and applies to all instruments filed in the records maintained by the register of deeds regardless of when the instrument was presented for registration. A register of deeds may not refuse to accept a record for registration because a notarial seal does not satisfy the requirements of G.S. 10B-37. The presumption under this subsection is rebuttable and shall apply to all instruments whenever recorded. However, a court order finding the lack of a valid seal shall not affect the rights of a person who (i) records an interest in the real property described in the instrument before the finding of a lack of a valid seal and (ii) would otherwise have an enforceable interest in the real property. (1899, c. 235, s. 7; 1905, c. 414; Rev., s. 999; C.S., s. 3305; 1921, c. 91; 1939, c. 210, s. 2; 1967, c. 639, s. 1; 1969, c. 664, s. 2; 1973, c. 60; 2005-123, s. 2; 2006-59, s. 26; 2006-259, s. 52(a)-(b); 2006-264, s. 40(c); 2008-194, s. 7(a); 2012-18, s. 1.4; 2013-204, s. 1.14.)

§ 47-14.1. Repeal of laws requiring private examination of married women.

All deeds, contracts, conveyances, leaseholds or other instruments executed from and after February 7, 1945, shall be valid for all purposes without the separate, privy, or private examination of married woman where she is a party to or a grantor in such deed, contract, conveyance, leasehold or other instrument, and it shall not be necessary nor required that the separate or privy examination of such married woman be taken by the certifying officer. From and after February 7, 1945, all laws and clauses of laws contained in any section of the General Statutes requiring the privy or private examination of a married woman are hereby repealed. (1945, c. 73, s. 21; 1951, c. 893, s. 1.)

§ 47-15. Repealed by Session Laws 1985, c. 589, s. 26, effective January 1, 1986.

§ 47-16. Probate of corporate deeds, where corporation has ceased to exist.

It is competent for the clerk of the superior court in any county in this State, on proof before him upon the oath and examination of the subscribing witness to any contract or instrument required to be registered under the laws of this State, to adjudge and order that such contract or instrument be registered as by law provided, when such contract or instrument is signed by any corporation in its corporate name by its president, and when such corporation has been out of existence for more than 10 years when the said contract or instrument is offered for probate and registration, and when the grantee and those claiming under any such grantee have been in the uninterrupted possession of the property described in said contract or instrument since the date of its execution; and said contract or instrument so probated and registered shall be as effective to all intents and purposes as if signed, sealed, and acknowledged, or proven, as provided under the existing laws of this State. (1911, c. 44, s. 1; C.S., s. 3307.)

Article 1A.

Uniform Real Property Electronic Recording Act.

§ 47-16.1. Short title.

This Article may be cited as the Uniform Real Property Electronic Recording Act. (2005-391, s. 1.)

§ 47-16.2. Definitions.

In this Article:

(1) "Document" means information that is:

a. Inscribed on a tangible medium or that is stored in an electronic or other medium and is retrievable in perceivable form; and

b.   Eligible to be recorded in the land records maintained by the register of deeds.

(2)   "Electronic" means relating to technology having electrical, digital, magnetic, wireless, optical, electromagnetic, or similar capabilities.

(3)   "Electronic document" means a document that is received by the register of deeds in an electronic form.

(4)   "Electronic signature" means an electronic sound, symbol, or process attached to or logically associated with a document and executed or adopted by a person with the intent to sign the document.

(5)   "Person" means an individual, corporation, business trust, estate, trust, partnership, limited liability company, association, joint venture, public corporation, government, or governmental subdivision, agency, or instrumentality, or any other legal or commercial entity. (2005-391, s. 1.)

§ 47-16.3. Validity of electronic documents.

(a)   If a law requires, as a condition for recording, that a document be an original, be on paper or another tangible medium, or be in writing, the requirement is satisfied by an electronic document satisfying this Article.

(b)   If a law requires, as a condition for recording, that a document be signed, the requirement is satisfied by an electronic signature.

(c)   A requirement that a document or a signature associated with a document be notarized, acknowledged, verified, witnessed, or made under oath is satisfied if the electronic signature of the person authorized to notarize, acknowledge, verify, witness, or administer the oath, and all other information required to be included, is attached to or logically associated with the document or signature. A physical or electronic image of a stamp, impression, or seal need not accompany an electronic signature. Nothing in this act shall prohibit the North Carolina Board of Examiners for Engineers and Surveyors from requiring that the image of a seal accompany any plat or map that is presented electronically for recording. (2005-391, s. 1.)

§ 47-16.4. Recording of documents.

(a)   In this section, "paper document" means a document that is received by the register of deeds in a form that is not electronic.

(b)   A register of deeds:

(1)   Who implements any of the functions listed in this section shall do so in compliance with standards adopted by the Secretary of State.

(2)   May receive, index, store, archive, and transmit electronic documents.

(3)   May provide for access to, and for search and retrieval of, documents and information by electronic means.

(4)   Who accepts electronic documents for recording shall continue to accept paper documents as authorized by law and shall place entries for both types of documents in the same index.

(5)   May convert paper documents accepted for recording into electronic form.

(6)   May convert into electronic form information recorded before the register of deeds began to record electronic documents.

(7)   May accept electronically any fee or tax that the register of deeds is authorized to collect.

(8)   May agree with other officials of this State or a political subdivision thereof on procedures or processes to facilitate the electronic satisfaction of conditions to recording and the electronic payment of fees and taxes. (2005-391, s. 1.)

§ 47-16.5. Administration and standards.

(a)   Standard-Setting Agency. - The Secretary of State shall adopt standards to implement this Article upon recommendation of the Electronic Recording Council. The Secretary of State may direct the Council to revise any portion of the recommended standards the Secretary deems inadequate or inappropriate. Technological standards and specifications adopted by the Secretary of State to implement this Article are engineering standards for the purposes of G.S. 150B-2(8a)h.

(b) Electronic Recording Council Created. - The Electronic Recording Council is created in the Department of the Secretary of State to advise and assist the Secretary of State in the adoption of standards to implement this Article. The Council shall review the functions listed in G.S. 47-16.4 and shall formulate and recommend to the Secretary standards for recording electronic documents and implementing the other functions listed in G.S. 47-16.4. The Council shall report its findings and recommendations to the Secretary of State at least once each calendar year. The Council shall advise the Secretary of State on a continuing basis of the need to adopt, amend, revise, or repeal standards. The Council may advise the Secretary of State on any other matter the Secretary refers to the Council.

(c) Council Membership, Terms, and Vacancies. - The Council shall consist of 13 members as follows:

(1) Seven members appointed by the North Carolina Association of Registers of Deeds. It is the intent of the General Assembly that the North Carolina Association of Registers of Deeds shall appoint as members a representative selection of registers of deeds from large, medium, and small counties, urban and rural counties, and the different geographic areas of this State.

(2) One member appointed by the North Carolina Bar Association.

(3) One member appointed by the North Carolina Society of Land Surveyors.

(4) One member appointed by the North Carolina Bankers Association.

(5) One member appointed by the North Carolina Land Title Association.

(6) One member appointed by the North Carolina Association of Assessing Officers.

(7) The Secretary of Cultural Resources or the Secretary's designee.

In making appointments to the Council, each appointing authority shall select appointees with the ability and commitment to fulfill the purposes of the Council.

Appointed members shall serve four-year terms, except that the initial appointments by the North Carolina Bar Association, the North Carolina Bankers Association, the North Carolina Association of Assessing Officers, and three of the initial appointments by the North Carolina Association of Registers of Deeds shall be for two years. All initial terms shall commence on the effective date of this Article. Members shall serve until their successors are appointed. An appointing authority may reappoint a member for successive terms. A vacancy on the Council shall be filled in the same manner in which the original appointment was made, and the term shall be for the balance of the unexpired term.

(d) Council Meetings and Officers. - The Secretary of State shall call the first meeting of the Council. At the first meeting and biennially thereafter, the Council shall elect from its membership a chair and a vice-chair to serve two-year terms. Meetings may be called by the chair, the vice-chair, or the Secretary of State. Meetings shall be held as often as necessary, but at least once a year.

(e) Council Compensation. - None of the members of the Council shall receive compensation for serving on the Council, but Council members shall receive per diem, subsistence, and travel expenses in accordance with G.S. 138-5 and G.S. 138-6, as applicable.

(f) Staff and Other Assistance. - As soon as practicable and as needed thereafter, the Council shall identify the information technology expertise it needs and report its needs to the Secretary of State. The Council shall also report any other expertise needed to fulfill its responsibilities. The Secretary of State shall provide professional and clerical staff and other services and supplies, including meeting space, as needed for the Council to carry out its duties in an effective manner. The Secretary of State may appoint additional committees to advise and assist the Council in its work.

The Council shall consult with the North Carolina Local Government Information Systems Association, and may consult with any other person the Council deems appropriate, to advise and assist the Council in its work.

(g) Uniformity of Standards. - To keep the standards and practices of registers of deeds in this State in harmony with the standards and practices of recording offices in other jurisdictions that enact substantially this Article and to keep the technology used by registers of deeds in this State compatible with technology used by recording offices in other jurisdictions that enact substantially this Article, the Secretary of State and the Council shall consider all of the following in carrying out their responsibilities under this Article, so far as is consistent with its purposes, policies, and provisions:

(1)   Standards and practices of other jurisdictions.

(2)   The most recent standards adopted by national standard-setting bodies, such as the Property Records Industry Association.

(3)   The views of interested persons and other governmental officials and entities.

(4)   The needs of counties of varying size, population, and resources.

(5)   Standards requiring adequate information security protection to ensure that electronic documents are accurate, authentic, adequately preserved, and resistant to tampering. (2005-391, s. 1.)

§ 47-16.6. Uniformity of application and construction.

In applying and construing this Article, consideration shall be given to promoting uniformity of interpretation of the Uniform Real Property Electronic Recording Act among states that enact it. (2005-391, s. 1.)

§ 47-16.7. Relation to Electronic Signatures in Global and National Commerce Act.

This Article modifies, limits, and supersedes the federal Electronic Signatures in Global and National Commerce Act (15 U.S.C. § 7001, et seq.) but does not modify, limit, or supersede section 101(c) of that act (15 U.S.C. § 7001(c)) or authorize electronic delivery of any of the notices described in section 103(b) of that act (15 U.S.C. § 7003(b)). (2005-391, s. 1.)

Article 2.

Registration.

§ 47-17. Probate and registration sufficient without livery of seizin, etc.

All deeds, contracts or leases, before registration, except those executed prior to January 1, 1870, shall be acknowledged by the grantor, lessor or the person executing the same, or their signature proven on oath by one or more witnesses in the manner prescribed by law, and all deeds executed and registered according to law shall be valid, and pass title and estates without livery of seizin, attornment or other ceremony. (29, Ch. II, c. 3; 1715, c. 7; 1756, c. 58, s. 3; 1838-9, c. 33; R.C., c. 37, s. 1; Code, s. 1245; 1885, c. 147, s. 3; 1905, c. 277; Rev., s. 979; C.S., s. 3308.)

§ 47-17.1. Documents registered or ordered to be registered in certain counties to designate draftsman; exceptions.

The register of deeds of any county in North Carolina shall not accept for registration, nor shall any judge order registration pursuant to G.S. 47-14, of any deeds or deeds of trust, executed after January 1, 1980, unless the first page of the deeds or deeds of trust bears an entry showing the name of either the person or law firm who drafted the instrument. (1953, c. 1160; 1955, cc. 54, 59, 87, 88, 264, 280, 410, 628, 655; 1957, cc. 431, 469, 932, 982, 1119, 1290; 1959, cc. 266, 312, 548, 589; 1961, cc. 789, 1167; 1965, cc. 160, 597, 830; 1967, cc. 42, 139; c. 639, s. 2; c. 658; 1969, c. 10; 1971, c. 46; 1973, cc. 65, 283, 342; 1979, c. 703; 1981, c. 362, ss. 1, 2; 2011-351, s. 3.)

§ 47-17.2. Assignments of mortgages, deeds of trust, or other agreements pledging real property as security.

It shall not be necessary in order to effect a valid assignment of a note and deed of trust, mortgage, or other agreement pledging real property or an interest in real property as security for an obligation, to record a written assignment in the office of the register of deeds in the county in which the real property is located. A transfer of the promissory note or other instrument secured by the deed of trust, mortgage, or other security interest that constitutes an effective assignment under the law of this State shall be an effective assignment of the deed of trust, mortgage, or other security instrument. The assignee of the note shall have the right to enforce all obligations contained in the promissory note or other agreement, and all the rights of the assignor in the deed of trust, mortgage, or other security instrument, including the right to substitute the trustee named in any deed of trust, and to exercise any power of sale contained in the instrument without restriction. The provisions of this section do not preclude the recordation of a written assignment of a deed of trust, mortgage, or other security instrument, with or without the promissory note or other instrument that it secures, provided that the assignment complies with applicable law. (1993, c. 288, s. 4.)

§ 47-18. Conveyances, contracts to convey, options and leases of land.

(a)   No (i) conveyance of land, or (ii) contract to convey, or (iii) option to convey, or (iv) lease of land for more than three years shall be valid to pass any property interest as against lien creditors or purchasers for a valuable consideration from the donor, bargainer or lesser but from the time of registration thereof in the county where the land lies, or if the land is located in more than one county, then in each county where any portion of the land lies to be effective as to the land in that county. Unless otherwise stated either on the registered instrument or on a separate registered instrument duly executed by the party whose priority interest is adversely affected, (i) instruments registered in the office of the register of deeds shall have priority based on the order of registration as determined by the time of registration, and (ii) if instruments are registered simultaneously, then the instruments shall be presumed to have priority as determined by:

(1)   The earliest document number set forth on the registered instrument.

(2)   The sequential book and page number set forth on the registered instrument if no document number is set forth on the registered instrument.

The presumption created by this subsection is rebuttable.

(b)   This section shall not apply to contracts, leases or deeds executed prior to March 1, 1885, until January 1, 1886; and no purchase from any such donor, bargainor or lessor shall avail or pass title as against any unregistered deed executed prior to December 1, 1885, when the person holding or claiming under such unregistered deed shall be in actual possession and enjoyment of such land, either in person or by his tenant, at the time of the execution of such second deed, or when the person claiming under or taking such second deed had at the time of taking or purchasing under such deed actual or constructive notice of such unregistered deed, or the claim of the person holding or claiming thereunder. (Code, s. 1245; 1885, c. 147, s. 1; Rev., s. 980; C.S., s. 3309; 1959, c. 90; 1975, c. 507; 2003-219, s. 2; 2005-212, s. 2.)

§ 47-18.1. Registration of certificate of corporate merger, consolidation, or conversion.

(a) If title to real property in this State is vested by operation of law in another entity upon the merger, consolidation, or conversion of an entity, such vesting is effective against lien creditors or purchasers for a valuable consideration from the entity formerly owning the property, only from the time of registration of a certificate thereof as provided in this section, in the county where the land lies, or if the land is located in more than one county, then in each county where any portion of the land lies to be effective as to the land in that county.

(b) The Secretary of State shall adopt uniform certificates of merger, consolidation, or conversion, to be furnished for registration, and shall adopt such fees as are necessary for the expense of such certification. If the entity involved is not a domestic entity, a similar certificate by any competent authority in the jurisdiction of incorporation or organization may be registered in accordance with this section.

(c) A certificate of the Secretary of State prepared in accordance with this section shall be registered by the register of deeds in the same manner as deeds, and for the same fees, but no formalities as to acknowledgment, probate, or approval by any other officer shall be required. The name of the entity formerly owning the property shall appear in the "Grantor" index, and the name of the entity owning the property by virtue of the merger, consolidation, or conversion shall appear in the "Grantee" index. (1967, c. 950, s. 3; 1991, c. 645, s. 2(b); 1999-369, s. 5.1.)

§ 47-18.2. Registration of Inheritance and Estate Tax Waiver.

An Inheritance and Estate Tax Waiver or other consent to transfer issued by the Secretary of Revenue bearing the signature of the Secretary of Revenue or the official facsimile signature of the Secretary of Revenue may be registered by the Register of Deeds in the county or counties where the real estate described in the Inheritance and Estate Tax Waiver or consent to transfer is located in the same manner as deeds, and for the same fees, but no formalities as to acknowledgement, probate, or approval by an officer shall be required. The name of the decedent owning the real property at death shall appear in the "Grantor" index. Nothing herein shall require a personal representative or other person interested in the decedent's estate to register Inheritance and Estate Tax Waivers or consents to transfer. (1987, c. 548, s. 3.)

§ 47-18.3. Execution of corporate instruments; authority and proof.

(a)   Notwithstanding anything to the contrary in the bylaws or articles of incorporation, when it appears on the face of an instrument registered in the office of the register of deeds that the instrument was signed in the ordinary course of business on behalf of a domestic or foreign corporation by its chairman, president, chief executive officer, a vice-president or an assistant vice-president, treasurer, or chief financial officer, such an instrument shall be as valid with respect to the rights of innocent third parties as if executed pursuant to authorization from the board of directors, unless the instrument reveals on its face a potential breach of fiduciary obligation. The subsection shall not apply to parties who had actual knowledge of lack of authority or of a breach of fiduciary obligation.

(b)   Any instrument registered in the office of the register of deeds, appearing on its face to be executed by a corporation, foreign or domestic, and bearing a seal which purports to be the corporate seal, setting forth the name of the corporation engraved, lithographed, printed, stamped, impressed upon, or otherwise affixed to the instrument, is prima facie evidence that the seal is the duly adopted corporate seal of the corporation, that it has been affixed as such by a person duly authorized so to do, that the instrument was duly executed and signed by persons who were officers or agents of the corporation acting by authority duly given by the board of directors, and that any such instrument is the act of the corporation, and shall be admissible in evidence without further proof of execution.

(c) Nothing in this section shall be deemed to exclude the power of any corporate representatives to bind the corporation pursuant to express, implied, inherent or apparent authority, ratification, estoppel, or otherwise.

(d) Nothing in this section shall relieve corporate officers from liability to the corporation or from any other liability that they may have incurred from any violation of their actual authority.

(e) Any corporation may convey an interest in real property which is transferable by instrument which is duly executed by either an officer, manager, or agent of said corporation and has attached thereto a signed and attested resolution of the board of directors of said corporation authorizing the said officer, manager, or agent to execute, sign, seal, and attest deeds, conveyances, or other instruments. This section shall be deemed to have been complied with if an attested resolution is recorded separately in the office of the register of deeds in the county where the land lies, which said resolution shall be applicable to all deeds executed subsequently thereto and pursuant to its authority. Notwithstanding the foregoing, this section shall not require a signed and attested resolution of the board of directors of the corporation to be attached to an instrument or separately recorded in the case of an instrument duly executed by the corporation's chairman, president, chief executive officer, a vice-president, assistant vice-president, treasurer, or chief financial officer. All deeds, conveyances, or other instruments which have been heretofore or shall be hereafter so executed shall, if otherwise sufficient, be valid and shall have the effect to pass the title to the real or personal property described therein. (1991, c. 647, s. 2; 1999-221, s. 4.)

§ 47-19. Unregistered deeds prior to January, 1920, registered on affidavit.

Any person holding any unregistered deed or claiming title thereunder, executed prior to the first day of January, 1920, may have the same registered without proof of the execution thereof by making an affidavit, before the officer having jurisdiction to take probate of such deed, that the grantor, bargainor or maker of such deed, and the witnesses thereto, are dead or cannot be found, that he cannot make proof of their handwriting, and that affiant believes such deed to be a bona fide deed and executed by the grantor therein named. Said affidavit shall be written upon or attached to such deed, and the same, together with such deed, shall be entitled to registration in the same manner and with the same effect as if proved in the manner prescribed by law for other deeds. (1885,

c. 147, s. 2; 1905, c. 277; Rev., s. 981; 1913, c. 116; 1915, cc. 13, 90; C.S., s. 3310; Ex. Sess. 1924, c. 56; 1951, c. 771.)

§ 47-20. Deeds of trust, mortgages, conditional sales contracts, assignments of leases and rents; effect of registration.

(a)   No deed of trust or mortgage of real or personal property, or of a leasehold interest or other chattel real, or conditional sales contract of personal property in which the title is retained by the vendor, shall be valid to pass any property as against lien creditors or purchasers for a valuable consideration from the grantor, mortgagor or conditional sales vendee, but from the time of registration thereof as provided in this Article; provided however that any transaction subject to the provisions of the Uniform Commercial Code (Chapter 25 of the General Statutes) is controlled by the provisions of that act and not by this section. Unless otherwise stated either on the registered instrument or on a separate registered instrument duly executed by the party whose priority interest is adversely affected, (i) instruments registered in the office of the register of deeds shall have priority based on the order of registration as determined by the time of registration, and (ii) if instruments are registered simultaneously, then the instruments shall be presumed to have priority as determined by:

(1)   The earliest document number set forth on the registered instrument.

(2)   The sequential book and page number set forth on the registered instrument if no document number is set forth on the registered instrument.

The presumption created by this subsection is rebuttable.

(b)   For purposes of this section and G.S. 47-20.1, the following definitions apply:

(1)   "Rents, issues, or profits" means all amounts payable by or on behalf of any lessee, tenant, or other person having a possessory interest in real estate on account of or pursuant to any written or oral lease or other instrument evidencing a possessory interest in real property or pursuant to any form of tenancy implied by law, and all amounts payable by or on behalf of any licensee or permittee or other person occupying or using real property under license or permission from the owner or person entitled to possession. The term shall not include farm products as defined in G.S. 25-9-102(34), timber, the proceeds

from the sale of farm products or timber, or the proceeds from the recovery or severance of any mineral deposits located on or under real property.

(2) "Assignment of leases, rents, issues, or profits" means every document assigning, transferring, pledging, mortgaging, or conveying an interest in leases, licenses to real property, and rents, issues, or profits arising from real property, whether set forth in a separate instrument or contained in a mortgage, deed of trust, conditional sales contract, or other deed or instrument of conveyance.

(3) "Collateral assignment" means any assignment of leases, rents, issues, or profits made and delivered in connection with the grant of any mortgage, or the execution of any conditional sales contract or deed of trust or in connection with any extension of credit made against the security of any interest in real property, where the assignor retains the right to collect or to apply such lease revenues, rents, issues, or profits after assignment and prior to default.

(c) The recording of a written document in accordance with G.S. 47-20.1 containing an assignment of leases, rents, issues, or profits arising from real property shall be valid and enforceable from the time of recording to pass the interest granted, pledged, assigned, or transferred as against the assignor, and shall be perfected from the time of recording against subsequent assignees, lien creditors, and purchasers for a valuable consideration from the assignor.

(d) Where an assignment of leases, rents, issues, or profits is a collateral assignment, after a default under the mortgage, deed of trust, conditional sales contract, or evidence of indebtedness which such assignment secures, the assignee shall thereafter be entitled, but not required, to collect and receive any accrued and unpaid or subsequently accruing lease revenues, rents, issues, or profits subject to the assignment, without need for the appointment of a receiver, any act to take possession of the property, or any further demand on the assignor. Unless otherwise agreed, after default the assignee shall be entitled to notify the tenant or other obligor to make payment to him and shall also be entitled to take control of any proceeds to which he may be entitled. The assignee must proceed in a commercially reasonable manner and may deduct his reasonable expenses of realization from the collections.

(e) This section shall not exclude other methods of creating, perfecting, collecting, sequestering, or enforcing a security interest in rents, issues, or profits provided by the law of this State. (1829, c. 20; R.C., c. 37, s. 22; Code, s. 1254; Rev., s. 982; 1909, c. 874, s. 1; C.S., s. 3311; 1953, c. 1190, s. 1; 1959,

c. 1026, s. 2; 1965, c. 700, s. 8; 1967, c. 562, s. 5; 1991, c. 234, s. 1; 2000-169, s. 35; 2003-219, s. 3; 2005-212, s. 3.)

§ 47-20.1. Place of registration; real property.

To be validly registered pursuant to G.S. 47-20, a deed of trust or mortgage of real property must be registered in the county where the land lies, or if the land is located in more than one county, then the deed of trust or mortgage must be registered in each county where any portion of the land lies in order to be effective as to the land in that county. (1953, c. 1190, s. 2.)

§ 47-20.2. Place of registration; personal property.

(a)   As used in this section:

(1)   "Mortgage" includes a deed of trust and a conditional sales contract; unless subject to the filing requirements of Article 9 of the Uniform Commercial Code (Chapter 25) and duly filed pursuant thereto;

(2)   "Mortgagor" includes a grantor in a deed of trust and a conditional sales vendee.

(b)   To be validly registered pursuant to G.S. 47-20, a mortgage of personal property must be registered as follows:

(1)   If the mortgagor is an individual:

a.   Who resides in this State, the mortgage must be registered in the county where the mortgagor resides when the mortgage is executed.

b.   Who resides outside this State, the mortgage must be registered in each county in this State where any of the tangible mortgaged property is located at the time the mortgage is executed, in order to be effective as to such property; and if any of the mortgaged property consists of a chose in action which arises out of the business transacted at a place of business operated by the mortgagor in this State, then the mortgage must be registered in the county where such place of business is located.

(2) If the mortgagor is a partnership, either limited or unlimited:

a. Which has a principal place of business in this State, the mortgage must be registered in the county where such place of business is located at the time the mortgage is executed.

b. Which does not have a principal place of business in this State but has any place of business in this State, the mortgage must be registered in every county in this State where any such place of business is located at the time the mortgage is executed. Where such mortgage is registered in one or more of such counties but is not registered in every county required under this subsection, it shall, nevertheless, be effective as to the property in every county in which it is registered.

c. Which has no place of business in the State, the mortgage must be registered in every county in this State where a partner resides at the time the mortgage is executed. Where such mortgage is registered in one or more of such counties but is not registered in every county required under this subsection, it shall, nevertheless, be effective as to the property in every county in which it is registered.

d. Which has no place of business in this State, and no partner residing in this State, the mortgage must be registered in each county in this State where any of the mortgaged property is located when the mortgage is executed, in order to be effective as to the property in such county.

(3) If the mortgagor is a domestic corporation:

a. Which has a registered office in this State, the mortgage must be registered in the county where such registered office is located when the mortgage is executed.

b. Which having been formed prior to July 1, 1957, has no such registered office but does have a principal office in this State as shown by its certificate of incorporation, or amendment thereto, or legislative charter, the mortgage must be registered in the county where the principal office is said to be located by such certificate of incorporation, or amendment thereto, or legislative charter when the mortgage is executed.

(4) If the mortgagor is a foreign corporation:

a. Which has a registered office in this State, the mortgage must be registered in the county where such registered office is located when the mortgage is executed.

b. Which, having been domesticated prior to July 1, 1957, has no such registered office in this State, but does have a principal office in this State, the mortgage must be registered in the county where the principal office is said to be located by the statement filed with the Secretary of State in its application for permission to do business in this State or other document filed with the Secretary of State showing the location of such principal office in this State when the mortgage is executed.

c. Which has not been domesticated in this State, the mortgage must be registered in the same county or counties as a mortgage executed by a nonresident individual.

(5) If the personal property concerned is a vehicle required to be registered under the motor vehicle laws of the State of North Carolina, then the provisions of this section shall not apply but the security interest arising from the deed of trust, mortgage, conditional sales contract, or lease intended as security of such vehicle may be perfected by recordation in accordance with the provisions of G.S. 20-58 through 20-58.10. (1953, c. 1190, s. 2; 1957, c. 979, ss. 1, 2; 1961, c. 835, s. 12; 1965, c. 700, s. 8.)

§ 47-20.3. Place of registration; instruments covering both personal property and real property.

To be validly registered pursuant to G.S. 47-20, a mortgage, deed of trust or conditional sales contract, or any combination of these, of both personal property and real property must be registered pursuant to the provisions of G.S. 47-20.1 for the real property covered by the instrument and pursuant to the provisions of G.S. 47-20.2 for the personal property covered by the instrument, and in each case the registration must be indexed in the records designated for the particular type of property involved. (1953, c. 1190, s. 2.)

§ 47-20.4. Place of registration; chattel real.

To be validly registered pursuant to G.S. 47-20, a deed of trust or mortgage of a leasehold interest or other chattel real must be registered in the county where the land involved lies, or if the land involved is located in more than one county, then the deed of trust or mortgage must be registered in each county where any portion of the land involved lies in order to be effective as to the land in that county. (1959, c. 1026, s. 1.)

§ 47-20.5. Real property; effectiveness of after-acquired property clause.

(a)   As used in this section, "after-acquired property clause" means any provision or provisions in an instrument which create a security interest in real property acquired by the grantor of the instrument subsequent to its execution.

(b)   As used in this section, "after-acquired property," and "property subsequently acquired" mean any real property which the grantor of a security instrument containing an after-acquired property clause acquires subsequent to the execution of such instrument, and in which the terms of the after-acquired property clause would create a security interest.

(c)   An after-acquired property clause is effective to pass after-acquired property as between the parties to the instrument containing such clause, but shall not be effective to pass title to after-acquired property as against lien creditors or purchasers for a valuable consideration from the grantor of the instrument unless and until such instrument has been registered or reregistered at or subsequent to the time such after-acquired property is acquired by such grantor and the deed to the grantor of the after-acquired property is registered.

(d)   In lieu of reregistering the instrument containing the after-acquired property clause as specified in subsection (c), such instrument may be made effective to pass title to after-acquired property as against lien creditors and purchasers for a valuable consideration from the grantor of the instrument by registering a notice of extension as specified in subsection (e) at or subsequent to the time of acquisition of the after-acquired property by the grantor.

(e)   The notice of extension shall

(1)   Show that effective registration of the after-acquired property clause is extended,

(2) Include the names of the parties to the instrument containing the after-acquired property clause,

(3) Refer to the book and page where the instrument containing the after-acquired property clause is registered, and

(4) Be signed by the grantee or the person secured by the instrument containing the after-acquired property clause or his successor in interest.

(f) The register of deeds shall index the notice of extension in the same manner as the instrument containing the after-acquired property clause.

(g) Except as provided in subsection (h) of this section, no instrument which has been heretofore executed or registered and which contains an after-acquired property clause shall be effective to pass title to after-acquired property as against lien creditors or purchasers for a valuable consideration from the grantor of such instrument unless and until such instrument or a notice of extension thereof has been registered or reregistered as herein provided.

(h) Notwithstanding the provisions of this section with respect to registration, reregistration and registration of notice of extension, an after-acquired property clause in an instrument which creates a security interest made by a public utility as defined in G.S. 62-3(23) or a natural gas company as defined in section 2(6) of the Natural Gas Act, 15 U.S.C.A. 717a(6), or by an electric or telephone membership corporation incorporated or domesticated in North Carolina shall be effective to pass after-acquired property as against lien creditors or purchasers for a valuable consideration from the grantor of the instrument from the time of original registration of such instrument. (1967, c. 861, s. 1; 1969, c. 813, ss. 1-3; 1997-386, s. 1.)

§ 47-20.6. Affidavit for permanent attachment of titled manufactured home to real property.

(a) If the owner of real property or the owner of the manufactured home who has entered into a lease with a primary term of at least 20 years for the real property on which the manufactured home is affixed has surrendered the title to a manufactured home that is placed on the real property and the title has been cancelled by the Division of Motor Vehicles under G.S. 20-109.2, the owner, or the secured party having the first security interest in the manufactured home at time of surrender, shall record the affidavit described in G.S. 20-109.2 with the office of the register of deeds of the county where the real property is located. Upon recordation, the affidavit shall be indexed on the grantor index in the name of the owner of the manufactured home and on the grantee index in the name of the secured party or lienholder, if any.

(b) After the affidavit is recorded, the manufactured home becomes an improvement to real property. Any lien on the manufactured home shall be perfected and given priority in the manner provided for a lien on real property.

(c) Following recordation of the affidavit, all existing liens on the real property are considered to include the manufactured home. Thereafter, no conveyance of any interest, lien, or encumbrance shall attach to the manufactured home, unless the interest, lien, or encumbrance is applicable to the real property on which the home is located and is recorded in the office of the register of deeds of the county where the real property is located in accordance with the applicable sections of this Chapter.

(d) The provisions of this section control over the provisions of G.S. 25-9-334 relating to the priority of a security interest in fixtures, as applied to manufactured homes. (2001-506, s. 3; 2003-400, s. 2.)

§ 47-20.7. Declaration of intent to affix manufactured home; transfer of real property with manufactured home attached.

(a) A person who owns real property on which a manufactured home has been or will be placed or the owner of a manufactured home who has entered into a lease with a primary term of at least 20 years for the real property on which the manufactured home has been or will be placed, as defined in G.S. 105-273(13), and either where the manufactured home has never been titled by the Division of Motor Vehicles or where the title to the manufactured home has been surrendered and cancelled by the Division prior to January 1, 2002, may record in the office of the register of deeds of the county where the real property is located a declaration of intent to affix the manufactured home to the property and may convey or encumber the real property, including the manufactured home, by a deed, deed of trust, or other instrument recorded in the office of the register of deeds.

(b) The declaration of intent, deed, deed of trust, or other instrument shall contain a description of the manufactured home, including the name of the manufacturer, the model name, if applicable, the serial number, and a statement of the owner's intention that the manufactured home be treated as property.

(c) On or after the filing of the instrument with the office of the register of deeds pursuant to subsection (a) of this section, the manufactured home placed, or to be placed, on the property becomes an improvement to real property. Any lien on the manufactured home shall be perfected and have priority in the manner provided for a lien on real property.

(d) The provisions of this section control over the provisions of G.S. 25-9-334 relating to the priority of a security interest in fixtures, as applied to manufactured homes. (2001-506, s. 3; 2003-400, s. 3.)

§ 47-21. Blank or master forms of mortgages, etc.; embodiment by reference in instruments later filed.

It shall be lawful for any person, firm or corporation to have a blank or master form of mortgage, deed of trust, or other instrument conveying an interest in, or creating a lien on, real and/or personal property, filed, indexed and recorded in the office of the register of deeds. When any such blank or master form is filed, the register of deeds shall record it and shall index it in the manner now provided by law for the indexing of instruments recorded in the office of the register of deeds, except that the name of the person, firm or corporation whose name appears on such blank or master form shall be inserted in the indices as grantor and also as grantee. The fee for filing, recording and indexing such blank or master form shall be that for recording instruments in general, as provided in G.S. 161-10(a)(1).

When any deed, mortgage, deed of trust, or other instrument conveying an interest in, or creating a lien on, real and/or personal property, refers to the provisions, terms, covenants, conditions, obligations, or powers set forth in any such blank or master form recorded as herein authorized, and states the office of recordation of such blank or master form, book and page where same is recorded such reference shall be equivalent to setting forth in extenso in such deed, mortgage, deed of trust, or other instrument conveying an interest in, or creating a lien on, real and/or personal property, the provisions, terms, covenants, conditions, obligations and powers set forth in such blank or master form. Provided this section shall not apply to Alleghany, Ashe, Avery, Beaufort, Bladen, Camden, Carteret, Chowan, Cleveland, Columbus, Dare, Gates, Granville, Guilford, Halifax, Iredell, Jackson, Martin, Moore, Perquimans, Sampson, Stanly, Swain, Transylvania, Vance, Washington and Watauga Counties. (1935, c. 153; 1971, c. 156; 2001-390, s. 4.)

§ 47-22. Counties may provide for photographic or photostatic registration.

The board of county commissioners of any county is hereby authorized and empowered to provide for photographic or photostatic recording of all instruments filed in the office of the register of deeds and in other offices of such county where said board may deem such recording feasible. The board of county commissioners may also provide for filing such copies of said instruments in loose-leaf binders. (1941, c. 286; 1971, c. 1185, s. 12.)

§ 47-23. Repealed by Session Laws 1953, c. 1190, s. 3.

§ 47-24. Conditional sales or leases of railroad property.

When any railroad equipment and rolling stock is sold, leased or loaned on the condition that the title to the same, notwithstanding the possession and use of the same by the vendee, lessee, or bailee, shall remain in the vendor, lessor or bailor until the terms of the contract, as to the payment of the installments, amounts or rentals payable, or the performance of other obligations thereunder, shall have been fully complied with, such contract shall be invalid as to any subsequent judgment creditor, or any subsequent purchaser for a valuable consideration without notice, unless -

(1)   The same is evidenced by writing duly acknowledged before some person authorized to take acknowledgments of deeds.

(2)   Such writing is registered as mortgages are registered, in the office of the register of deeds in at least one county in which such vendee, lessee or bailee does business.

(3)   Each locomotive or car so sold, leased or loaned has the name of the vendor, lessor, or bailor, or the assignee of such vendor, lessor or bailor plainly marked upon both sides thereof, followed by the word owner, lessor, bailor or assignee as the case may be.

This section shall not apply to or invalidate any contract made before the twelfth day of March, 1883. (1883, c. 416; Code, s. 2006; Rev., s. 984; 1907, c. 150, s. 1; C.S., s. 3313.)

§ 47-25. Marriage settlements.

All marriage settlements and other marriage contracts, whereby any money or other estate is secured to the wife or husband, shall be proved or acknowledged and registered in the same manner as deeds for lands, and shall be valid against creditors and purchasers for value only from registration. (1785, c. 238; R.C., c. 37, ss. 24, 25; 1871-2, c. 193, s. 12; Code, ss. 1269, 1270, 1281; 1885, c. 147; Rev., s. 985; C.S., s. 3314.)

§ 47-26. Deeds of gift.

All deeds of gift of any estate of any nature shall within two years after the making thereof be proved in due form and registered, or otherwise shall be void, and shall be good against creditors and purchasers for value only from the time of registration. (1789, c. 315, s. 2; R.C., c. 37, s. 18; Code, s. 1252; 1885, c. 147; Rev., s. 986; C.S., s. 3315.)

§ 47-27. Deeds of easements.

All persons, firms, or corporations now owning or hereafter acquiring any deed or agreement for rights-of-way and easements of any character whatsoever shall record such deeds and agreements in the office of the register of deeds of the county where the land affected is situated. Where such deeds and agreements may have been acquired, but no use has been made thereof, the person, firm, or corporation holding such instrument, or any assignment thereof, shall not be required to record them until within 90 days after the beginning of the use of the easements granted thereby. If after 90 days from the beginning of the easement granted by such deeds and agreements the person, firm, or corporation holding such deeds or agreements has not recorded the same in the office of the register of deeds of the county where the land affected is situated, then the grantor in the said deed or agreement may, after 10 days' notice in writing served and returned by the sheriff or other officer of the county upon the said person, firm, or corporation holding such lease or agreement, file a copy of the said lease or agreement for registration in the office of the register of deeds of the county where the original should have been recorded, but such copy of the lease or agreement shall have attached thereto the written notice above referred to, showing the service and return of the sheriff or other officer. The registration of such copy shall have the same force and effect as the original would have had if recorded: Provided, said copy shall be duly probated before being registered.

Nothing in this section shall require the registration of the following classes of instruments or conveyances, to wit:

(1)   It shall not apply to any deed or instrument executed prior to January 1, 1910.

(2)   It shall not apply to any deed or instrument so defectively executed or witnessed that it cannot by law be admitted to probate or registration, provided that such deed or instrument was executed prior to the ratification of this section.

(3)   It shall not apply to decrees of a competent court awarding condemnation or confirming reports of commissioners, when such decrees are on record in such courts.

(4)   It shall not apply to local telephone companies, operating exclusively within the State, or to agreements about alleyways.

The failure of electric companies or power companies operating exclusively within this State or electric membership corporations, organized pursuant to Chapter 291 of the Public Laws of 1935 [G.S. 117-6 through 117-27], to record any deeds or agreements for rights-of-way acquired subsequent to 1935, shall not constitute any violation of any criminal law of the State of North Carolina.

No deed, agreement for right-of-way, or easement of any character shall be valid as against any creditor or purchaser for a valuable consideration but from the registration thereof within the county where the land affected thereby lies.

From and after July 1, 1959, the provisions of this section shall apply to require the Department of Transportation to record as herein provided any deeds of easement, or any other agreements granting or conveying an interest in land which are executed on or after July 1, 1959, in the same manner and to the same extent that individuals, firms or corporations are required to record such easements. (1917, c. 148; 1919, c. 107; C.S., s. 3316; 1943, c. 750; 1959, c. 1244; 1973, c. 507, s. 5; 1977, c. 464, s. 34.)

§ 47-28. Powers of attorney.

(a) Recording required for powers of attorney affecting real property:

(1) Before any transfer of real property executed by an attorney-in-fact empowered by a power of attorney governed by Article 1, Article 2, or Article 2A of Chapter 32A of the General Statutes, the power of attorney or a certified copy of the power of attorney shall be registered in the office of the register of deeds of the county in which the principal is domiciled or where the real property lies. If the principal is not a resident of North Carolina, the power of attorney or a certified copy of the power of attorney may be recorded in any county in the State wherein the principal owns real property or has a significant business reason for registering in the county.

(2) If the real property lies in more than one county or in a county other than where the principal is domiciled, the power of attorney or a certified copy of the power of attorney shall be registered in the office of the register of deeds in one of the counties, and the instrument of transfer shall refer to the recordation specifically by reference to the book, page, and county where recorded.

(3) Any instrument subject to the provisions of G.S. 47-17.2, 47-18, or 47-20 and signed by an attorney-in-fact and recorded in a county other than the county where a power of attorney is recorded in this State shall include the recording information, including book, page, and county for the power of attorney.

(4) The failure to comply with the provisions of this subsection shall not affect the sufficiency, validity, or enforceability of the instrument but shall constitute an infraction.

(b) If the instrument of conveyance is recorded prior to the registration of the power of attorney or a certified copy of the power of attorney pursuant to subsection (a) of this section, the power of attorney or a certified copy of the power of attorney may be registered in the office of the register of deeds as provided in subsection (a) of this section thereafter provided that the attorney-in-fact was empowered at the time of the original conveyance. Notwithstanding the provisions of subsection (a) of this section, no conveyance shall be rendered invalid by the recordation of the power of attorney or a certified copy of the power of attorney after the instrument of conveyance, and the registration shall relate back to the date and time of registration of the instrument of conveyance.

(c) The provisions of subsection (a) of this section shall apply to all real property transfers utilizing an authority under any power of attorney whether made on or after April 1, 2013, and the provisions of subsection (b) of this section shall apply to all real property transfers utilizing an authority under any power of attorney whether made before, on, or after April 1, 2013. (Code, s. 1249; 1899, c. 235, s. 15; Rev., s. 987; C.S., s. 3317; 2013-204, s. 1.15.)

§ 47-29. Recording of bankruptcy records.

A copy of the petition with the schedules omitted beginning a proceeding under the United States Bankruptcy Act, or of the decree of adjudication in such proceeding, or of the order approving the bond of the trustee appointed in such proceeding, shall be recorded in the office of any register of deeds in North Carolina, and it shall be the duty of the register of deeds, on request, to record the same. The register of deeds shall be entitled to the same fees for such registration as he is now entitled to for recording conveyances. (1939, c. 254.)

§ 47-29.1. Recordation of environmental notices.

(a) A permit for the disposal of waste on land shall be recorded as provided in G.S. 130A-301.

(a1) The disposal of land clearing and inert debris in a landfill with a disposal area of 1/2 acre or less pursuant to G.S. 130A-301.1 shall be recorded as provided in G.S. 130A-301.1(c).

(a2) A Notice of Open Dump shall be recorded as provided in G.S. 130A-301(f).

(a3) Expired pursuant to Session Laws 1995, c. 502, s. 4, as amended by Session Laws 2001-357, s. 2, effective September 30, 2003.

(a4) The disposal of on-site demolition debris from the decommissioning of manufacturing buildings, including electric generating stations, shall be recorded as provided in G.S. 130A-301.3.

(b) An inactive hazardous substance or waste disposal site shall be recorded as provided in G.S. 130A-310.8.

(c) A Notice of Brownfields Property shall be recorded as provided in G.S. 130A-310.35.

(d) A Notice of Oil or Hazardous Substance Discharge Site shall be recorded as provided in G.S. 143-215.85A.

(e) A Notice of Dry-Cleaning Solvent Remediation shall be recorded as provided in G.S. 143-215.104M.

(f) A Notice of Contaminated Site shall be recorded as provided in G.S. 143B-279.10.

(g) A Notice of Residual Petroleum shall be recorded as provided in G.S. 143B-279.11.

(h) A land-use restriction that provides for the maintenance of stormwater best management practices or site consistency with approved stormwater project plans shall be recorded as provided in G.S. 143-214.7(c1). (1995, c. 502, s. 2.1; 1997-330, s. 1; 2001-357, s. 2; 2001-384, s. 10; 2006-246, s. 16(a); 2013-55, s. 3; 2013-410, s. 16.3.)

§ 47-30. Plats and subdivisions; mapping requirements.

(a) Size Requirements. - All land plats presented to the register of deeds for recording in the registry of a county in North Carolina after September 30, 1991, having an outside marginal size of either 18 inches by 24 inches, 21 inches by 30 inches, or 24 inches by 36 inches, and having a minimum one and one-half inch border on the left side and a minimum one-half inch border on the other sides shall be deemed to meet the size requirements for recording under this section. Where size of land areas, or suitable scale to assure legibility require, plats may be placed on two or more sheets with appropriate match lines. Counties may specify either:

(1)   Only 18 inches by 24 inches;

(2)   A combination of 18 inches by 24 inches and 21 inches by 30 inches;

(3)   A combination of 18 inches by 24 inches and 24 inches by 36 inches; or

(4)   A combination of all three sizes.

Provided, that all registers of deeds where specific sizes other than the combination of all three sizes have been specified, shall be required to submit said size specifications to the North Carolina Association of Registers of Deeds for inclusion on a master list of all such counties. The list shall be available in each register of deeds office by October 1, 1991. For purposes of this section, the terms "plat" and "map" are synonymous.

(b)   Plats to Be Reproducible. - Each plat presented for recording shall be a reproducible plat, either original ink on polyester film (mylar), or a reproduced drawing, transparent and archival (as defined by the American National Standards Institute), and submitted in this form. The recorded plat must be such that the public may obtain legible copies. A direct or photographic copy of each recorded plat shall be placed in the plat book or plat file maintained for that purpose and properly indexed for use. In those counties in which the register has made a security copy of the plat from which legible copies can be made, the original may be returned to the person indicated on the plat.

(c)   Information Contained in Title of Plat. - The title of each plat shall contain the following information: property designation, name of owner (the name of owner shall be shown for indexing purposes only and is not to be construed as title certification), location to include township, county and state, the date or dates the survey was made; scale or scale ratio in words or figures and bar graph; name and address of surveyor or firm preparing the plat.

(d) Certificate; Form. - There shall appear on each plat a certificate by the person under whose supervision the survey or plat was made, stating the origin of the information shown on the plat, including recorded deed and plat references shown thereon. The ratio of precision before any adjustments must be shown. Any lines on the plat that were not actually surveyed must be clearly indicated and a statement included revealing the source of information. Where a plat consists of more than one sheet, only one sheet must contain the certification and all other sheets must be signed and sealed.

The certificate required above shall include the source of information for the survey and data indicating the ratio of precision of the survey before adjustments and shall be in substantially the following form:

"I, _____, certify that this plat was drawn under my supervision from an actual survey made under my supervision (deed description recorded in Book ____, page ____, etc.) (other); that the boundaries not surveyed are clearly indicated as drawn from information found in Book ____, page ____; that the ratio of precision as calculated is 1: ____; that this plat was prepared in accordance with G.S. 47-30 as amended. Witness my original signature, registration number and seal this ____ day of ____, A.D., ____.

Seal or Stamp

_____

                                          Surveyor

                                          Registration Number"

Nothing in this requirement shall prevent the recording of a map that was prepared in accordance with a previous version of G.S. 47-30 as amended, properly signed, and notarized under the statutes applicable at the time of the signing of the map. However, it shall be the responsibility of the person presenting the map to prove that the map was so prepared.

(e) Method of Computation. - An accurate method of computation shall be used to determine the acreage and ratio of precision shown on the plat. Area by estimation is not acceptable nor is area by planimeter, area by scale, or area copied from another source, except in the case of tracts containing inaccessible sections or areas. In such case the surveyor may make use of aerial photographs or other appropriate aids to determine the acreage of any inaccessible areas when the areas are bounded by natural and visible monuments. In such case the methods used must be stated on the plat and all accessible areas of the tract shall remain subject to all applicable standards of this section.

(f) Plat to Contain Specific Information. - Every plat shall contain the following specific information:

(1) An accurately positioned north arrow coordinated with any bearings shown on the plat. Indication shall be made as to whether the north index is true, magnetic, North Carolina grid ("NAD 83" or "NAD 27"), or is referenced to old deed or plat bearings. If the north index is magnetic or referenced to old deed or plat bearings, the date and the source (if known) the index was originally determined shall be clearly indicated.

(2) The azimuth or course and distance of every property line surveyed shall be shown. Distances shall be in feet or meters and decimals thereof. The number of decimal places shall be appropriate to the class of survey required.

(3) All plat distances shall be by horizontal or grid measurements. All lines shown on the plat shall be correctly plotted to the scale shown. Enlargement of portions of a plat are acceptable in the interest of clarity, where shown as inserts. Where the North Carolina grid system is used the grid factor shall be shown on the face of the plat. If grid distances are used, it must be shown on the plat.

(4) Where a boundary is formed by a curved line, the following data must be given: actual survey data from the point of curvature to the point of tangency shall be shown as standard curve data, or as a traverse of bearings and distances around the curve. If standard curve data is used the bearing and distance of the long chord (from point of curvature to point of tangency) must be shown on the plat.

(5) Where a subdivision of land is set out on the plat, all streets and lots shall be accurately plotted with dimension lines indicating widths and all other information pertinent to reestablishing all lines in the field. This shall include

bearings and distances sufficient to form a continuous closure of the entire perimeter.

(6)   Where control corners have been established in compliance with G.S. 39-32.1, 39-32.2, 39-32.3, and 39-32.4, as amended, the location and pertinent information as required in the reference statute shall be plotted on the plat. All other corners which are marked by monument or natural object shall be so identified on all plats, and where practical all corners of adjacent owners along the boundary lines of the subject tract which are marked by monument or natural object shall be shown.

(7)   The names of adjacent landowners, or lot, block, parcel, subdivision designations or other legal reference where applicable, shall be shown where they could be determined by the surveyor.

(8)   All visible and apparent rights-of-way, watercourses, utilities, roadways, and other such improvements shall be accurately located where crossing or forming any boundary line of the property shown.

(9)   Where the plat is the result of a survey, one or more corners shall, by a system of azimuths or courses and distances, be accurately tied to and coordinated with a horizontal control monument of some United States or State Agency survey system, such as the North Carolina Geodetic Survey where the monument is within 2,000 feet of the subject property. Where the North Carolina Grid System coordinates of the monument are on file in the North Carolina Geodetic Survey Section in the Division of Emergency Management of the Department of Public Safety, the coordinates of both the referenced corner and the monuments used shall be shown in X (easting) and Y (northing) coordinates on the plat. The coordinates shall be identified as based on "NAD 83," indicating North American Datum of 1983, or as "NAD 27," indicating North American Datum of 1927. The tie lines to the monuments shall also be sufficient to establish true north or grid north bearings for the plat if the monuments exist in pairs. Within a previously recorded subdivision that has been tied to grid control, control monuments within the subdivision may be used in lieu of additional ties to grid control. Within a previously recorded subdivision that has not been tied to grid control, if horizontal control monuments are available within 2,000 feet, the above requirements shall be met; but in the interest of bearing consistency with previously recorded plats, existing bearing control should be used where practical. In the absence of grid control, other appropriate natural monuments or landmarks shall be used. In all cases, the tie lines shall be sufficient to

accurately reproduce the subject lands from the control or reference points used.

(10)   A vicinity map (location map) shall appear on the plat.

(11)   Notwithstanding any other provision contained in this section, it is the duty of the surveyor, by a certificate on the face of the plat, to certify to one of the following:

a.   That the survey creates a subdivision of land within the area of a county or municipality that has an ordinance that regulates parcels of land;

b.   That the survey is located in a portion of a county or municipality that is unregulated as to an ordinance that regulates parcels of land;

c.   Any one of the following:

1.   That the survey is of an existing parcel or parcels of land and does not create a new street or change an existing street;

2.   That the survey is of an existing building or other structure, or natural feature, such as a watercourse; or

3.   That the survey is a control survey.

d.   That the survey is of another category, such as the recombination of existing parcels, a court-ordered survey, or other exception to the definition of subdivision;

e.   That the information available to the surveyor is such that the surveyor is unable to make a determination to the best of the surveyor's professional ability as to provisions contained in (a) through (d) above.

However, if the plat contains the certificate of a surveyor as stated in a., d., or e. above, then the plat shall have, in addition to said surveyor's certificate, a certification of approval, or no approval required, as may be required by local ordinance from the appropriate government authority before the plat is presented for recordation. If the plat contains the certificate of a surveyor as stated in b. or c. above, nothing shall prevent the recordation of the plat if all other provisions have been met.

(g) Recording of Plat. - In certifying a plat for recording pursuant to G.S. 47-30.2, the Review Officer shall not be responsible for reviewing or certifying as to any of the following requirements of this section:

(1) Subsection (b) of this section as to archival.

(2) Repealed by Session Laws 1997-309, s. 2.

(3) Subsection (e) of this section.

(4) Subdivisions (1) through (10) of subsection (f) of this section.

A plat, when certified pursuant to G.S. 47-30.2 and presented for recording, shall be recorded in the plat book or plat file and when so recorded shall be duly indexed. Reference in any instrument hereafter executed to the record of any plat herein authorized shall have the same effect as if the description of the lands as indicated on the record of the plat were set out in the instrument.

(h) Nothing in this section shall be deemed to prevent the filing of any plat prepared by a registered land surveyor but not recorded prior to the death of the registered land surveyor. However, it is the responsibility of the person presenting the map to the Review Officer pursuant to G.S. 47-30.2 to prove that the plat was so prepared. For preservation these plats may be filed without signature, notary acknowledgement or probate, in a special plat file.

(i) Nothing in this section shall be deemed to invalidate any instrument or the title thereby conveyed making reference to any recorded plat.

(j) The provisions of this section shall not apply to boundary plats of areas annexed by municipalities nor to plats of municipal boundaries, whether or not required by law to be recorded.

(k) The provisions of this section shall apply to all counties in North Carolina.

(l) This section does not apply to the registration of highway right-of-way plans provided for in G.S. 136-19.4 or G.S. 136-89.184, nor to the registration of roadway corridor official maps provided for in Article 2E of Chapter 136 of the General Statutes.

(m)   Maps attached to deeds or other instruments and submitted for recording in that form must be no larger than 8 1/2 inches by 14 inches and comply with either this subsection or subsection (n) of this section. Such a map shall either (i) have the original signature of a registered land surveyor and the surveyor's seal as approved by the State Board of Registration for Professional Engineers and Land Surveyors, or (ii) be a copy of a map, already on file in the public records, that is certified by the custodian of the public record to be a true and accurate copy of a map bearing an original personal signature and original seal. The presence of the original personal signature and seal shall constitute a certification that the map conforms to the standards of practice for land surveying in North Carolina, as defined in the rules of the North Carolina State Board of Registration for Professional Engineers and Land Surveyors.

(n)   A map that does not meet the requirements of subsection (m) of this section may be attached to a deed or other instrument submitted for recording in that form for illustrative purposes only if it meets both of the following requirements:

(1)   It is no larger than 8 1/2 inches by 14 inches.

(2)   It is conspicuously labelled, "THIS MAP IS NOT A CERTIFIED SURVEY AND HAS NOT BEEN REVIEWED BY A LOCAL GOVERNMENT AGENCY FOR COMPLIANCE WITH ANY APPLICABLE LAND DEVELOPMENT REGULATIONS."

(o)   The requirements of this section regarding plat size, reproducible form, and evidence of required certifications shall be met with respect to a plat that is an "electronic document," as that term is defined in G.S. 47-16.2(3), if all of the following conditions have been met:

(1)   The register of deeds has authorized the submitter to electronically register the electronic document.

(2)   The plat is submitted by a United States federal or a state governmental unit or instrumentality or a trusted submitter. For purposes of this subsection, "a trusted submitter" means a person or entity that has entered into a memorandum of understanding regarding electronic recording with the register of deeds in the county in which the electronic document is to be submitted.

(3)   Evidence of required certifications appear on the digitized image of the document as it will appear on the public record.

(4) With respect to a plat submitted by a trusted submitter, the digitized image of the document as it will appear on the public record contains the submitter's name in the following completed statement on the first page of the document image: "Submitted electronically by _____ (submitter's name) in compliance with North Carolina statutes governing recordable documents and the terms of the submitter agreement with the _____ (insert county name) County Register of Deeds.

(5) Except as otherwise provided in this subsection, the digitized image of the plat conforms to all other applicable laws and rules that prescribe recordation. (1911, c. 55, s. 2; C.S., s. 3318; 1923, c. 105; 1935, c. 219; 1941, c. 249; 1953, c. 47, s. 1; 1959, c. 1235, ss. 1, 3A, 3.1; 1961, cc. 7, 111, 164, 199, 252, 660, 687, 932, 1122; 1963, c. 71, ss. 1, 2; cc. 180, 236; c. 361, s. 1; c. 403; 1965, c. 139, s. 1; 1967, c. 228, s. 2; c. 394; 1971, c. 658; 1973, cc. 76, 848, 1171; c. 1262, s. 86; 1975, c. 192; c. 200, s. 1; 1977, c. 50, s. 1; c. 221, s. 1; c. 305, s. 2; c. 771, s. 4; 1979, c. 330, s. 1; 1981, c. 138, s. 1; c. 140, s. 1; c. 479; 1983, c. 473; 1987, c. 747, s. 20; 1989, c. 727, s. 218(6); 1991, c. 268, s. 3; 1993, c. 119, ss. 1, 2; 1997-309, s. 2; 1997-443, s. 11A.119(a); 1998-228, ss. 11, 12; 1999-456, s. 59; 2000-140, s. 93.1(b); 2001-424, s. 12.2(b); 2008-225, s. 9; 2010-180, s. 1; 2011-246, s. 7; 2012-142, s. 12.4(f).)

§ 47-30.1. Plats and subdivisions; alternative requirements.

In a county to which the provisions of G.S. 47-30 do not apply, any person, firm or corporation owning land may have a plat thereof recorded in the office of the register of deeds if such land or any part thereof is situated in the county, upon proof upon oath by the surveyor making such plat or under whose supervision such plat was made that the same is in all respects correct according to the best of his knowledge and belief and was prepared from an actual survey by him made, or made under his supervision, giving the date of such survey, or if the surveyor making such plat is dead, or where land has been sold and conveyed according to an unrecorded plat, upon the oath of a duly licensed surveyor that said map is in all respects correct according to the best of his knowledge and belief and that the same was actually and fully checked and verified by him, giving the date on which the same was verified and checked. (1961, c. 534, s. 1; c. 985.)

§ 47-30.2. Review Officer.

(a) The board of commissioners of each county shall, by resolution, designate by name one or more persons experienced in mapping or land records management as a Review Officer to review each map and plat required to be submitted for review before the map or plat is presented to the register of deeds for recording. Each person designated a Review Officer shall, if reasonably feasible, be certified as a property mapper pursuant to G.S. 147-54.4. A resolution designating a Review Officer shall be recorded in the county registry and indexed on the grantor index in the name of the Review Officer.

(b) The Review Officer shall review expeditiously each map or plat required to be submitted to the Officer before the map or plat is presented to the register of deeds for recording. The Review Officer shall certify the map or plat if it complies with all statutory requirements for recording.

Except as provided in subsection (c) of this section, the register of deeds shall not accept for recording any map or plat required to be submitted to the Review Officer unless the map or plat has the certification of the Review Officer affixed to it. A certification shall be in substantially the following form:

State of North Carolina

County of

I, _____, Review Officer of _____ County, certify that the map or plat to which this certification is affixed meets all statutory requirements for recording.

_____

Review Officer

Date_____

(c) A map or plat must be presented to the Review Officer unless one or more of the following conditions are applicable:

(1) The certificate required by G.S. 47-30(f)(11) shows that the map or plat is a survey within the meaning of G.S. 47-30(f)(11)b. or c.

(2) The map or plat is exempt from the requirements of G.S. 47-30 pursuant to G.S. 47-30(j) or (l).

(3) The map is an attachment that is being recorded pursuant to G.S. 47-30(n). (1997-309, s. 3; 1998-228, s. 13.)

§ 47-31. Certified copies may be registered; used as evidence.

(a) A duly certified copy of any deed or writing required or allowed to be registered may be registered in any county. The register of deeds may rely on the record keeper's certification on a presented document that the document is a certified copy and is not required to further verify the proof or acknowledgement otherwise required by G.S. 47-14 or to determine whether the document has been changed or altered after it was certified. The registered or duly certified copy of any deed or writing that has been registered in the county where the land is situate may be given in evidence in any court of the State.

(b) Instruments registered pursuant to this section prior to July 6, 1993 that were not further certified pursuant to G.S. 47-14 at the time of registration are hereby validated. (1858-9, c. 18, s. 2; Code, s. 1253; Rev., s. 988; C. S., s. 3319; 1993, c. 288, ss. 2, 3; 2008-194, s. 7(b).)

§ 47-32. Photographic copies of plats, etc.

After January 1, 1960, in all special proceedings in which a map shall be filed as a part of the papers, such map shall meet the specifications required for recording of maps in the office of the register of deeds, and the clerk of superior court may certify a copy thereof to the register of deeds of the county in which said lands lie for recording in the Map Book provided for that purpose; and the clerk of superior court may have a photographic copy of said map made on a sheet of the same size as the leaves in the book in which the special proceeding is recorded, and when made, may place said photographic copy in said book at the end of the report of the commissioner or other document referring to said map.

The provisions of this section shall not apply to the following counties: Alexander, Alleghany, Ashe, Beaufort, Camden, Clay, Franklin, Granville, Greene, Harnett, Hertford, Hoke, Hyde, Jackson, Jones, Lee, Lincoln, Madison, Martin, Northampton, Pamlico, Pasquotank, Pender, Person, Pitt, Richmond, Robeson, Rockingham, Sampson, Scotland, Surry, Swain, Vance, Warren, Washington, Watauga and Yadkin. (1931, c. 171; 1959, c. 1235, ss. 2, 3A, 3.1; 1961, cc. 7, 111, 164, 252, 697, 932, 1122; 1963, c. 71, s. 3; c. 236; c. 361, s. 2; 1965, c. 139, s. 2; 1971, c. 1185, s. 13; 1977, c. 111; c. 221, s. 2; 1981, c. 138, s. 1; c. 140, s. 1; 1985, c. 32, s. 1.)

§ 47-32.1. Photostatic copies of plats, etc.; alternative provisions.

In a county to which the provisions of G.S. 47-32 do not apply, the following alternative provisions shall govern photostatic copies of plats filed in special proceedings:

In all special proceedings in which a plat, map or blueprint shall be filed as a part of the papers, the clerk of the superior court may have a photostatic copy of said plat, map or blueprint made on a sheet of the same size as the leaves in the book in which the special proceeding is recorded, and when made, shall place said photostatic copy in said book at the end of the report of the commissioners or other document referring to said plat, map or blueprint. (1961, c. 535, s. 1; 1971, c. 1185, s. 14.)

§ 47-32.2. Violation of § 47-30 or § 47-32 a misdemeanor.

Any person, firm or corporation willfully violating the provisions of G.S. 47-30 or G.S. 47-32 shall be guilty of a Class 3 misdemeanor and upon conviction shall be subject only to a fine of not less than fifty dollars ($50.00) nor more than five hundred dollars ($500.00).

The provisions of this section shall not apply to the following counties: Alexander, Alleghany, Ashe, Beaufort, Camden, Clay, Franklin, Granville, Greene, Harnett, Hertford, Hoke, Hyde, Jackson, Jones, Lee, Lincoln, Madison, Martin, Northampton, Pamlico, Pasquotank, Pender, Person, Pitt, Richmond, Robeson, Rockingham, Sampson, Scotland, Surry, Swain, Vance, Warren,

Washington, Watauga and Yadkin. (1959, c. 1235, ss. 3, 3A, 3.1; 1961, cc. 7, 111, 164, 252; c. 535, s. 1; cc. 687, 932, 1122; 1963, c. 236; c. 361, s. 3; 1965, c. 139, s. 3; 1977, c. 110; c. 221, s. 3; 1981, c. 138, s. 1; c. 140, s. 1; 1985, c. 32, s. 2; 1993, c. 539, s. 408; 1994, Ex. Sess., c. 24, s. 14(c).)

§ 47-33. Certified copies of deeds made by alien property custodian may be registered.

Any copy of a deed made, or purporting to be made, by the United States alien property custodian duly certified pursuant to title twenty-eight, section six hundred sixty-one of United States Code by the department of justice of the United States, with its official seal impressed thereon, when the said certified copy reveals the fact that the execution of the original was acknowledged by the alien property custodian before a notary public of the District of Columbia, and that the official seal of the alien property custodian by recital was affixed or impressed on the original, and further reveals it to have been approved, as to form, by general counsel, and the copy also shows that the original was signed and approved by the acting chief, division of trusts, and was witnessed by two witnesses, shall, when presented to the register of deeds of any county wherein the land described therein purports to be situate, be recorded by the register of deeds of such county without other or further proof of the execution and/or delivery of the original thereof, and the same when so recorded shall be indexed and cross-indexed by the register of deeds as are deeds made by individuals upon the payment of the usual and lawful fees for the registration thereof. (1937, c. 5, s. 1.)

§ 47-34. Certified copies of deeds made by alien property custodian admissible in evidence.

The record of all such recorded copies of such instruments authorized in G.S. 47-33 shall be received in evidence in all the courts of this State and the courts of the United States in the trial of any cause pending therein, the same as though and with like effect as if the original thereof had been probated and recorded as required by the law of North Carolina, and the record in the office of register of deeds of such recorded copy of such an instrument shall be presumptive evidence that the original of said copy was executed and delivered to the vendee, or vendees therein named, and that the original thereof has been lost or unintentionally destroyed without registration, and in the absence of legal proof to the contrary said so registered copy shall be conclusive evidence that the United States alien property custodian conveyed the lands and premises described in said registered copy to the vendees therein named, as said copy reveals, and title to such land shall pass by such recorded instrument. (1937, c. 5, s. 2.)

§ 47-35. Register to fill in deeds on blank forms with lines.

Registers of deeds shall, in registering deeds and other instruments, where printed skeletons or forms are used by the register, fill all spaces left blank in such skeletons or forms by drawing or stamping a line or lines in ink through such blank spaces. (1911, c. 6, s. 1; C.S., s. 3320.)

§ 47-36. Errors in registration corrected on petition to clerk.

Every person who discovers that there is an error in the registration of his grant, conveyance, bill of sale or other instrument of writing, may prefer a petition to the clerk of the superior court of the county in which said writing is registered, in the same manner as is directed for petitioners to correct errors in grants or patents, and if on hearing the same before said clerk it appears that errors have been committed, the clerk shall order the register of the county to correct such errors and make the record conformable to the original. The petitioner must notify his grantor and every person claiming title to or having lands adjoining those mentioned in the petition, 30 days previous to preferring the same. Any person dissatisfied with the judgment may appeal to the superior court as in other cases. (1790, c. 326, ss. 2, 3, 4; R.C., c. 37, s. 28; Code, s. 1266; Rev., s. 1008; C.S., s. 3321.)

§ 47-36.1. Correction of errors in recorded instruments.

(a) Notwithstanding G.S. 47-14 and G.S. 47-17, notice of typographical or other minor error in a deed or other instrument recorded with the register of deeds may be given by recording an affidavit. If an affidavit is conspicuously identified as a corrective or scrivener's affidavit in its title, the register of deeds shall index the name of the affiant, the names of the original parties in the instrument, the recording information of the instrument being corrected, and the original parties as they are named in the affidavit. A copy of the previously recorded instrument to which the affidavit applies may be attached to the affidavit and need not be a certified copy. To the extent the correction is inconsistent with the originally recorded instrument, and only to that extent, notice of the corrective information as provided by the affiant in the corrective affidavit is deemed to have been given as of the time the corrective affidavit is registered. Nothing in this section invalidates or otherwise alters the legal effect of any instrument of correction authorized by statute in effect on the date the instrument was registered.

(b) Nothing in this section requires that an affidavit be attached to an original or certified copy of a previously recorded instrument that is unchanged but rerecorded. Nothing in this section requires that an affidavit be attached to a previously recorded instrument with a copy of a previously recorded instrument that includes identified corrections or an original execution by a party or parties of the corrected instrument after the original recording, with proof or acknowledgment of their execution of the correction of the instrument.

(c) If the corrective affidavit is solely made by a notary public in order to correct a notarial certificate made by that notary public that was attached to an instrument already recorded with the register of deeds, the notary public shall complete the corrective affidavit identifying the correction and may attach a new acknowledgment completed as of the date the original acknowledgment took place, which shall be deemed attached to the original recording, and the instrument's priority shall remain the date and time originally recorded. The provisions of this subsection shall apply to corrective affidavits filed prior to, on, or after April 1, 2013. (1985 (Reg. Sess., 1986), c. 842, s. 1; 1987, c. 360, s. 1; 2008-194, s. 7(c); 2013-204, s. 1.16.)

Article 3.

Forms of Acknowledgment, Probate and Order of Registration.

§ 47-37: Repealed by Session Laws 2005-123, s. 3, effective October 1, 2005.

§ 47-37.1. Other forms of proof.

(a) The proof and acknowledgment forms set forth in this Article are not exclusive. Without regard to whether an instrument presented for registration was signed by an individual acting in his or her own right or by an individual acting in a representative or fiduciary capacity, a notarial certificate that complies with the provisions of Part 6 of Article 1 of Chapter 10B shall be deemed a sufficient form of probate or acknowledgment for purposes of this Chapter. Use of a notarial certificate that satisfies the requirements of Part 6 of Article 1 of Chapter 10B shall not be grounds for a register of deeds to refuse to accept a record for registration.

(b) When an instrument presented for registration purports to be signed by an individual in a representative or fiduciary capacity, the acknowledgment or proof of that individual's signature may:

(1) State that the individual signed the instrument in a representative or fiduciary capacity.

(2) State that the individual who signed the instrument in a representative or fiduciary capacity had due authority to do so.

(3) Identify the represented person or the fiduciary capacity.

(c) This section relates only to the form of proof or acknowledgment. The capacity and authority of the individual who signs an instrument presented for registration are governed by other provisions of law.

(d) This section applies to proofs and acknowledgments made before, on, or after December 1, 2005. (2005-391, s. 9; 2006-59, s. 27.)

§ 47-38. Acknowledgment by grantor.

When properly completed, a certificate in substantially the following form may be used and shall be sufficient under the law of this State to satisfy the requirements for a notarial certificate for one or more individuals, acting in his, her, or their own right or, whether or not so stated in the notarial certificate, in a representative or fiduciary capacity, including one or more individuals acting on behalf of an unincorporated association, as an officer or director of a corporation, as a partner of a general or limited partnership, as a manager or member of a limited liability company, as the trustee of a trust, as the personal representative of a decedent's estate, as an agent or attorney in fact for another, as the guardian of a minor or an incompetent, or as a public official. The authorization of the form in this section does not preclude the use of other forms. This section applies to notarial certificates made before, on, and after December 1, 2005.

North Carolina, _____ County.

I (here give the name of the official and his official title), do hereby certify that (here give the name of the individual whose acknowledgment is being taken) personally appeared before me this day and acknowledged the due execution of the foregoing instrument. Witness my hand and (where an official seal is required by law) official seal this the _____ day of _____ (year).

(Official seal.)

_____

(Signature of officer.)

(Title)

(Rev., s. 1002; C.S., s. 3323; 1945, c. 73, s. 13; 1977, c. 375, s. 12; 2006-59, s. 28.)

§ 47-39. Repealed by Session Laws 1977, c. 375, s. 16, effective January 1, 1978.

§ 47-40. Husband's acknowledgment and wife's acknowledgment before the same officer.

Where the instrument is acknowledged by both husband and wife or by other grantor before the same officer the form of acknowledgment shall be in substance as follows:

I (here give name of official and his official title), do hereby certify that (here give names of the grantors whose acknowledgment is being taken) personally appeared before me this day and acknowledged the due execution of the foregoing (or annexed) instrument.

(1899, c. 235, s. 8; 1901, c. 299; Rev., s. 1004; C.S., s. 3325; 1945, c. 73, s. 15.)

§ 47-41: Repealed by Session Laws 1991, c. 647, s. 3.

§ 47-41.01. Corporate conveyances.

(a)   The following forms of probate for deeds and other conveyances executed by a corporation shall be deemed sufficient, but shall not exclude other forms of probate which would be deemed sufficient in law.

(b)   If the deed or other instrument is executed by an official of the corporation, signing the name of the corporation by him in his official capacity, or any other agent authorized by resolution pursuant to G.S. 47-18.3(e), is sealed with its common or corporate seal, and is attested by another person who is an attesting official of the corporation, the following form of acknowledgment is sufficient:

_____

(State and county, or other

description of place where

acknowledgment is taken)

I,_____ ,

_____ ,

(Name of officer taking acknowledgment) (Official title of officer taking acknowledgment) certify that _____ personally came before

(Name of attesting official)

me this day and acknowledged that he (or she) is _____

(Title of attesting official)

of_____, a corporation, and that by authority duly

(Name of corporation)

given and as the act of the corporation, the foregoing instrument was signed in its name by its_____,

(Title of official)

sealed with its corporate seal, and attested by himself (or herself) as its

_____

(Title of attesting official)

Witness my hand and official seal, this the _____ day of

_____,

(Month)

_____

(Year)

_____

(Signature of officer taking acknowledgment)

(Official seal, if officer taking acknowledgment has one)

My commission expires _____

(Date of expiration of commission as notary public)

(c) If the deed or other instrument is executed by an official of the corporation, signing the name of the corporation in his official capacity, or any other agent authorized by resolution pursuant to G.S. 47-18.3(e) the following form of acknowledgment is sufficient:

(State and county, or other description of place where acknowledgment is taken)

I,_____ ,
_____,

(Name of officer taking acknowledgment) (Official title of officer taking acknowledgment)

certify that _____ personally came before

(Name of official)

me this day and acknowledged that he (or she) is _____

(Title of official)

of_____, a corporation, and that he/she, as

_____, being authorized to do so, executed the

(Title of official)

foregoing on behalf of the corporation.

Witness my hand and official seal, this the _____ day of

_____,

(Month)

_____

(Year)

_____

(Signature of officer taking acknowledgment)

(Official seal, if officer taking

acknowledgment has one)

My commission expires _____

(Date of expiration of commission as

notary public)

(d) For purposes of this section:

(1) The words "a corporation" following the blank for the name of the corporation may be omitted when the name of the corporation ends with the word "Corporation" or "Incorporated."

(2) The words "My commission expires" and the date of expiration of the notary public's commission may be omitted except when a notary public is the officer taking the acknowledgment. The fact that these words and this date may be located in a position on the form different from the position indicated in this subsection does not by itself invalidate the form.

(3) The phrase "and official seal" and the seal itself may be omitted when the officer taking the acknowledgment has no seal or when such officer is the

clerk, assistant clerk, or deputy clerk of the superior court of the county in which the deed or other instrument acknowledged is to be registered.

(4)   The official of the corporation is the corporation's chairman, president, chief executive officer, a vice-president or an assistant vice-president, treasurer, or chief financial officer, or any other agent authorized by resolution pursuant to G.S. 47-18.3(e).

(5)   The attesting official of the corporation is the corporation's secretary or assistant secretary, trust officer, assistant trust officer, associate trust officer, or in the case of a bank, its secretary, assistant secretary, cashier or assistant cashier.

(6)   The phrase "sealed with its corporate seal" may be omitted if the seal of the corporation has not been affixed to the instrument being acknowledged.

(e)   The forms of probate set forth in this section may be modified and adopted for use in the probate of deeds and other conveyances and instruments executed by entities other than corporations, including general and limited partnerships, limited liability companies, trusts, and unincorporated associations. This subsection applies to notarial certificates and forms of probate made before, on, or after December 1, 2005. (1991, c. 647, s. 4; 1995 (Reg. Sess., 1996), c. 742, s. 18; 1999-221, s. 1; 2006-59, s. 29.)

§ 47-41.02. Other forms of probate for corporate conveyances.

(a)   The following forms of probate for deeds and other conveyances executed by a corporation shall also be deemed sufficient but shall not exclude other forms of probate which would be deemed sufficient in law.

(b)   If the instrument is executed by the president or presiding member or trustee and two other members of the corporation, and sealed with the common seal, the following form shall be sufficient:

North Carolina, _____ County.

This _____ day of _____ A.D._____, personally came before me (here give the name and official title of the officer who signs this certificate) A.B. (here give the name of the subscribing witness), who, being by me duly sworn, says that he knows the common seal of the (here give the name of the corporation), and is also acquainted with C.D., who is the president (or presiding member or trustee), and also with E.F. and G.H., two other members of said corporation; and that he, the said A.B., saw the said president (or presiding member or trustee) and the two said other members sign the said instrument, and saw the said president (or presiding member or trustee) affix the said common seal of said corporation thereto, and that he, the said subscribing witness, signed his name as such subscribing witness thereto in their presence. Witness my hand and (when an official seal is required by law) official seal, this ____ day of _____ (year).

(Official seal.)

_____

                                                                    (Signature of officer.)

(c)   If the deed or other instrument is executed by the president, presiding member or trustee of the corporation, and sealed with its common seal, and attested by its secretary or assistant secretary, either of the following forms of proof and certificate thereof shall be deemed sufficient:

North Carolina, _____ County.

This _____ day of _____, A.D. _____, personally came before me (here give name and official title of the officer who signs the certificate) A.B. (here give the name of the attesting secretary or assistant secretary), who, being by me duly sworn, says that he knows the common seal of (here give the name of the corporation), and is acquainted with C.D., who is the president of said corporation, and that he, the said A.B., is the secretary (or assistant secretary) of the said corporation, and saw the said president sign the foregoing (or annexed) instrument, and saw the said common seal of said corporation affixed to said instrument by said president (or that he, the said A.B., secretary or assistant secretary as aforesaid, affixed said seal to said instrument), and that he, the said A.B., signed his name in attestation of the execution of said instrument in the presence of said president of said corporation. Witness my hand and (when an official seal is required by law) official seal, this the _____ day of _____ (year).

(Official seal.)

(Signature of officer.)

North Carolina, _____ County.

This is to certify that on the _____ day of _____, _____, before me personally came _____ (president, vice-president, secretary or assistant secretary, as the case may be), with whom I am personally acquainted, who, being by me duly sworn, says that _____ is the president (or vice-president), and _____ is the secretary (or assistant secretary) of the _____, the corporation described in and which executed the foregoing instrument; that he knows the common seal of said corporation; that the seal affixed to the foregoing instrument is said common seal, and the name of the corporation was subscribed thereto by the said president (or vice-president), and that said president (or vice-president) and secretary (or assistant secretary) subscribed their names thereto, and said common seal was affixed, all by order of the board of directors of said corporation, and that the said instrument is the act and deed of said corporation. Witness my hand and (when an official seal is required by law) official seal, this the _____ day of _____ (year).

(Official seal.)

(Signature of officer.)

(d)   If the deed or other instrument is executed by the signature of the president, vice-president, presiding member or trustee of the corporation, and sealed with its common seal and attested by its secretary or assistant secretary, the following form of proof and certificate thereof shall be deemed sufficient:

This ____ day of ____, A.D. ____, personally came before me (here give name and official title of officer who signs the certificate) A.B., who, being by me duly sworn, says that he is president (vice-president, presiding member or trustee) of the ____ Company, and that the seal affixed to the foregoing (or annexed) instrument in writing is the corporate seal of said company, and that said writing was signed and sealed by him in behalf of said corporation by its authority duly given. And the said A.B. acknowledged the said writing to be the act and deed of said corporation.

(Official seal.)

(Signature of officer.)

(e) All corporate conveyances probated and recorded prior to February 14, 1939, wherein the same was attested by the assistant secretary, instead of the secretary, and otherwise regular, are hereby validated as if attested by the secretary of the corporation.

(f) The following forms of probate for contracts in writing for the purchase of personal property by corporations providing for a lien on the property or the retention of a title thereto by the vendor as security for the purchase price or any part thereof, or chattel mortgages, chattel deeds of trust, and conditional sales of personal property executed by a corporation shall be deemed sufficient but shall not exclude other forms of probate which would be deemed sufficient in law:

(Signature of officer.)

(g) All deeds and other conveyances executed on or before April 12, 1974, by the president, any vice-president, assistant vice-president, manager, comptroller, treasurer, assistant treasurer, trust officer or assistant trust officer, or chairman or vice-chairman of a corporation are hereby validated to the extent that such deeds or other conveyances were otherwise properly executed, probated, and recorded.

(h) The forms of probate set forth in this section may be modified and adopted for use in the probate of deeds and other conveyances and instruments executed by entities other than corporations, including general and limited partnership, limited liability companies, trusts, and unincorporated associations. This subsection applies to notarial certificates and forms of probate made before, on, or after December 1, 2005. (1991, c. 647, s. 5; 1991 (Reg. Sess., 1992), c. 1030, s. 14; 1999-456, s. 59; 2006-59, s. 30.)

§ 47-41.1. Corporate seal.

All documents, including but not limited to deeds, deeds of trust, and mortgages, required or permitted by law to be executed by corporations, shall be legally valid and binding when a legible corporate stamp which is a facsimile of its seal is used in lieu of an imprinted or embossed corporate seal. (1971, c. 340, s. 1.)

§ 47-41.2. Technical defects.

(a) Technical defects, including technical defects under G.S. 10B-68, and errors or omissions in a form of probate or other notarial certificate, shall not affect the sufficiency, validity, or enforceability of the form of probate or the notarial certificate or the related instrument or document. A register of deeds may not refuse to accept an instrument or document for registration because of technical defects, errors, or omissions in a form of probate or other notarial certificate.

(b) This section does not apply to the requirements for registration contained in G.S. 47-14(a) and a register of deeds shall not accept for registration an instrument that does not comply with the requirements of G.S. 47-14(a). (2006-59, s. 31; 2006-199, s. 3; 2013-204, s. 1.17.)

§ 47-42. Attestation of bank conveyances by secretary or cashier.

(a) Repealed by Session Laws 2002-26, s. 1.

(b) All deeds and conveyances executed prior to February 14, 1939, by banking corporations, where the cashier of said banking corporation has attested said instruments, which deeds and conveyances are otherwise regular, are hereby validated.

(c) All deeds and conveyances executed by a banking corporation on or after October 1, 1999, that complied with G.S. 47-18.3 are hereby validated. (1939, c. 20, s. 21/2; 1957, c. 783, s. 4; 2002-26, s. 1.)

§ 47-43. Form of certificate of acknowledgment of instrument executed by attorney-in-fact.

When an instrument purports to be signed by parties acting through another by virtue of the execution of a power of attorney, the following form of certificate shall be deemed sufficient, but shall not exclude other forms which would be deemed sufficient in law:

North Carolina, _____ County.

I (here give name of the official and his official title), do hereby certify that (here give name of attorney-in-fact), attorney-in-fact for (here give names of parties who executed the instrument through attorney-in-fact), personally appeared before me this day, and being by me duly sworn, says that he executed the foregoing and annexed instrument for and in behalf of (here give names of parties who executed the instrument through attorney-in-fact), and that his authority to execute and acknowledge said instrument is contained in an instrument duly executed, acknowledged, and recorded in the office of (here insert name of official in whose office power of attorney is recorded, and the county and state of recordation), on the (day of month, month, and year of recordation), and that this instrument was executed under and by virtue of the authority given by said instrument granting him power of attorney; that the said (here give name of attorney-in-fact) acknowledged the due execution of the foregoing and annexed instrument for the purposes therein expressed for and in behalf of the said (here give names of parties who executed the instrument through attorney-in-fact).

WITNESS my hand and official seal, this _____ day of _____, (year) ____

(Official seal.)

_____

Signature of Officer

(1941, c. 238.)

§ 47-43.1. Execution and acknowledgment of instruments by attorneys or attorneys-in-fact.

When an instrument purports to be executed by parties acting through another by virtue of a power of attorney, it shall be sufficient if the attorney or attorney-in-fact signs such instrument either in the name of the principal by the attorney or attorney-in-fact or signs as attorney or attorney-in-fact for the principal; and if such instrument purports to be under seal, the seal of the attorney-in-fact shall be sufficient. For such instrument to be executed under seal, the power of attorney must have been executed under seal. (1949, c. 66, s. 1.)

§ 47-43.2. Officer's certificate upon proof of instrument by subscribing witness.

When the execution of an instrument is proved by a subscribing witness as provided by G.S. 47-12, the certificate required by G.S. 47-13.1 shall be in substantially the following form:

STATE OF _____

(Name of state)

_____ COUNTY

I, _____, a
_____

(Name of officer taking proof)   (Official title of officer taking proof)

of _____ COUNTY, _____,
certify that

(Name of state)

_____ personally appeared before me this day,

(Name of subscribing witness)

and being duly sworn, stated that in his presence

_____

(Name of maker)

(signed the foregoing instrument) (acknowledged the execution of the foregoing instrument.) (Strike out the words not applicable.)

WITNESS my hand and official seal, this the _____ day of_____,

(Month)

_____

(Year)

_____

(Signature of officer taking proof)

_____

(Official title of officer taking proof)

My commission expires
_____

(Date of expiration of officer's commission)

Provided, however, that when instruments have been recorded upon proof of execution of the instrument by certificate of a judicial officer, showing that execution was proven by oath and examination of the subscribing witness, the date of such examination, and the signature of the officer taking the proof, such proof of execution shall be deemed sufficient on all instruments filed for registration prior to March 15, 1961. (1951, c. 379, s. 3; 1953, c. 1078, s. 3; 1955, c. 1345, s. 6; 1961, c. 237; 1999-456, s. 59.)

§ 47-43.3. Officer's certificate upon proof of instrument by proof of signature of maker.

When the execution of an instrument is proved by proof of the signature of the maker as provided by G.S. 47-12.1 or as provided by G.S. 47-13, the certificate required by G.S. 47-13.1 shall be in substantially the following form:

STATE OF_____

(Name of state)

_____ COUNTY

I, _____, a
   _____
              (Name of officer taking proof)   (Official title of officer taking proof)

of_____ COUNTY, _____,
certify that

                                    (Name of state)
_____ personally appeared before me this day,

         (Name of person familiar with

              maker's handwriting)

and being duly sworn, stated that he knows the handwriting of _____

(Name of maker)

and that the signature to the foregoing instrument is the signature of
_____

(Name of maker)

WITNESS my hand and official seal, this the ____ day of _____,
____

(Year)   (Month)

_____

(Signature of officer taking proof)

_____

(Official title of officer taking proof)

My commission expires _____

(Date of expiration of officer's commission)

(1951, c. 379, s. 3; 1999-456, s. 59.)

§ 47-43.4. Officer's certificate upon proof of instrument by proof of signature of subscribing witness.

When the execution of an instrument is proved by proof of the signature of a subscribing witness as provided by G.S. 47-12.1, the certificate required by G.S. 47-13.1 shall be in substantially the following form:

STATE OF _____

(Name of state)

_____ COUNTY

I, _____, a
_____
(Name of officer taking proof)   (Official title of officer taking proof)

of _____ COUNTY, _____, certify that

(Name of state)

_____ personally appeared before me this day, and

(Name of person familiar with

handwriting of subscribing witness)

being duly sworn, stated that he knows the handwriting of
_____,

(Name of subscribing witness)

and that the signature of _____ as a subscribing witness to the

(Name of subscribing witness)

foregoing instrument is the signature of

_____

(Name of subscribing witness)

WITNESS my hand and official seal, this the ____ day of _____,
_____

(Month)

(Year)

_____

(Signature of officer taking proof)

_____

(Official title of officer taking proof)

My commission expires

_____

(Date of expiration of officer's commission)

(1951, c. 379, s. 3; 1999-456, s. 59.)

§ 47-44. Clerk's certificate upon probate by justice of peace or magistrate.

When the proof or acknowledgment of any instrument is had before a justice of the peace of some other state or territory of the United States, or before a magistrate of this State, but of a county different from that in which the instrument is offered for registration, the form of certificate as to his official position and signature shall be substantially as follows:

North Carolina _____ County.

I, A.B. (here give name and official title of a clerk of a court of record), do hereby certify that C.D. (here give the name of the justice of the peace or magistrate taking the proof, etc.), was at the time of signing the foregoing (or annexed) certificate an acting justice of the peace or magistrate in and for the county of _____ and State (or territory) of_____,

and that his signature thereto is in his own proper handwriting.

In witness whereof, I hereunto set my hand and official seal, this_____ day of_____, A.D. _____

(Official seal.)

_____

(Signature of officer.)

(1899, c. 235, s. 8; Rev., s. 1006; C.S., s. 3327; 1971, c. 1185, s. 15.)

§ 47-45. Clerk's certificate upon probate by nonresident official without seal.

When the proof or acknowledgment of any instrument is had before any official of some other state, territory or country and such official has no official seal, then the certificate of such official shall be accompanied by the certificate of a clerk of a court of record of the state, territory or country in which the official taking the proof or acknowledgment resides, of the official position and signature of such official; such certificate of the clerk shall be under his hand and official seal and shall be in substance as follows:

_____County.

I, A.B. (here give name and official title of the clerk of a court of record as provided herein), do hereby certify that C.D. (here give name of the official taking the proof, etc.) was at the time of signing the foregoing (or annexed) certificate (here give the official title of the officer taking proof, etc.) in and for the county of _____ and state of _____ (or other political division of the state, territory or country, as the case may be), and that his signature thereto is in his own proper handwriting.

In witness whereof, I hereunto set my hand and official seal, this _____day of_____, A.D._____

(Official seal.)

_____

(Signature of Clerk.)

(1899, c. 235, s. 8; Rev., s. 1007; C.S., s. 3328.)

§ 47-46: Repealed by Session Laws 2005-123, s. 4, effective October 1, 2005.

§ 47-46.1. Notice of satisfaction of deed of trust, mortgage, or other instrument.

No particular phrasing is required for a notice of satisfaction pursuant to G.S. 45-37(a)(5) as it was prior to October 1, 2005, a satisfaction of a security instrument under G.S. 45-36.10, or a trustee's satisfaction under G.S. 45-36.20. The following form, when properly completed, is sufficient to satisfy the requirements (i) for a notice of satisfaction under G.S. 45-37(a)(5) as it was in effect prior to October 1, 2005, (ii) for a satisfaction under G.S. 45-36.10 if the form is signed and acknowledged by the secured creditor, and (iii) for a trustee's satisfaction under G.S. 45-36.20 if the security instrument is a deed of trust and the form is signed and acknowledged by the trustee:

North Carolina, _____ County.

I, _____ (name of trustee or mortgagee), certify that the debt or other obligation in the amount of _____ secured by the (deed of trust)(mortgage)(other instrument) executed by _____ (grantor)(mortgagor), _____ (trustee)(leave blank if mortgage), and _____ (beneficiary)(mortgagee), and recorded in _____ County at _____ (book and page) was satisfied on _____ (date of satisfaction).

                                                    (Signature of trustee or mortgagee)

(Acknowledgment before officer authorized to take acknowledgments)

My commission expires _____ (Date of expiration of official's commission).

(1987, c. 405, s. 2; c. 662, s. 4; 1989, c. 434, s. 2; 2005-123, s. 5; 2006-264, s. 82(a).)

§ 47-46.2. Certificate of satisfaction of deed of trust, mortgage, or other instrument.

No particular phrasing is required for a certification of satisfaction pursuant to G.S. 45-37(a)(6) as it was in effect prior to October 1, 2005, or for a satisfaction of a security instrument under G.S. 45-36.10. The following form, when properly completed, is sufficient to satisfy the requirements (i) for a certificate of satisfaction under G.S. 45-37(a)(6) as it was in effect prior to October 1, 2005, and (ii) for a satisfaction of a security instrument under G.S. 45-36.10 when signed and acknowledged by the secured creditor:

CERTIFICATE OF SATISFACTION

North Carolina, _____ County.

I, _____ (name of owner of the note or other indebtedness secured by the deed of trust or mortgage), certify that I am the owner of the indebtedness secured by the hereafter described deed of trust or mortgage and that the debt or other obligation in the amount of _____ secured by the (deed of trust)(mortgage)(other instrument) executed by _____ (grantor)(mortgagor),

_____ (trustee)(leave blank if mortgage), and _____ (beneficiary)(mortgagee), and recorded in _____ County at _____ (book and page) was satisfied on _____ (date of satisfaction). I request that this certificate of satisfaction be recorded and the above-referenced security instrument be canceled of record.

(Signature of owner of note)

[Acknowledgment before officer authorized to take acknowledgments]. (1995, c. 292, s. 3; 2005-123, s. 5; 2006-226, s. 27(a); 2006-264, s. 82(a).)

§ 47-46.3. Affidavit of lost note.

No particular phrasing is required for an affidavit of lost note pursuant to G.S. 45-36(a)(6) as it was in effect prior to October 1, 2005. The following form, when properly completed, is sufficient to satisfy the requirements for an affidavit of lost note under G.S. 45-37(a)(6) as it was in effect prior to October 1, 2005.

AFFIDAVIT OF LOST NOTE

[Name of affiant] personally appeared before me in _____ County, State of _____, and having been duly sworn (or affirmed) made the following affidavit:

1. The affiant is the owner of the note or other indebtedness secured by the deed of trust, mortgage, or other instrument executed by _____ (grantor, mortgagor), _____ (trustee), and _____ (beneficiary, mortgagee), and recorded in _____ County at _____ (book and page); and

2. The note or other indebtedness has been lost and after the exercise of due diligence cannot be located.

3. The affiant certifies that all indebtedness secured by the deed of trust, mortgage, or other instrument was satisfied on _____, _____ (date of satisfaction), and the affiant is responsible for cancellation of the same.

_____

(Signature of affiant)

Sworn to (or affirmed) and subscribed before me this ____ day of _____, _____.

[Signature and seal of notary public or other official authorized to administer oaths]. (1995, c. 292, s. 4; 1995 (Reg. Sess., 1996), c. 604, s. 2; c. 742, s. 19; 1999-456, s. 59; 2005-123, s. 6.)

Article 4.

Curative Statutes; Acknowledgments; Probates; Registration.

§ 47-47. Defective order of registration; "same" for "this instrument".

Where instruments were admitted to registration prior to March 2, 1905, and the clerk's order for the registration used the word "same" in place of "this instrument," the said registrations are good and valid. (1905, c. 344; Rev., s. 1010; C.S., s. 3329.)

§ 47-48. Clerks' and registers of deeds' certificate failing to pass on all prior certificates.

When it appears that the clerk of the superior court, register of deeds, or other officer having the power to probate or certify deeds, in passing upon deeds or other instruments, and the certificates thereto, having more than one certificate of the same or a different date, by other officer or officers taking acknowledgment or probating the same, has in his certificate or order mentioned only one or more of the preceding or foregoing certificates or orders, but not all of them, but has admitted the same deed or other instrument to probate or recordation, it shall be conclusively presumed that all the certificates of said deed or instrument necessary to the admission of same to probate or recordation have been passed upon, and the certificate of said clerk, register of deeds, or other probating or certifying officer shall be deemed sufficient and the probate, certification and recordation of said deed or instrument is hereby made and declared valid for all intents and purposes. The provisions of this section shall apply to all instruments recorded in any county of this State prior to April 1, 2013. (1917, c. 237; C.S., s. 3330; 1945, c. 808, s. 1; 1965, c. 1001; 1971, c. 11; 1973, c. 1402; 1987, c. 360, s. 2; 2013-204, s. 1.18.)

§ 47-49. Defective certification or adjudication of clerk, etc., admitting to registration.

In all cases where, prior to January 1, 1919, instruments by law required or authorized to be registered, with certificates showing the acknowledgment or proof of execution thereof as required by the laws of the State of North Carolina, have been ordered registered by the clerk of the superior court or other officer qualified to pass upon probates and admit instruments to registration, and actually put upon the books in the office of the register of deeds as if properly proven and ordered to be registered, all such probates and registrations are hereby validated and made as good and sufficient as though such instruments had been in all respects properly proved and recorded, notwithstanding the failure of clerks or other officers qualified to pass upon the proofs or acknowledgments of instruments and to admit such instruments to registration to adjudge or certify that said instruments were duly proven, and notwithstanding the failure of such officers to adjudge or certify that the certificates of proof or acknowledgments of said instruments were correct or in due form. (1919, c. 248; C.S., s. 3331.)

§ 47-50. Order of registration omitted.

In all cases prior to October 1, 2005, where it appears from the records of the office of the register of deeds of any county in this State that the execution of a deed of conveyance or other instrument by law required or authorized to be registered was duly signed and acknowledged as required by the laws of the State of North Carolina, and the clerk of the superior court of such county or other officer authorized to pass upon acknowledgments and to order registration of instruments has failed either to adjudge the correctness of the acknowledgment or to order the registration thereof, or both, such registrations are hereby validated and the instrument so appearing in the office of the register of deeds of such county shall be effective to the same extent as if the clerk or other authorized officer had properly adjudged the correctness of the acknowledgment and had ordered the registration of the instrument. (1911, cc. 91, 166; 1913, c. 61; Ex. Sess. 1913, c. 73; 1915, c. 179, s. 1; C.S., s. 3332; 1941, cc. 187, 229; 1949, c. 493; 1957, c. 314; 1961, c. 79; 1981, c. 812; 1993, c. 80, s. 1; 2013-204, s. 1.19.)

§ 47-50.1. Register's certificate omitted.

In all cases prior to October 1, 2005, where it appears from the records of the office of the register of deeds of any county in this State that the execution of a deed of conveyance or other instrument by law required or authorized to be registered was duly signed and acknowledged as required by the laws of this State, and the register of deeds has failed to certify the correctness of the acknowledgment as required by G.S. 47-14(a), the registrations are hereby validated and the instrument so appearing in the office of the register of deeds of that county is effective to the same extent as if the register of deeds had properly certified the correctness of the acknowledgment. (2004-199, s. 17; 2013-204, s. 1.20.)

§ 47-51. Official deeds omitting seals.

All deeds executed prior to April 1, 2013, by any sheriff, commissioner, receiver, executor, executrix, administrator, administratrix, or other officer authorized to execute a deed by virtue of his office or appointment, in which the officer has omitted to affix his seal after his signature, shall not be invalid on account of the omission of such seal. (1907, c. 807; 1917, c. 69, s. 1; C.S., s. 3333; Ex. Sess. 1924, c. 64; 1941, c. 13; 1955, c. 467, ss. 1, 2; 1959, c. 408; 1971, c. 14; 1973, c. 1207, s. 1; 1983, c. 398, s. 2; 1985, c. 70, s. 2; 1987, c. 277, s. 2; 1989, c. 390, s. 2; 1991, c. 489, s. 2; 2013-204, s. 1.21.)

§ 47-52. Defective acknowledgment on old deeds validated.

The clerk of the superior court may order registered any deed, or other conveyance of land, in all cases where the instrument and probate bears date prior to January 1, 1907, where the acknowledgment, private examination, or other proof of execution, has been taken or had before a notary public residing in the county where the land is situate, where said officer failed to affix his official seal, and where the certificate of said officer appears otherwise to be genuine. (1933, c. 439.)

§ 47-53. Probates omitting official seals, etc.

In all cases where the acknowledgment, private examination, or other proof of the execution of any deed, mortgage, or other instrument authorized or required to be registered has been taken or had by or before any commissioner of affidavits and deeds of this State, or clerk or deputy clerk of a court of record, or notary public of this or any other state, territory, or district, and such deed, mortgage, or other instrument has heretofore been recorded in any county in this State, but such commissioner, clerk, deputy clerk, or notary public has omitted to attach his or her official or notarial seal thereto, or if omitted, to insert his or her name in the body of the certificate, or if omitted, to sign his or her name to such certificate, if the name of such officer appears in the body of said certificate or is signed thereto, or it does not appear of record that such seal was attached to the original deed, mortgage, or other instrument, or such commissioner, clerk, deputy clerk, or notary public has certified the same as under his or her "official seal," or "notarial seal," or words of similar import, and no such seal appears of record or where the officer uses "notarial" in his or her certificate and signature shows that "C.S.C.," or "clerk of superior court," or similar exchange of capacity, and the word "seal" follows the signature, then all such acknowledgments, private examinations or other proofs of such deeds, mortgages, or other instruments, and the registration thereof, are hereby made in all respects valid and binding. The provisions of this section apply to acknowledgments, private examinations, or proofs taken prior to April 1, 2013. Provided, this section does not apply to pending litigation. (Rev., s. 1012; 1907, cc. 213, 665, 971; 1911, c. 4; 1915, c. 36; C.S., s. 3334; 1929, c. 8, s. 1; 1945, c. 808, s. 2; 1951, c. 1151, s. 1; 1965, c. 500; 1983, c. 398, s. 3; 1985, c. 70, s. 3; 1987, c. 277, s. 3; 1989, c. 390, s. 3; 1991, c. 489, s. 3; 2013-204, s. 1.22.)

§ 47-53.1. Acknowledgment omitting seal of clerk or notary public.

Where any person has taken an acknowledgment as either a notary public or a clerk of a superior court, deputy clerk of a superior court, or assistant clerk of a superior court and has failed to affix his or her seal and this acknowledgment has been otherwise duly probated and recorded then this acknowledgment is hereby declared to be sufficient and valid. This section applies only to those deeds and other instruments acknowledged prior to April 1, 2013. (1951, c. 1151, s. 1A; 1953, c. 1307; 1963, c. 412; 1975, c. 878; 1983, c. 398, s. 4; 1985, c. 70, s. 4; 1987, c. 277, s. 4; 1989, c. 390, s. 4; 1991, c. 489, s. 4; 2004-199, s. 18; 2013-204, s. 1.23.)

§ 47-54. Registration by register's deputies or clerks.

All registrations of instruments heretofore made in the office of register of deeds of the several counties by the register's deputy or clerk, and signed in the name of the register of deeds by the deputy or clerk, or signed by the deputy in his own name and not in the name of the register of deeds, when such registrations are in all other respects regular, are hereby validated and declared to be of the same force and effect as if signed in the name of the register of deeds by such register. (1911, c. 184, s. 1; C.S., s. 3335; 1953, c. 849; 1963, c. 203.)

§ 47-54.1. Registration by register's assistants or deputies.

All registrations of instruments heretofore made in the office of register of deeds of the several counties by the register's assistant or deputy, and signed in the name of the register of deeds by the assistant or deputy, and initialed by the assistant or deputy, instead of being signed by them as assistant or deputy, when such registrations are in all other respects regular, are hereby validated and declared to be of the same force and effect as if signed by the assistant or deputy in the respective capacity. (1991 (Reg. Sess., 1992), c. 877, s. 1.)

§ 47-55. Before officer in wrong capacity or out of jurisdiction.

All deeds, conveyances, or other instruments permitted by law to be registered in this State, which have been probated or ordered to be registered previous to January 1, 1913, before any officer of this or any other state or country, authorized by law to take acknowledgments or to order registration, where the certificate of the probate or order of registration is sufficient in form, but appears to have been certified by the officer in some capacity other than that in which such officer was authorized to act, or appears to have been made out of the county or district authorized by law, but within the State, and where the instrument with such certificate has been recorded in the proper county, are hereby declared to have been duly proved, probated and recorded, and to be valid. (Rev., ss. 1017, 1030; 1913, c. 125, s. 1; C.S., s. 3336.)

§ 47-56. Before justices of peace, where clerk's certificate or order of registration defective.

In every case where it appears from the record of the office of any register of deeds in this State that a justice of the peace in this State or any other state of the United States, has taken and certified the proof of any instrument required by the law to be registered, or the privy examination of a married woman thereto, and the deed and certificate have been registered prior to the first day of January, 1963, in the county where the lands described in the instrument are located, without a certificate or with a defective certificate of the clerk of the official character of the justice, or as to the genuineness of his signature, or without the order of registration of the clerk, or his adjudication of due probate, or with a defective adjudication thereof, such proofs, certificates and registration are hereby validated. (1907, c. 83, s. 1; C.S., s. 3337; 1951, c. 35; 1963, c. 1014.)

§ 47-57. Probates on proof of handwriting of maker refusing to acknowledge.

All registrations of instruments, prior to February 5, 1897, permitted or required by law to be registered, which were ordered to registration upon proof of the handwriting of the grantor or maker who refused to acknowledge the execution, are hereby validated. (1897, c. 28; Rev., s. 1026; C.S., s. 3338.)

§ 47-58. Before judges of Supreme Court or superior courts or clerks before 1889.

Wherever the judges of the Supreme Court or the superior court, or the clerks or deputy clerks of the superior court, or courts of pleas and quarter sessions, mistaking their powers, have essayed previously to the first day of January, 1889, to take the probate of any instrument required or allowed by law to be registered, and the privy examination of femes covert, whose names are signed to such deeds, and have ordered said deeds to registration, and the same have been registered, all such probates, privy examinations and registrations are validated. (1871-2, c. 200, s. 1; Code, s. 1260; 1889, c. 252; 1891, c. 484; Rev., s. 1009; C.S., s. 3339.)

§ 47-59. Before clerks of inferior courts.

All probates and orders of registration made by and taken before any clerk of any inferior or criminal court prior to the twentieth day of February, 1885, and valid in form and substance, shall be valid and effectual, and all deeds, mortgages or other instruments requiring registration, registered upon such probate and order of registration, shall be valid. This section shall apply only to the counties of Ashe, Beaufort, Bertie, Buncombe, Cumberland, Duplin, Edgecombe, Granville, Greene, Halifax, Hertford, Iredell, Lenoir, Martin, Mecklenburg, New Hanover, Northampton, Robeson and Wayne. This section applies to probates and private examinations taken before the clerks of the criminal court of Buncombe prior to February second, 1893. (1885, cc. 105, 108; 1889, cc. 143, 463; Rev., ss. 1020, 1021; C.S., s. 3340.)

§ 47-60. Order of registration by judge, where clerk party.

All deeds, mortgages or other instruments which prior to the twentieth day of January, 1893, have been probated by a justice of the peace and ordered to registration by a judge of the superior court or justice of the Supreme Court, to which clerks of the superior court are parties, are hereby confirmed, and the probates and orders for registration declared to be valid. (1893, c. 3, s. 2; Rev., s. 1011; C.S., s. 3342.)

§ 47-61. Order of registration by interested clerk.

The probate and registration of all deeds, mortgages and other instruments requiring registration prior to the fifteenth day of January, 1935, to which the clerks of the superior courts are parties, or in which they have an interest, and which have been registered on the order of such clerks or their deputies, or by assistant clerks of the superior courts, on proof of acknowledgment taken before such clerks, assistant clerks, deputy clerks, justices of the peace or notaries public, be, and the same are declared valid. (1891, c. 102; 1899, c. 258; 1905, c. 427; Rev., s. 1015; 1907, c. 1003, s. 2; Ex. Sess. 1908, c. 105, s. 1; C.S., s. 3343; 1935, c. 235.)

§ 47-62. Probates before interested notaries.

The proof and acknowledgment of instruments required by law to be registered in the office of the register of deeds of a county, and all privy examinations of a feme covert to such instruments made before any notary public on or since March 11, 1907, are hereby declared valid and sufficient, notwithstanding the notary may have been interested as attorney, counsel or otherwise in such instruments. (Ex. Sess. 1908, c. 105, s. 2; C.S., s. 3344.)

§ 47-63. Probates before officer of interested corporation.

In all cases when acknowledgment or proof of any conveyance has been taken before a clerk of superior court, magistrate or notary public, who was at the time a stockholder or officer in any corporation, bank or other institution which was a party to such instrument, the certificates of such clerk, magistrate, or notary public shall be held valid, and are so declared. (Rev., s. 1015; 1907, c. 1003, s. 1; C.S., s. 3345; 1971, c. 1185, s. 16.)

§ 47-64. Probates before officers, stockholders or directors of corporations.

No acknowledgment or proof of execution, including privy examination of married women, of any deed, mortgage or deed of trust to which instrument a corporation is a party shall be held invalid by reason of the fact that the officer taking such acknowledgment, proof or privy examination was an officer, stockholder, or director in said corporation; but such proofs and acknowledgments and the registration thereof, if in all other respects valid, are declared to be valid. Nor shall the registration of any such instrument ordered to be registered be held invalid by reason of the fact that the clerk or deputy clerk ordering the registration was an officer, stockholder or director in any corporation which is a party to any such instrument. (Ex. Sess. 1913, c. 41; C.S., s. 3346; 1929, c. 24, s. 1; 1943, c. 135; 1945, c. 860; 2013-204, s. 1.24.)

§ 47-65. Clerk's deeds, where clerk appointed himself to sell.

All deeds made by any clerk of the superior court of any county or his deputy, prior to the first day of January, 1905, in any proceeding before him in which he has appointed himself or his deputy to make the sale of real property or other property are hereby validated. (1911, c. 146, s. 1; C.S., s. 3347.)

§ 47-66. Certificate of wife's "previous" examination.

All probates of deeds, letters of attorney or other instruments requiring registration to which married women were parties, had and taken prior to the fourteenth day of February, 1893, in which probate it appears that such married women were "previously examined" instead of "privately examined," are hereby validated and confirmed. (1893, c. 130; Rev., s. 1016; C.S., s. 3348.)

§ 47-67. Probates of husband and wife in wrong order.

All probates prior to March 6, 1893, of instruments executed by a husband and wife in which the probate as to the husband has been taken before or subsequent to the privy examination of his wife are validated. (1893, c. 293; Rev., s. 1017; C.S., s. 3349.)

§ 47-68. Probates of husband and wife before different officers.

Where, prior to the second day of March, 1895, the probate of a deed or other instrument, executed by husband and wife, has been taken as to the husband and the wife by different officers having the power to take probates of deeds, whether both officers reside in this State or one in this State and the other in another state, or foreign country, the said probate, in the cases mentioned, shall be valid to all intents and purposes, and all deeds and other instruments required to be registered, and which have been ordered to registration by the proper officer in this State, and upon such probate or probates, and have been registered, shall be taken and considered as duly registered, and the word "probate," as used in this section, shall include privy examination of the wife. (1895, c. 120; Rev., s. 1018; 1907, c. 34, s. 1; C.S., s. 3350.)

§ 47-69. Wife free trader; no examination or husband's assent.

In all cases prior to the twenty-fourth day of September, 1913, where a married woman who was at the time a free trader by her husband's consent has executed and delivered a deed conveying her land, without her privy examination having been taken, and without the written assent of her husband other than his written assent contained in the instrument making her a free trader, such deed shall be valid and effectual to convey her land as if she had been, at the time of the execution and delivery of such deed, a feme sole. This section does not validate such deed where it would affect the title to land or property of purchasers or their grantees or assignees from such married woman and free trader subsequent to the execution of such deed. (Ex. Sess. 1913, c. 54, s. 1; C.S., s. 3351.)

§ 47-70. By president and attested by treasurer under corporate seal.

All deeds and conveyances for lands in this State, made by any corporation of this State, which have heretofore been proved or acknowledged before any notary public in any other state, or before any commissioner of deeds and affidavits for the State of North Carolina in any other state, and sealed with the common seal of the corporation and attested by the treasurer, are hereby ratified and declared to be good and valid deeds for all purposes. Where such deeds have been executed for the corporation by its president and attested, sealed and acknowledged or probated as aforesaid, and the acknowledgment or probate has been duly adjudged sufficient by any deputy clerk and ordered registered, the acknowledgment, probate and registration are ratified, and said deed is declared valid. Such deeds, or certified copies thereof, may be used as evidence of title to the lands therein conveyed in the trial of any suits in any of the courts of this State where the title of said lands shall come in controversy. (1905, c. 307; Rev., s. 1028; C.S., s. 3352.)

§ 47-71. By president and attested by witness before January, 1900.

Any deed or conveyance for land in this State, made prior to January 1, 1900, by the president of any corporation duly chartered under the laws of this State, and attested by a witness, is hereby declared to be a good and valid deed by such corporation for all purposes, and shall be admitted to probate and registration and shall pass title to the property therein conveyed to the grantee as fully as if said deed were executed according to provisions and forms of law in force in this State at the date of the execution of said deed. (1909, c. 859, s. 1; C.S., s. 3353.)

§ 47-71.1. Corporate seal omitted prior to January 1, 2000.

Any corporate deed, or conveyance of land in this State, made prior to January 1, 2000, which is defective only because the corporate seal is omitted therefrom is hereby declared to be a good and valid conveyance by such corporation for all purposes and shall be sufficient to pass title to the property therein conveyed as fully as if the said conveyance were executed according to the provisions and forms of law in force in this State at the date of the execution of such conveyance. (1957, c. 500, s. 1; 1963, c. 1015; 1969, c. 815; 1971, c. 61; 1973,

c. 479; 1977, c. 538; 1981, c. 191, s. 1; 1983, c. 398, s. 5; 1985, c. 70, s. 5; 1987, c. 277, s. 5; 1989, c. 390, s. 5; 1991, c. 489, s. 5; 2013-204, s. 1.25.)

§ 47-72. Corporate name not affixed, but signed otherwise prior to April 1, 2013.

In all cases prior to April 1, 2013, where any deed conveying lands purported to be executed by a corporation, but the corporate name was in fact not affixed to said deed, but same was signed by the president and secretary of said corporation, or by the president and two members of the governing body of said corporation, and said deed has been registered in the county where the land conveyed by said deed is located, said defective execution above described shall be and the same is hereby declared to be in all respects valid, and such deed shall be deemed to be in all respects the deed of said corporation. (1919, c. 53, s. 1; C.S., s. 3354; 1927, c. 126; 1963, c. 1094; 1973, c. 118, s. 1; 2013-204, s. 1.26.)

§ 47-73. Probated and registered on oath of subscribing witness.

In all cases prior to the first day of January, 1919, where any deed conveying lands was executed by a corporation, and said deed was probated and ordered registered upon the oath and examination of a subscribing witness, by the clerk of the superior court of the county in which the land conveyed by said deed is located, and said deed has been duly registered by the register of deeds of said county, such probate and order of registration shall be, and the same is hereby, declared to be in all respects valid. (1919, c. 53, s. 2; C.S., s. 3355.)

§ 47-74. Certificate alleging examination of grantor instead of witness.

Wherever any deed of conveyance registered prior to January 1, 1886, purports to have been attested by two witnesses and in the certificate of probate and acknowledgment it is stated that the execution of such deed was proven by the oath and examination of one of the grantors in said deed instead of either of the witnesses named, all such probates and certificates are hereby validated and confirmed, and any such deed shall be taken and considered as duly acknowledged and probated. (1925, c. 84.)

§ 47-75. Proof of corporate articles before officer authorized to probate.

All proofs of articles of agreement for the creation of corporations which were, prior to the eighteenth day of February, 1901, made before any officer who was at that time authorized by the law to take proofs and acknowledgments of deeds and mortgages, are ratified. (1901, c. 170; Rev., s. 1027; C.S., s. 3356.)

§ 47-76. Before officials of wrong state.

In all cases where the acknowledgment, examination and probate of any deed, mortgage, power of attorney or other instrument required or authorized to be registered has been taken before any judge, clerk of a court of record, notary public having a notarial seal, mayor of a city having a seal, or justice of the peace of a state other than the state in which the grantor, maker or subscribing witness resided at the time of the execution, acknowledgment, examination or probate thereof, and such acknowledgment, examination or probate is in other respects according to law, and such instrument has been duly ordered to registration and has been registered, then such acknowledgment, examination, probate and registration are hereby in all respects made valid and binding. This section applies to probates and acknowledgments of deputy clerks of other states when such probate and acknowledgment has been attested by the official seal of said office and adjudged sufficient and in due form of law by the clerk of the court in the state where the instrument is required to be registered. (1905, c. 505; Rev., s. 1013; C.S., s. 3357.)

§ 47-77. Before notaries and clerks in other states.

All deeds and conveyances made for lands in this State which have, previous to February 15, 1883, been proved before a notary public or clerk of a court of record, or before a court of record, not including mayor's court, of any other state, where such proof has been duly certified by such notary or clerk under his official seal, or the seal of the court, or in accordance with the act of Congress regulating the certifying of records of the courts of one state to another state, or under the seal of such courts, and such deed or conveyance, with the certificate, has been registered in the office of register of deeds in the book of records thereof for the county in which such lands were situate at the time of such registration, are declared to be validly registered, and the proof and registration is adjudged valid. All deeds and conveyances so proved, certified and registered, or certified copies of the same, may be used as evidence of title for the lands on the trial of any suit in any courts where title to the lands come into controversy. (1883, c. 129, ss. 1, 2; Code, ss. 1262, 1263; 1885, c. 11; Rev., ss. 1022, 1023; 1915, c. 213; C.S., s. 3358.)

§ 47-78. Acknowledgment by resident taken out-of-state.

When prior to the ninth day of March, 1895, a deed or mortgage executed by a resident of this State has been proved or acknowledged by the maker thereof before a notary public of any other state of the United States, and has been ordered to be registered by the clerk of the superior court of the county in which the land conveyed is situated, and said deed or mortgage has been registered, such registration is valid. (1895, c. 181; Rev., s. 1019; C.S., s. 3359.)

§ 47-79. Before deputy clerks of courts of other states.

Where any deed or conveyance of lands in this State, executed prior to January 1, 1923, has been acknowledged by the grantor or the privy examination of any married woman has been taken before the deputy clerk of a court of record of any other state, and the certificate of acknowledgment and privy examination is otherwise sufficient under the laws of this State, except that it appears to have been signed in the name of the clerk of said court, by the deputy clerk, and the seal of the court has been affixed thereto, and such certificate has been duly approved by the clerk of the superior court of this State in the county where the lands conveyed are situated and the instrument ordered to be recorded, such certificate and probate and the registration made thereon are validated, and the conveyance, if otherwise sufficient, is declared valid. (1913, c. 57, ss. 1, 2; C.S., s. 3360; 1951, c. 1134, s. 1.)

§ 47-80. Sister state probates without Governor's authentication.

In all cases where any deed concerning lands or any power of attorney for the conveyance of the same, or any other instrument required or allowed to be registered, has been, prior to the twenty-ninth day of January, 1901, acknowledged by the grantor therein, or proved and the private examination of any married woman, who was a party thereto, taken according to law, before any judge of a supreme, superior or circuit court of any other state or territory of the United States where the parties to such instrument resided, and the certificate of such judge as to such acknowledgment, probate or private examination, and also the certificate of the secretary of state of said state or territory instead of the Governor thereof (as required by the laws of this State then in force) that the judge, before whom the acknowledgment or probate and private examination were taken, was at the time of taking the same a judge as aforesaid, are attached to said deed, or other instrument, and the said deed or other instrument, having said certificates attached, has been exhibited before the former judge of probate, or the clerk of the superior court of the county in which the property is situated, and such acknowledgment, or probate and private examination have been adjudged by him to be sufficient and said deed or other instrument ordered to be registered and has been registered accordingly, such probate and registration shall be valid. Nothing herein contained affects the rights of third parties who are purchasers for value, without notice, from the grantor in such deed or other instrument. (1901, c. 39; Rev., s. 1014; C.S., s. 3361.)

§ 47-81. Before commissioners of deeds.

Any deed or other instrument permitted by law to be registered, and which has prior to the third day of March, 1913, been proved or acknowledged before a commissioner of deeds, is validated; and its registration is authorized and validated. (1913, c. 39, s. 2; C.S., s. 3362.)

§ 47-81.1. Before commissioner of oaths.

All deeds, mortgages or other instruments required to be registered, which prior to March 5, 1943, have been probated by a commissioner of oaths and ordered registered, are hereby validated and confirmed as properly probated and registered instruments. (1943, c. 471, s. 2.)

§ 47-81.2. Before United States Army, etc., officers, and other service members.

In all cases where instruments and writings have been proved or acknowledged before any commissioned officer of the United States Army, Navy, Air Force, Marine Corps, or Coast Guard or any officer of the United States Merchant Marine having the rank of lieutenant, senior grade, or higher, such proofs or acknowledgments, where valid in other respects, are hereby ratified, confirmed and declared valid. All proofs or acknowledgments made by any military personnel authorized by the Congress of the United States are hereby ratified, confirmed, and declared valid and shall not require the affixation of a seal where valid in other respects. (1943, c. 159, s. 2; 2011-183, s. 32; 2013-204, s. 1.27.)

§ 47-82. Foreign probates omitting seals.

In all cases where the acknowledgment, privy examination or other proof of the execution of any instrument authorized or required to be registered has been taken by or before any ambassador, minister, consul, vice-consul, vice-consul general or commercial agent of the United States in any country beyond the limits of the United States, and such instrument has heretofore been recorded in any county in this State, but the official before whom it was taken has omitted to attach his seal of office, or it does not appear of record that such seal was attached to the instrument, or such official has certified the same as under his "official seal" or seal of his office, or words of similar import, and no such seal appears of record, then all such acknowledgments, privy examinations or other proof of such instruments, and the registration thereof, are hereby made in all respects valid, and such instruments, after the ratification hereof, shall be competent to be read in evidence. (1913, c. 69, s. 1; C.S., s. 3363.)

§ 47-83. Before consuls general.

Any deed or other instrument permitted by law to be registered, and which has prior to the thirteenth day of October, 1913, been proved or acknowledged before a "consul general," is validated; and its registration is authorized and validated. (Ex. Sess. 1913, c. 72, s. 2; C.S., s. 3364.)

§ 47-84. Before vice-consuls and vice-consuls general.

The order for registration by the clerk of the superior court and the registration thereof of all deeds of conveyance and other instruments in any county of this State prior to January 1, 1905, upon the certificate of any vice-consul or vice-consul general of the United States residing in a foreign country, certifying in due form under his name and the official seal of the United States consul or United States consul general of the same place and country where such vice-consul or vice-consul general resided and acted, that he has taken the proof or acknowledgments of the parties to such instruments, together with the privy examinations of married women parties thereto, are hereby, together with such proof and acknowledgments, privy examinations and certificates, validated. (1905, c. 451, s. 2; Rev., s. 1024; C.S., s. 3365.)

§ 47-85. Before masters in chancery.

All probates, acknowledgments, and private examinations of deeds and conveyances of land heretofore taken before masters in equity or masters in chancery in any other state are declared to be valid, and all registrations of such deeds or conveyances upon such probates, acknowledgments and private examinations, or any of them, are hereby declared to be sufficient. All such deeds and conveyances and registration thereof, and all certified copies of such registrations, shall be received in evidence or otherwise used in the same manner and with the same force and effect as other deeds and conveyances with probates, acknowledgments, or private examinations made in accordance with provisions of statutes of this State in force at the time and as registrations thereof and certified copies of such registrations. Nothing in this section contained shall have effect to deprive anyone of any legal rights acquired, before its passage, from the grantors in such deeds or conveyances subsequently to their execution, where the deeds or conveyances by which such rights were acquired have been duly acknowledged or probated and registered. (1911, c. 10; C.S., s. 3366.)

§ 47-85.1. Further as to acknowledgments, etc., before masters in chancery.

All probates, acknowledgments and privy examinations of deeds, mortgages and conveyances of land, which prior to January 1, 1948 have been taken before masters in equity or masters in chancery in any other state, are hereby declared to be valid, and all registrations of such deeds, mortgages or conveyances upon such probates, acknowledgments and private examinations, or any of them are hereby declared to be sufficient and valid. All such deeds and conveyances and registration thereof, and all certified copies of such registrations shall be received in evidence or otherwise used in the same manner and with the same force and effect as other deeds, mortgages and conveyances with probates, acknowledgments, or private examinations made in accordance with the provisions of statutes and laws of this State in force at the time, and as registrations thereof and certified copies of such registrations. (1953, c. 1136.)

§ 47-86. Validation of probate of deeds by clerks of courts of record of other states, where official seal is omitted.

In all cases where, prior to the first day of January, 1891, the acknowledgment, privy examination of a married woman, or other proof of the execution of any deed, mortgage, or other instrument authorized to be registered has been taken before a clerk of a court of record in another state, and such clerk has failed or neglected to affix his official seal to his certificate of such acknowledgment, privy examination, or other proof of execution, of such deed, mortgage or other instrument, or where such court had no official seal and no official seal was affixed to such certificate by reason of that fact, and such deed, mortgage, or other instrument has been ordered to registration by the clerk of the superior court of any county in this State and has been registered, the probate of any and every such deed, mortgage, or other instrument authorized to be registered shall be and hereby is to all intents and purposes validated. (1921, c. 15, ss. 1, 2; C.S., s. 3366(a).)

§ 47-87. Validation of probates by different officers of deeds by wife and husband.

In all cases where, prior to the second day of March, 1895, the acknowledgment, privy examination of a married woman, or other proof of the execution of any deed, mortgage, or other instrument, authorized to be registered, executed by husband and wife, has been taken as to the husband and wife in different states and by different officers having power to take acknowledgments, any and every such acknowledgment, privy examination of a married woman, or other proof of execution, and the probate of any and every such deed, mortgage or other instrument shall be and hereby is, to all intents and purposes validated. (1921, c. 19, ss. 1, 4; C.S., s. 3366(b).)

§ 47-88. Registration without formal order validated.

In all cases where the acknowledgment, privy examination of a married woman, or other proof of the execution of any deed, mortgage or other instrument, authorized to be registered, has been taken before a commissioner in another state appointed by the probate judge of any county of this State, under the provisions of section 20 of Chapter 35 of Battle's Revisal, during the time said Chapter remained in force and effect, and such commissioner has certified to such acknowledgment, privy examination or other proof, and has returned such deed, mortgage or other instrument to said probate judge, with his certificate endorsed thereon, and such deed, mortgage or other instrument, together with such certificate, has been registered, without any adjudication or order of registration by such probate judge, the probate and registration of any and every such deed shall be, and hereby are, to all intents and purposes validated. (1921, c. 19, ss. 2, 4; C.S., s. 3366(c).)

§ 47-89. Same subject.

In all cases where any deed, mortgage or other instrument has heretofore been acknowledged or probated in accordance with the provisions of G.S. 47-87 and 47-88, and such deed, mortgage or other instrument has been registered, without any order of registration by the probate judge or clerk of the superior court appearing thereon, the probate and registration of any and every such deed, mortgage or other instrument shall be, and hereby is, to all intents and purposes validated. (1921, c. 19, ss. 3, 4; C.S., s. 3366(d).)

§ 47-90. Validation of acknowledgments taken by notaries public holding other office.

In every case where deeds or other instruments have been acknowledged before a notary public, when the notary public, at the time was also holding some other office, and the deed or other instrument has been duly probated and recorded, such acknowledgment taken by such notary public is hereby declared to be sufficient and valid. (1921, c. 21; C.S., s. 3366(e).)

§ 47-91. Validation of certain probates of deeds before consular agents of the United States.

In all cases where the acknowledgment, privy examination of a married woman, or other proof of the execution of any deed, mortgage or other instrument authorized or required to be registered has been taken before any consular agent of the United States, during the time Chapter 35 of Battle's Revisal remained in force and effect, and such acknowledgment, privy examination, or other proof of the execution of such deed, mortgage, or other instrument is in other respects regular and in proper form, and such deed, mortgage, or other instrument has been duly ordered to registration and registered in the proper county, the acknowledgment, probate, and registration of any and every such deed, mortgage, or other instrument is hereby validated as fully and to the same effect as though such acknowledgment, privy examination, or other proof of execution had been taken before one of the officers named in subsection five of section two of said Chapter 35 of Battle's Revisal. (1921, c. 157; C.S., s. 3366(f).)

§ 47-92. Probates before stockholders and directors of banks.

No acknowledgment or proof of execution, including privy examination of married women, of any mortgage, or deed of trust executed to secure the payment of any indebtedness to any banking corporation shall be held invalid by reason of the fact that the officer taking such acknowledgment, proof, or privy examination was a stockholder or director in such banking corporation. (1923, c. 17; C.S., s. 3366(g); 2013-204, s. 1.28.)

§ 47-93. Acknowledgments taken by stockholder, officer, or director of bank.

No acknowledgment or proof of execution, including privy examination of married women, of any mortgage or deed of trust executed to secure the payment of any indebtedness to any banking corporation shall be held invalid by reason of the fact that the officer taking such acknowledgment, proof, or privy examination was a stockholder, officer, or director in such banking corporation. (Ex. Sess. 1924, c. 68; 2013-204, s. 1.29.)

§ 47-94. Acknowledgment and registration by officer or stockholder in building and loan or savings and loan association.

All acknowledgments and proofs of execution, including privy examination of married women, of any mortgage or deed of trust executed to secure the payment of any indebtedness to any State or federal building and loan or savings and loan association shall not be, nor held to be, invalid by reason of the fact that the clerk of the superior court, justice of the peace, notary public, or other officer taking such acknowledgment, proof of execution or privy examination, was an officer or stockholder in such building and loan association; but such proofs and acknowledgments of all such instruments, and the registration thereof, if in all other respects valid, are hereby declared to be valid.

Nor shall the registration of any such mortgage or deed of trust ordered to be registered by the clerk of the superior court, or by any deputy or assistant clerk of the superior court, be or held to be invalid by reason of the fact that the clerk of the superior court, or deputy, or assistant clerk of the superior court, ordering such mortgages or deeds of trust to be registered was an officer or stockholder in any State or federal building and loan or savings and loan association, whose indebtedness is secured in and by such mortgage or deed of trust. (Ex. Sess. 1924, c. 108; 1929, c. 146, s. 1; 1959, c. 489; 2013-204, s. 1.30.)

§ 47-95. Acknowledgments taken by notaries interested as trustee or holding other office.

In every case where deeds and other instruments have been acknowledged and privy examination of wives had before notaries public, or justices of the peace, prior to October 1, 1991, when the notary public or justice of the peace at the time was interested as trustee in said instrument or at the time was also holding some other office, and the deed or other instrument has been duly probated and recorded, such acknowledgment and privy examination taken by such notary public or justice of the peace is hereby declared to be sufficient and valid. (1923, c. 61; C.S., s. 3366(h); 1931, cc. 166, 438; 1939, c. 321; 1955, c. 696; 1957, c. 1270; 1959, c. 81; 1969, c. 639, s. 1; 1975, c. 320, s. 1; 2013-204, s. 1.31.)

§ 47-96. Validation of instruments registered without probate.

In every case where it shall appear from the records in the office of the register of deeds of any county in the State that any instrument of writing required or allowed by law to be registered prior to January 1, 1869, without any acknowledgment, proof, privy examination, or probate, or upon a defective acknowledgment, proof, privy examination, or probate, the record of such instrument may, notwithstanding, be read in evidence in any of the courts of this State, if otherwise competent. (1923, c. 215, s. 1; C.S., s. 3366(i).)

§ 47-97. Validation of corporate deed with mistake as to officer's name.

In all cases where the deed of a corporation executed before April 1, 2013, is properly executed, properly recorded and there is error in the probate of said corporation's deed as to the name or names of the officers in said probate, said deed shall be construed to be a deed of the same force and effect as if said probate were in every way proper. (1933, c. 412, s. 1; 2013-204, s. 1.32.)

§ 47-97.1. Validation of corporate deeds containing error in acknowledgment or probate.

In all cases where the deed of a corporation executed and filed for registration prior to April 1, 2013, is properly executed and properly recorded and there is error in the acknowledgment or probate of said corporation's deed as to the name or names of the officer or officers named therein and error as to the title or titles of the officer or officers named therein, said deed shall be construed to be a deed of the same force and effect as if said probate or acknowledgment were in every way proper. (1951, c. 825; 2013-204, s. 1.33.)

§ 47-98. Registration on defective probates beyond State.

In every case where it shall appear from the records in the office of the register of deeds of any county in this State that any instrument required or allowed by law to be registered, bearing date prior to the year 1835, executed by any person or persons residing in any of the United States, other than this State, or in any of the territories of the United States, or in the District of Columbia, has been proven or acknowledged, or the privy examination of any feme covert taken thereto, before any officer or person authorized by any of the laws of this State in force prior to the said year 1835 to take such proofs, privy examinations and acknowledgments, and the said instrument has been registered in the proper county without the certificate of the Governor of the state or territory in which such proofs, acknowledgments or privy examinations were taken, or of the Secretary of State of the United States, when such certificate or certificates were required, as to the official character of the person taking such acknowledgment, proof or privy examination, as aforesaid, and without an order of registration made by a court or judge in this State having jurisdiction to make such order, then and in all such cases such proofs, privy examinations, acknowledgments and registrations are hereby in all respects fully validated and confirmed and declared to be sufficient in law, and such instruments so registered may be read in evidence in any of the courts of this State. (1923, c. 215, ss. 2, 3; C.S., s. 3366(j).)

§ 47-99. Certificates of clerks without seal.

All certificates of acknowledgment and all verifications of pleadings, affidavits, and other instruments executed by clerks of the superior court of the State prior to March 1, 1945, and which do not bear the official seal of such clerks, are hereby validated in all cases in which the instruments bearing such acknowledgment or certification are filed or recorded in any county in the State other than the county in which the clerk executing such certificates of acknowledgment or verifications resides, and such acknowledgments and verifications are hereby made and declared to be binding, valid and effective to the same extent and in the same manner as if said official seal had been affixed. (1925, c. 248; 1945, c. 798.)

§ 47-100. Acknowledgments taken by officer who was grantor.

In all cases where a deed or deeds dated prior to the first day of January, 1980, purporting to convey lands, have been registered in the office of the register of deeds of the county where the lands conveyed in said deed or deeds are located, prior to said first day of January, 1980, and the acknowledgments or proof of execution of such deed or deeds has been taken as to some of the grantors by an officer who was himself one of the grantors named in such deed or deeds, such defective execution, acknowledgment and proof of execution and probate of such deed or deeds thereon and the registration thereof as above described, shall be, and the same are hereby declared to be in all respects valid, and such deed or deeds shall be declared to be in all respects duly executed, probated and recorded to the same effect as if such officer taking such proof or acknowledgment of execution had not been named as a grantor therein, or in anywise interested therein. (1929, c. 48, s. 1; 1953, c. 986; 1991 (Reg. Sess., 1992), c. 1030, s. 51.8.)

§ 47-101. Seal of acknowledging officer omitted; deeds made presumptive evidence.

In all cases where deeds appear to have been executed for land prior to January 1, 1900, and appear to have been recorded in the offices of the registers of deeds in the proper counties in this State, and the same appear to have been acknowledged before commissioners of affidavits (or deeds) of North Carolina, residing in the District of Columbia or elsewhere in the different states, or appear to have been recorded without any certificate being recorded on the record of such deed or deeds, such record or records shall be presumptive evidence of the execution of such deed or deeds by the grantor or the grantors to the grantee or grantees therein named for the lands therein described, and the record of such deed or deeds may be offered or read in evidence upon the trial or hearing of any cause in any of the courts of this State as if the same had been properly probated and recorded: Provided, however, that nothing herein contained shall prevent such record or records from being attacked for fraud, and provided further that this section shall not apply to creditors or purchasers, but as to them the same shall stand as if this section had not been passed, and shall only apply to deeds executed prior to January 1, 1900. (1929, c. 14, s. 1.)

§ 47-102. Absence of notarial seal.

Any deed executed prior to October 1, 2005, and duly acknowledged before a North Carolina notary public, and the probate recites "witness my hand and notarial seal," or words of similar import, and no seal was affixed to the said deed, shall be ordered registered by the clerk of the superior court of the county in which the land lies, upon presentation to him: Provided, the probate is otherwise in due form. (1935, c. 130; 1943, c. 472; 1945, c. 808, s. 3; 2013-204, s. 1.34.)

§ 47-103. Deeds probated and registered with notary's seal not affixed, validated.

Any deed conveying or affecting real estate executed prior to January 1, 1932, and ordered registered and recorded in the county in which the land lies prior to said date, from which deed and the acknowledgment and privy examination thereof the seal of the notary public taking the acknowledgment or privy examination of the grantor or grantors thereof was omitted, is hereby declared to be sufficient and valid, and the probate and registration thereof are hereby in all respects validated and confirmed to the same effect as if the seal of said notary was affixed to the acknowledgment or privy examination thereof. (1941, c. 20.)

§ 47-104. Acknowledgments of notary holding another office.

In every case where deeds or other instruments have been acknowledged before a notary public, when the notary public at the time was also holding some other office, and the deed or other instrument has been duly probated and recorded, such acknowledgment taken by such notary public is hereby declared to be sufficient and valid. (1935, c. 133; 1937, c. 284.)

§ 47-105. Acknowledgment and private examination of married woman taken by officer who was grantor.

In all cases where a deed or deeds of mortgages or other conveyances of land dated prior to the first day of January, 1926, purporting to convey lands have been registered in the office of the register of deeds of the county where the lands conveyed in said deeds are located prior to said first day of January, 1926, and the acknowledgments or proof of execution of such deed or deeds and the private examination of any married woman who is a grantor in such deed or deeds have been taken as to some of the grantors, and the private examination of any married woman grantor in such deed has been taken by an officer who was himself one of the grantors named in such deed or deeds, such defective execution, acknowledgment, proof of execution and the private examination of such married woman, evidenced by the certificate thereof on such deed and the registration thereof as above described and set forth, shall be and the same are hereby declared to be in all respects valid, and such deed or deeds or other conveyances of land are declared to be in all respects duly executed, probated and recorded to the same effect as if such officer taking such proof or acknowledgment of execution or taking the private examination of such married woman and certifying thereto upon such deed or deeds had not been named as grantor therein and had not been interested therein in any way whatsoever. (1937, c. 91.)

§ 47-106. Certain instruments in which clerk of superior court was a party, validated.

In all cases where a deed, or other conveyance of land dated prior to the first day of January, 1918, purporting to convey land, wherein the grantor or one of the grantors therein was at the time clerk of the superior court of the county where the land purporting to be conveyed was located, was acknowledged, proof of execution, privy examination of a married woman, and, or, order of registration had and taken before a deputy clerk of the superior court of said county, and the instrument registered upon the order of said deputy clerk of the superior court in the office of the register of deeds of said county, within two years from the date of said instrument, such instrument and its probate are hereby in all respects validated and confirmed; and such instrument, together with such defective acknowledgment, proof of execution, privy examination of a married woman, order of registration, and the certificate of such deputy clerk of the superior court, and the registration thereof, are hereby declared in all respects to be valid and binding upon the parties of such instrument and their privies, and such instrument so probated and recorded together with its certificates may be read in evidence as a muniment of title, for all intents and purposes, in any of the courts of this State. (1939, c. 261.)

§ 47-107. Validation of probate and registration of certain instruments where name of grantor omitted from record.

Whenever any deed, deed of trust, conveyance or other instrument permitted by law to be registered in this State has been registered for a period of 21 years or more and a clerk of the superior court or a register of deeds has adjudged the certificate of the officer before whom the acknowledgment was taken to be in due form and correct and has ordered the instrument to be recorded, but the name of a grantor which appears in the body of the instrument and as a signer of the instrument has been omitted from the record of the certificate of the officer before whom the acknowledgment was taken, such deed, deed of trust, conveyance or other instrument shall be conclusively presumed to have been duly acknowledged, probated and recorded; provided this presumption shall not affect litigation instituted within 21 years after date of registration. (1941, c. 30; 1971, c. 825.)

§ 47-108. Acknowledgments before notaries under age.

All acts of notaries public for the State of North Carolina who were not yet 21 years of age at the time of the performance of such acts are hereby validated; and in every case where deeds or other instruments have been acknowledged before such notary public who was not yet 21 years of age at the time of taking of said acknowledgment, such acknowledgment taken before such notary public is hereby declared to be sufficient and valid. (1941, c. 233.)

§ 47-108.1. Certain corporate deeds, etc., declared validly admitted to record.

Deeds, conveyances and other instruments of writing of corporations entitled to registration, which have been heretofore duly executed in the manner required by law, by the proper officers of the corporation, and which have prior to March 8, 1943, been admitted to registration, on the acknowledgment or proof of the proper executing officer, in the manner required by law, shall be, and the same are hereby declared to be, in all respects validly admitted to record, although such officer at the date of such acknowledgment or proof had ceased to be an officer of such corporation, or such corporation at the date of such acknowledgment or proof had ceased to exist. (1943, c. 598.)

§ 47-108.2. Acknowledgments and examinations before notaries holding some other office.

In every case where deeds or other instruments have been acknowledged, and where privy examination of wives had, before a notary public, when the notary public at the time was also holding some other office, and the deed or other instrument has been otherwise duly probated and recorded, such acknowledgment taken by, and such privy examination had before such notary public is hereby declared to be sufficient and valid. (1945, c. 149.)

§ 47-108.3. Validation of acts of certain notaries public prior to November 26, 1921.

In all cases where prior to November 26, 1921, instruments by law, or otherwise, required, permitted or authorized to be registered, certified, probated, recorded or filed with certificates of notaries public showing the acknowledgments or proofs of execution thereof as required by the laws of the State of North Carolina have been registered, certified, probated, recorded or filed, such registration, certifications, probates, recordations and filings are hereby validated and made as good and sufficient as though such instruments had been in all respects properly registered, certified, probated, recorded or filed, notwithstanding there are no records in the office of the Governor of the State of North Carolina or in the office of the clerk of the superior court of the county in which such notaries public were to act that such persons acting as such notaries public had ever been appointed or subscribed written oaths or received any certificates or commissions or were qualified as notaries public at the time of the performance of the acts hereby validated. (1947, c. 102.)

§ 47-108.4. Acknowledgments, etc., of instruments of married women made since February 7, 1945.

All acknowledgments, probates and registrations of instruments wherein any married woman was a grantor, including deeds and mortgages on land, made since February 7, 1945, are hereby validated, approved and declared of full force and effect. (1947, c. 991, s. 2.)

§ 47-108.5. Validation of certain deeds executed in other states where seal omitted.

All deeds to lands in North Carolina, executed prior to January 1, 1991, without seal attached to the maker's name, which deeds were acknowledged in another state, the laws of which do not require a seal for the validity of a conveyance of real property located in that state, and which deeds have been duly recorded in this State, shall be as valid to all intents and purposes as if the same had been executed under seal. (1949, cc. 87, 296; 1959, c. 797; 1983, c. 398, s. 6; 1985, c. 70, s. 6; 1987, c. 277, s. 6; 1989, c. 390, s. 6; 1991, c. 489, s. 6.)

§ 47-108.6. Validation of certain conveyances of foreign dissolved corporations.

In all cases when, prior to April 1, 2013, any dissolved foreign corporation has, prior to its dissolution, by deed of conveyance purported to convey real property in this State, and said instrument recites a consideration, is signed by the proper officers in the name of said corporation, sealed with the corporate seal and duly registered in the office of the register of deeds of the county where the land described in said instrument is located, but there is error in the attestation clause and acknowledgment in failing to identify the officers signing said deed and to recite that authority was duly given and that the same was the act of said corporation, said deed shall be construed to be a deed of the same force and effect as if said attestation clause and acknowledgment were in every way proper. (1949, c. 1212; 2013-204, s. 1.35.)

§ 47-108.7. Validation of acknowledgments, etc., by deputy clerks of superior court.

All acts heretofore performed by deputy clerks of the superior court in taking acknowledgments, examining witnesses and probating wills, deeds and other instruments required or permitted by law to be recorded are hereby validated: Provided, nothing in this section shall affect pending litigation. (1949, c. 1072.)

§ 47-108.8. Acts of registers of deeds or deputies in recording plats and maps by certain methods validated.

All acts heretofore performed by a register of deeds, or a deputy register of deeds in recording plats and maps by transcribing a correct copy thereof or permanently attaching the original to the records in a book designated "Book of Plats" is hereby validated the same as if said plats had been recorded as required by G.S. 47-30: Provided, however, that nothing herein contained shall affect pending litigation. (1949, c. 1073.)

§ 47-108.9. Validation of probate of instruments pursuant to § 47-12.

The probates of all instruments taken on and after February 7, 1945, in accordance with the provisions of G.S. 47-12, as amended by section 11 of Chapter 73 of the Session Laws of 1945 and section 1 of Chapter 991 of the Session Laws of 1947 and as further amended by sections 2 and 3 of Chapter 815 of the Session Laws of 1949, are hereby in all respects validated; provided, however, that this section shall not apply to pending litigation. (1949, c. 815, s. 3.)

§ 47-108.10. Validation of registration of plats upon probate in accordance with § 47-30.

The registration of all plats which have prior to February 6, 1953, been admitted to registration upon probate thereof, in accordance with the provisions of G.S. 47-30 as amended by section 1 of Chapter 47 of the Session Laws of 1953, is hereby validated. (1953, c. 47, s. 2.)

§ 47-108.11. Validation of recorded instruments where seals have been omitted.

In all cases of any deed, deed of trust, mortgage, lien or other instrument authorized or required to be registered in the office of the register of deeds of any county in this State where it appears of record or it appears that from said instrument, as recorded in the office of the register of deeds of any county in the State, there has been omitted from said recorded or registered instrument the word "seal," "notarial seal" and that any of said recorded or registered instruments shows or recites that the grantor or grantors "have hereunto fixed or set their hands and seals" and the signature of the grantor or grantors appears without a seal thereafter or on the recorded or registered instrument or in all cases where it appears there is an attesting clause which recites "signed, sealed and delivered in the presence of," and the signature of the grantor or grantors appears on the recorded or registered instrument without any seal appearing thereafter or of record, then all such deeds, mortgages, deeds of trust, liens or other instruments, and the registration of same in the office of the register of deeds, are hereby declared to be in all respects valid and binding and are hereby made in all respects valid and binding to the same extent as if the word "seal" or "notarial seal" had not been omitted, and the registration and recording of such instruments in the office of the register of deeds in any county in this State are hereby declared to be valid, proper, legal and binding registrations.

This section shall not apply in any respect to any instrument recorded or registered subsequent to April 1, 2013, or to pending litigation or to any such instruments now directly or indirectly involved in pending litigation. (1953, c. 996; 1959, c. 1022; 1973, c. 519; c. 1207, s. 2; 1977, c. 165; 1979, 2nd Sess., c. 1185, s. 1; 1983, c. 398, s. 7; 1985, c. 70, s. 7; 1987, c. 277, s. 7; 1989, c. 390, s. 7; 1991, c. 489, s. 7; 1995, c. 163, s. 16; 1999-456, s. 12; 2013-204, s. 1.36.)

§ 47-108.12. Validation of instruments acknowledged before United States commissioners.

All deeds, mortgages, or other instruments permitted or required by law to be registered, which prior to January 1, 1933, have been proved or acknowledged before a United States commissioner, or U.S. commissioner, are hereby in all respects validated as to such proof or acknowledgment, and all registrations of such deeds or conveyances, upon such probates, acknowledgments and private examinations, or any of them, are hereby declared to be sufficient and validated. (1953, c. 987.)

§ 47-108.13. Validation of certain instruments registered prior to January 1, 1934.

In all cases where prior to January 1, 1934 instruments by law required or authorized to be registered show the signatures and seal of each of the grantors therein and further show that each of such grantors has appeared before or signed such instruments in the presence of a notary public, justice of the peace or other person duly authorized to take acknowledgments, and such instruments have been ordered registered by the clerk of the superior court or other officer qualified to pass upon probate and admit instruments to registration, and actually put on the books in the office of the register of deeds, as if properly acknowledged, all such instruments and their registrations are hereby validated and made as good and sufficient as though such instruments had been in all respects properly acknowledged: Provided, that this section shall not apply to any privy examination or acknowledgment of a married woman. (1953, c. 1334.)

§ 47-108.14. Conveyances by the United States acting by and through the General Services Administration.

The United States of America, acting by and through the General Services Administration may convey lands and other property in the State of North Carolina which is transferable by deed, quitclaim deed, or other means of conveyances without the Regional Director or other duly authorized agent acting for and on behalf of the United States of America, adopting or placing a "seal," in any form, after the signature of the grantor's agent, or elsewhere on said deed, quitclaim deed, or other instrument, and the conveyances of the United

States of America acting by and through the General Services Administration, and executed by its Regional Director or other duly authorized agent, although without a "seal" appearing thereon, shall be in all respects valid and binding to the same extent as if the word "seal" or some other type of seal, appeared after the signature of the grantor's agent, or elsewhere on said conveyances.

All conveyances prior to April 19, 1955, where any deed, quitclaim deed, or other instrument conveying land or other property in the State of North Carolina has been executed by the United States of America, by and through the General Services Administration, and said conveyances are authorized or required to be registered in the office of the register of deeds of any county in this State, and it appears from said instrument, or said instrument as recorded in the office of the register of deeds of any county in this State, that a seal has been omitted from said instruments, that notwithstanding the absence of a seal all such conveyances are hereby declared to be in all respects valid and binding to convey lands and property rights in the State of North Carolina to the grantees named therein, to the same extent as if the word "seal," or a seal in some other form, had appeared after the signature of the grantor's agent, or elsewhere on said conveyances, and the registration and recording of such conveyances in the office of the register of deeds in all counties in this State are hereby declared to be valid, proper, legal and binding registrations to the same extent as if such conveyances were executed under seal. (1955, c. 629, s. 1.)

§ 47-108.15. Validation of registration of instruments filed before order of registration.

All deeds, deeds of trust, mortgages, chattel mortgages, contracts and all other instruments required or permitted by law to be registered which have heretofore been accepted for filing and registration by registers of deeds on a date preceding the date of the clerk's order of registration are hereby validated, approved, confirmed and declared to be valid, proper, legal and binding registrations to the same extent as if such instruments had been accepted for filing and registration on the date of or subsequent to the date of the clerk's order of registration. (1957, c. 1430.)

§ 47-108.16. Validation of certain deeds executed by nonresident banks.

All deeds and other conveyances of land in this State executed on behalf of banks not incorporated in the State of North Carolina, by a trust officer thereof, and properly recorded on or before December 31, 1963, which deeds are otherwise regular and valid, are hereby validated. (1965, c. 610.)

§ 47-108.17. Validation of certain deeds where official capacity not designated.

In all cases where an executor, executrix, administrator, administratrix, guardian or commissioner has executed a deed, deed of trust or other instrument of conveyance permitted by law to be registered in this State and the granting clause of the instrument sets forth the official capacity of the grantor, neither the failure to redesignate the grantor's official capacity following his or her signature nor the failure to designate the official capacity of the grantor in the acknowledgment of the instrument shall invalidate the conveyance provided the instrument is otherwise properly executed. (1973, c. 1220, s. 1.)

§ 47-108.18. Registration of certain instruments containing a notarial jurat validated.

A notarial jurat constitutes an acknowledgment in due form for all plats or maps that have heretofore been accepted for filing and registration under G.S. 47-30 as amended. No plat or map heretofore accepted for filing and registration, that contains a notarial jurat instead of an acknowledgment may be held to be improperly registered solely for lack of a proper acknowledgment. (1983, c. 391.)

§ 47-108.18A. Registration of certain instruments containing a notarial acknowledgment.

A notarial acknowledgment constitutes a jurat in due form for all instruments that have heretofore been accepted for filing and registration under this Chapter or which relate to real estate located within this State. (2013-204, s. 1.37.)

§ 47-108.18B. Registration of certain instruments containing a notarial jurat.

A notarial jurat constitutes an acknowledgment in due form for all instruments that have heretofore been accepted for filing and registration under this Chapter or which relate to real estate located within this State. (2013-204, s. 1.37.)

§ 47-108.19. Validation of certain maps and plats that cannot be copied.

All maps and plats registered before June 1, 1983, pursuant to G.S. 47-30 that met all of the requirements of that statute except that they were not on a material from which legible copies could be made or did not contain the original of the surveyor's signature and acknowledgment are declared to be valid registrations. (1983, c. 756.)

§ 47-108.20. Validation of certain recorded instruments that were not acknowledged.

All instruments recorded before April 1, 2013, that were not reexecuted and reacknowledged and that correct an obvious typographical or other minor error in a recorded instrument that was previously properly executed and acknowledged are declared to be valid instruments. (1985 (Reg. Sess., 1986), c. 842, s. 2; 2013-204, s. 1.38.)

§ 47-108.21. Sales for 1930 on dates other than first Monday in June validated.

All sales of land for failure to pay taxes held or conducted by any sheriff or any tax collector of any county, city, town, or other municipality during the year 1930, on any day subsequent to or other than the first Monday in June of said year, are hereby approved, confirmed, validated, and declared to be proper, valid, and legal sales of such land and legally binding in all respects, and all certificates of sale made and issued upon and in accordance with such sales are hereby approved and validated to all intents and purposes with such full force and legal effect as if said sales had been held and conducted on said first Monday of June, 1930. (1931, c. 160; 1971, c. 806, s. 1; 1987, c. 777, s. 4(1).)

§ 47-108.22. Tax sales for 1931-32 on day other than law provides and certificates validated.

All sales of land for failure to pay taxes held or conducted by any sheriff or any tax collector of any county, city, town, or other municipality during the years 1931 and 1932, on any day subsequent to or other than the first Monday in June of said year, are hereby approved, confirmed, validated, and declared to be proper, valid, and legal sales of such land and legally binding in all respects, and all certificates of sale made and issued upon and in accordance with such sales approved and validated to all intents and purposes with such full force and legal effect as if said sales had been held and conducted on said first Monday of June, 1931 and 1932. (1933, c. 177; 1971, c. 806, s. 1; 1987, c. 777, s. 4(1).)

§ 47-108.23. Tax sales for 1933-34 and certificates validated.

All sales of land for failure to pay taxes held or conducted by any sheriff or any tax collector of any county, city, town, or other municipality during the years 1933 and 1934, or on any date subsequent to or other than the date prescribed by law, and all certificates of sale executed and issued pursuant to and in accordance with such sales be and the same are hereby approved, confirmed, and validated and shall have the same force and legal effect as if said sales had been held and conducted on the date prescribed by law.

The board of county commissioners of any county or the governing board of any city, town, or other municipality may by resolution order the sheriff or tax collecting officer of the said county, city, town, or other municipality to advertise in the manner provided by law and sell all land for the taxes of any year levied by the said county, city, town, or other municipality, which land has not heretofore been legally sold for the failure to pay said taxes. The sale or sales herein authorized shall be held not later than the first Monday in September 1935, and certificates of sale shall be issued in accordance with and pursuant to said sale or sales in the same manner as if said sale or sales had been held and conducted as provided by law. Any sale held and conducted under the provisions of this paragraph and all certificates issued pursuant to such a sale shall be and the same are hereby approved, confirmed, and validated and shall have the same force and legal effect as if said sale had been held and conducted on the date prescribed by law.

All actions instituted in any county, city, town, or other municipality for the foreclosure of certificates of sale issued for the taxes of the years 1927, 1928, 1929, 1930, 1931 and 1932 subsequent to October 1, 1934, and all such actions instituted before October 1, 1935, shall be and the same are hereby approved, validated, and declared to be legally binding and of the same force and effect as if said actions were instituted prior to October 1, 1934: Provided, that this section shall not be construed to repeal any private or local act passed by the General Assembly of 1935. (1935, c. 331; 1971, c. 806, s. 1; 1987, c. 777, s. 4(1).)

§ 47-108.24. Notices of sale for taxes by publication validated.

All sales of real property under tax certificate foreclosures made between January 1, 1927, and March 13, 1937, where the original notice of sale was published for four successive weeks, and any notice of resale was published for two successive weeks, preceding said sales, whether the notice of sale was required to be published in a newspaper or at courthouse door, or both, shall be, and the same are in all respects validated as to publication of said notice: Provided said publication was completed as above set out within 10 days of the date of the sale.

The provisions of this section shall not apply to the Counties of Alleghany, Beaufort, Cabarrus, Camden, Carteret, Caswell, Currituck, Halifax, Harnett, Henderson, Hertford, Hyde, Iredell, Johnston, Jones, Macon, Mitchell, Moore, Nash, New Hanover, Perquimans, Pitt, Polk, Rowan, Rutherford, Scotland, Surry, Wake, Warren, Washington, and Wayne. (1937, c. 128; 1971, c. 806, s. 1; 1987, c. 777, s. 4(1).)

§ 47-108.25. Validation of sales and resales held pursuant to § 105-374.

All sales or resales held prior to April 14, 1951, pursuant to G.S. 105-374, where the advertisement was in accordance with G.S. 1-327 and 1-328 as provided by such sections prior to their repeal, are validated to the same extent as if such advertisement were in accordance with Article 29A of Chapter 1 of the General Statutes; and all such sales, where the provisions of G.S. 45-28 as to resales, as provided by such section prior to its repeal, were followed, are validated to the same extent as if the resale procedure provided for in Article 29A of Chapter 1 of the General Statutes had been followed. (1951, c. 1036, s. 2; 1971, c. 806, s. 1; 1987, c. 777, s. 4(1).)

§ 47-108.26. Validation of reconveyances of tax foreclosed property by county boards of commissioners.

The action of county boards of commissioners taken prior to March 20, 1951, reconveying tax foreclosed property by private sale to the former owners or other interested parties for amounts not less than such counties' interest therein is hereby ratified, confirmed, and validated. (1951, c. 300, s. 2; 1971, c. 806, s. 1; 1987, c. 777, s. 4.)

Article 5.

Registration of Official Discharges from the Armed Forces of the United States.

§ 47-109. Book for record of discharges in office of register of deeds; specifications.

There shall be provided, and at all times maintained, in the office of the register of deeds of each county in North Carolina a special and permanent book, in which shall be recorded official discharges from the United States Army, Navy, Marine Corps and other branches of the Armed Forces of the United States. The book shall be securely bound, and the pages of the book shall be printed in the form of discharge papers, with sufficient blank lines for the recording of such dates as may be contained in the discharge papers offered for registration. (1921, c. 198, s. 1; C.S., s. 3366(k); 1945, c. 659, s. 2; 2011-183, s. 34.)

§ 47-110. Registration of official discharge or certificate of lost discharge.

Upon the presentation to the register of deeds of any county of any official discharge, or official certificate of lost discharge, from the United States Army,

Navy, Marine Corps, or any other branch of the Armed Forces of the United States the register of deeds shall record the same without charge in the book provided for in G.S. 47-109. (1921, c. 198, s. 2; C.S., s. 3366(l); 1943, c. 599; 1945, c. 659, s. 1; 2011-183, s. 35.)

§ 47-111. Inquiry by register of deeds; oath of applicant.

If any register of deeds shall be in doubt as to whether or not any paper so presented for registration is an official discharge from the United States Army, Navy, Marine Corps, or any other branch of the Armed Forces of the United States or an official certificate of lost discharge, the register of deeds shall have power to examine, under oath, the person so presenting such discharge, or otherwise inquire into its validity; and every register of deeds to whom a discharge or certificate of lost discharge is presented for registration shall administer to the person offering such discharge or certificate of lost discharge for registration the following oath, to be recorded with and form a part of the registration of such discharge or certificate of lost discharge:

"I, _____, being duly sworn, depose and say that the foregoing discharge (or certificate of lost discharge) is the original discharge (or certificate of lost discharge) issued to me by the government of the United States; and that no alterations have been made therein by me, or by any person to my knowledge.

Subscribed and sworn to before me this _____ day of _____, _____"

(1921, c. 198, s. 3; C.S., s. 3366(m); 1999-456, s. 59; 2011-183, s. 36.)

§ 47-112. Forgery or alteration of discharge or certificate; punishment.

Any person who shall forge, or in any manner alter any discharge or certificate of lost discharge issued by the government of the United States, and offer the same for registration or secure the registration of the same under the provisions of this Article shall be guilty of a Class 1 misdemeanor. (1921, c. 198, s. 4; C.S., s. 3366(n); 1993, c. 539, s. 409; 1994, Ex. Sess., c. 24, s. 14(c).)

§ 47-113. Certified copy of registration.

Any person desiring a certified copy of any such discharge, or certificate of lost discharge, registered under the provisions of this Article shall apply for the same to the register of deeds of the county in which such discharge or certificate of lost discharge is registered. The register of deeds shall furnish certified copies of instruments registered under this Article without charge to any member or former member of the Armed Forces of the United States who applies therefor. (1921, c. 198, s. 5; C.S., s. 3366(o); 1945, c. 659, s. 3; 1969, c. 80, s. 11; 2011-183, s. 37.)

§ 47-113.1: Repealed by Session Laws 2003-248, s. 1, effective January 1, 2004.

§ 47-113.2. Restricting access to military discharge documents.

(a) All military discharge documents filed on or after January 1, 2004, shall be considered a public record, but for confidential safekeeping and restricted access to such documents, these documents will be filed with the registers of deeds in this State. These documents are exempt from public inspection and access except as allowed in subsections (b) and (m) of this section.

(b) Definitions:

(1) Authorized party. - Four categories of authorized parties are recognized with respect to access to military discharge documents under subsection (e) of this section:

a. The subject of the document or the subject's widow or widower.

b. Agents and representatives of the subject authorized in writing:

1. By the subject or subject's widow or widower in a notarized authorization,

2. By a court to represent subject, or

3. By the subject's executor acting on behalf of a deceased subject.

c. Authorized agents of the Division of Veterans Affairs, the United States Department of Veterans Affairs, the Department of Defense, or a court official with an interest in assisting the subject or the deceased subject's beneficiaries to obtain a benefit.

d. Agents or representatives of the North Carolina State Archives.

(2) Filing office. - The office where military discharge documents are recorded, registered, or filed in this State is the register of deeds.

(3) Military discharge document. - Any document that purports to represent a notice of separation from or service in the Armed Forces of the United States or armed forces of any state, including, but not limited to, Department of Defense Form 214 or 215, WD AGO 53, WD AGO 55, WD AGO 53-55, NAVMC 78-PD, and NAVPERS 553.

(c) A military discharge document shall be accepted for filing upon presentation in person.

(d) The filing officer may refuse to accept any document that is:

(1) Not submitted in person by an authorized party in accordance with subsection (b) of this section.

(2) Not an original, a carbon copy, or a photographic copy issued or certified by an agency of federal or State government.

(e) No copy of a military discharge document or any other information from such document filed after January 1, 2004, shall be made available other than in accordance with subsection (b) or (m) of this section.

(f) Certified copies of a military discharge document will be made available only in accordance with subsection (h) of this section and only by individual request.

(g) Uncertified copies of a military discharge document will be made available to an authorized party in accordance with subsection (b) of this section and only by individual request.

(h) The North Carolina Association of Registers of Deeds and the Division of Veterans Affairs shall adopt before January 1, 2004, such request forms and associated rules as are required to implement the provisions of this section. All filing offices shall use the forms and comply with the rules, as adopted.

(i) Completed request forms shall be maintained in the register of deeds for a period of one year.

(j) The request forms shall not be considered public records and are subject to the same restricted access as the military discharge document.

(k) In the event images of and the index to military discharge documents filed prior to January 1, 2004, have not been commingled with other publicly available document images and their index in a filing office, the images and the index will be maintained and are subject to all the provisions of this section that apply to newly filed documents.

(l) The register of deeds shall, to the greatest extent possible, take appropriate protective actions in accordance with any limitations determined necessary by the register of deeds with regard to records that were filed before January 1, 2004.

(m) Subsection (e) of this section shall not apply to images of military discharge documents that have been on file for over 80 years.

(n) There shall be no fee charged for filing military discharge documents or for providing certified copies of military discharge documents provided to those who have a right to access under subsection (e) of this section. Uncertified copy of a military discharge document that becomes public record under subsection (m) of this section is subject to fee as determined in G.S. 161-10(a)(11).

(o) Filing offices shall be responsible for the cost of compliance with this section.

(p) Recording officials shall not be liable for any damages that may result from good faith compliance with the provisions of this section.

(q) The words "register of deeds" appearing in this section shall be interpreted to mean "register of deeds, assistant register of deeds, or deputy register of deeds." (2003-248, s. 2; 2011-183, s. 38; 2011-246, s. 8; 2013-15, s. 1.)

§ 47-114. Payment of expenses incurred.

The county commissioners of each county are hereby authorized and empowered in their discretion to appropriate from the general fund of the county an amount sufficient to cover any additional expense incurred by the register of deeds of the county in carrying out the purposes of this Article. (1945, c. 659, s. 3 1/2.)

Article 6.

Registration and Execution of Instruments Signed under a Power of Attorney.

§ 47-115. Execution in name of either principal or attorney-in-fact; indexing in names of both.

Any instrument in writing executed by an attorney-in-fact shall be good and valid as the instrument of the principal, whether or not said instrument is signed and/or acknowledged in the name of the principal by the attorney-in-fact or by the attorney-in-fact designating himself as attorney-in-fact for the principal or acknowledged in the name of the attorney-in-fact without naming the principal from which it will appear that it was the purpose of the attorney-in-fact to be acting for and on behalf of the principal mentioned or referred to in the instrument. This section shall not affect any pending litigation or the status of any matter heretofore determined by the courts. This section shall apply to all such instruments heretofore or hereafter executed. Registers of deeds shall be required to index all such instruments filed for registration both in the name of the principal or principals executing the powers of appointment and in the name of the attorney-in-fact executing the instrument: Provided, that instruments heretofore registered and indexed only in the name of the attorney-in-fact shall be valid and in all respects binding upon the principal or principals insofar as validity of registration is concerned. (1945, c. 204; 1959, c. 210.)

§ 47-115.1. Repealed by Session Laws 1983, c. 626, s. 2, effective October 1, 1983.

Article 7.

Private Examination of Married Women Abolished.

§ 47-116. Transferred to G.S. 47-14.1 by Session Laws 1951, c. 893.

Article 8.

Memoranda of Leases and Options.

§ 47-117. Forms do not preclude use of others; adaptation of forms.

(a) The form prescribed in this Article does not exclude the use of other forms which are sufficient in law.

(b) The prescribed form may be adapted to fit the various situations in which the grantors or grantees are individuals, firms, associations, corporations, or otherwise, or combinations thereof. (1961, c. 1174.)

§ 47-118. Forms of registration of lease.

(a) A lease of land or land and personal property may be registered by registering a memorandum thereof which shall set forth:

(1) The names of the parties thereto;

(2) A description of the property leased;

(3) The term of the lease, including extensions, renewals and options to purchase, if any; and

(4) Reference sufficient to identify the complete agreement between the parties.

Such a memorandum may be in substantially the following form:

MEMORANDUM OF LEASE

_____

_____

(Name and address or description of lessor or lessors)

hereby lease(s) to
_____
,

(Name and address or description of lessee or lessees)

for a term beginning the _____ day of _____, _____

(Month)

(Year)

and continuing for a maximum period of _____, including extensions and renewals, if any, the following property:

(Here describe the property)

(If applicable: [There exists an option to purchase with respect to this leased property, in favor of the lessee which expires the ____ day of _____, _____, which

                                                                             (Month)

(Year)

is set forth at large in the complete agreement between the parties].)

The provisions set forth in a written lease agreement between the parties dated the ____ day of _____, _____, are hereby incorporated in this memorandum.

        (Month)   (Year)

_____ [Seal]

                                                   (Lessor)

_____ [Seal]

                                                   (Lessee)

(Acknowledgment as required by law.)

(b)   If the provisions of the lease make it impossible or impractical to state the maximum period of the lease because of conditions, renewals and extensions, or otherwise, then the memorandum of lease shall state in detail all provisions concerning the term of the lease as fully as set forth in the written lease agreement between the parties.

(c)   Registration of a memorandum of lease pursuant to subsections (a) and (b) of this section, shall have the same legal effect as if the written lease agreement had been registered in its entirety. (1961, c. 1174; 1999-456, s. 59.)

§ 47-119. Form of memorandum for option to purchase real estate.

An option to purchase real estate may be registered by registering a memorandum thereof which shall set forth:

(1)   The names of the parties thereto;

(2)   A description of the property which is subject to the option;

(3)   The expiration date of the option;

(4)   Reference sufficient to identify the complete agreement between the parties.

Such a memorandum may be in substantially the following form:

NORTH CAROLINA

_____ COUNTY

In consideration of , the
receipt_____

(Set out consideration)

of which is hereby acknowledged,
_____

(Name and address of person selling option)

does hereby give and grant to
_____

(Name and address of person buying option)

the right and option to purchase the following property:

(Here describe property)

This option shall expire on the _____ day of _____, _____.

The provisions set forth in a written option agreement between the parties dated the _____ day of _____, _____, are hereby incorporated in this memorandum.

Witness our hand(s) and seal(s) this _____ day of _____, _____

_____ (Seal)

_____ (Seal)

(1961, c. 1174; 1999-456, s. 59.)

§ 47-119.1. Form of memorandum for contract to purchase real estate.

A contract to convey real estate may be registered by registering a memorandum thereof which shall set forth all of the following:

(1)   The names of the parties thereto.

(2)   A description of the property which is subject to the contract.

(3)   The expiration date of the contract.

(4)   Reference sufficient to identify the complete agreement between the parties.

The memorandum may be in substantially the following form:

NORTH CAROLINA

_____ COUNTY

_____

(Name and address of person contracting to sell real estate)

and

_____

(Name and address of person contracting to purchase real estate)

have entered into a contract to sell and purchase the following property:

_____
_____

(Here describe property)

This contract provides for a closing date of the _____ day of _____, _____.

The provisions set forth in a written contract to convey real estate between the parties dated the _____ day of _____, _____, are hereby incorporated in this memorandum.

Witness our hand(s) and seal(s) this _____ day of _____, _____

(Seal)

(Seal)

[Acknowledgement notarial certificate by all parties, as provided by applicable law in order to register in the office of the register of deeds of the county in which the property is located.]

The titles of the contract and the parties thereto, as contained in the original written contract, may be substituted in lieu of the above references. (2011-351, s. 1.)

§ 47-120. Memorandum as notice.

Such memorandum of a lease, an option to purchase real estate, or a contract to convey real estate as proposed by G.S. 47-118, 47-119, or 47-119.1 when executed, acknowledged, delivered and registered as required by law, shall be as good and sufficient notice, and have the same force and effect as if the written lease, option to purchase real estate, or contract to convey had been registered in its entirety. However, it shall be conclusively presumed that the conditions of any contract to purchase that is the subject of a recorded memorandum under this section have been complied with or have expired and are no longer enforceable as against creditors or purchasers for valuable consideration who have recorded their interests after the memorandum from and after the expiration of 60 days from whichever of the following events occurs first:

(1) The closing date stated in the memorandum, or any recorded extension or renewal of the memorandum, signed by the parties and acknowledged before an officer authorized to take acknowledgements.

(2) The date when the conditions of the contract to convey, including payment of the last installment of earnest money or balance of purchase price (other than a purchase money note or deed of trust), and delivery of the deed from the seller to buyer were required by the terms of the recorded memorandum to have been performed, or the date of any recorded extension or renewal thereof signed by the parties and acknowledged before an officer authorized to take acknowledgements. (1961, c. 1174; 2011-351, s. 2.)

Chapter 47A.

Unit Ownership.

Article 1.

Unit Ownership Act.

§ 47A-1. Short title.

This Article shall be known as the "Unit Ownership Act." (1963, c. 685, s. 1; 1983, c. 624, s. 2.)

§ 47A-2. Declaration creating unit ownership; recordation.

Unit ownership may be created by an owner or the co-owners of a building by an express declaration of their intention to submit such property to the provisions of the Article, which declaration shall be recorded in the office of the register of deeds of the county in which the property is situated. (1963, c. 685, s. 2; 1983, c. 624, s. 2.)

§ 47A-3. Definitions.

Unless it is plainly evident from the context that a different meaning is intended, as used herein:

(1)   "Association of unit owners" means all of the unit owners acting as a group in accordance with the bylaws and declaration.

(1a)   "Building" means a building, or a group of buildings, each building containing one or more units, and comprising a part of the property; provided that the property shall contain not less than two units.

(2)   "Common areas and facilities," unless otherwise provided in the declaration or lawful amendments thereto, means and includes:

a.   The land on which the building stands and such other land and improvements thereon as may be specifically included in the declaration, except any portion thereof included in a unit;

b.   The foundations, columns, girders, beams, supports, main walls, roofs, halls, corridors, lobbies, stairs, stairways, fire escapes, and entrances and exits of the building;

c.   The basements, yards, gardens, parking areas and storage spaces;

d.   The premises for the lodging of janitors or persons in charge of property;

e.   Installations of central services such as power, light, gas, hot and cold water, heating, refrigeration, air conditioning and incinerating;

f. The elevators, tanks, pumps, motors, fans, compressors, ducts, and in general, all apparatus and installations existing for common use;

g. Such community and commercial facilities as may be provided for in the declaration; and

h. All other parts of the property necessary or convenient to its existence, maintenance and safety, or normally in common use.

(3) "Common expenses" means and includes:

a. All sums lawfully assessed against the unit owners by the association of unit owners;

b. Expenses of administration, maintenance, repair or replacement of the common areas and facilities;

c. Expenses agreed upon as common expenses by the association of unit owners;

d. Expenses declared common expenses by the provisions of this Article, or by the declaration or the bylaws;

e. Hazard insurance premiums, if required.

(4) "Common profits" means the balance of all income, rents, profits, and revenues from the common areas and facilities remaining after the deductions of the common expenses.

(5) "Condominium" means the ownership of single units in a multi-unit structure with common areas and facilities.

(6) "Declaration" means the instrument, duly recorded, by which the property is submitted to the provisions of this Article, as hereinafter provided, and such declaration as from time to time may be lawfully amended.

(7) "Limited common areas and facilities" means and includes those common areas and facilities which are agreed upon by all the unit owners to be reserved for the use of a certain number of units to the exclusion of the other

units, such as special corridors, stairways and elevators, sanitary services common to the units of a particular floor, and the like.

(8)   "Majority" or "majority of unit owners" means the owners of more than fifty percent (50%) of the aggregate interest in the common areas and facilities as established by the declaration assembled at a duly called meeting of the unit owners.

(9)   "Person" means individual, corporation, partnership, association, trustee, or other legal entity.

(10)   "Property" means and includes the land, the building, all improvements and structures thereon and all easements, rights and appurtenances belonging thereto, and all articles of personal property intended for use in connection therewith, which have been or are intended to be submitted to the provisions of this Article.

(11)   "Recordation" means to file of record in the office of the county register of deeds in the county where the land is situated, in the manner provided by law for recordation of instruments affecting real estate.

(12)   "Unit" or "condominium unit" means an enclosed space consisting of one or more rooms occupying all or a part of a floor or floors in a building of one or more floors or stories regardless of whether it be designed for residence, for office, for the operation of any industry or business, or for any other type of independent use and shall include such accessory spaces and areas as may be described in the declaration, such as garage space, storage space, balcony, terrace or patio, provided it has a direct exit to a thoroughfare or to a given common space leading to a thoroughfare.

(13)   "Unit designation" means the number, letter, or combination thereof designating the unit in the declaration.

(14)   "Unit owner" means a person, corporation, partnership, association, trust or other legal entity, or any combination thereof, who owns a unit within the building. (1963, c. 685, s. 3; 1969, c. 848; 1971, c. 418; 1983, c. 624, s. 2.)

§ 47A-4. Property subject to Article.

This Article shall be applicable only to property, the full owner or all of the owners of which submit the same to the provisions hereof by duly executing and recording a declaration as hereinafter provided. (1963, c. 685, s. 4; 1983, c. 624, s. 2.)

§ 47A-5. Nature and incidents of unit ownership.

Unit ownership as created and defined in this Article shall vest in the holder exclusive ownership and possession with all the incidents of real property. A condominium unit in the building may be individually conveyed, leased and encumbered and may be inherited or devised by will, as if it were solely and entirely independent of the other condominium units in the building of which it forms a part. Such a unit may be held and owned by more than one person either as tenants in common or tenants by the entirety or in any other manner recognized under the laws of this State. (1963, c. 685, s. 5; 1983, c. 624, s. 2.)

§ 47A-6. Undivided interests in common areas and facilities; ratio fixed in declaration; conveyance with unit.

(a)   Each unit owner shall be entitled to an undivided interest in the common areas and facilities in the ratio expressed in the declaration. Such ratio shall be in the approximate relation that the fair market value of the unit at the date of the declaration bears to the then aggregate fair market value of all the units having an interest in said common areas and facilities.

(b)   The ratio of the undivided interest of each unit owner in the common areas and facilities as expressed in the declaration shall have a permanent character and shall not be altered except with the unanimous consent of all unit owners expressed in an amended declaration duly recorded.

(c)   The undivided interest in the common areas and facilities shall not be separated from the unit to which it appertains and shall be deemed conveyed or encumbered with the unit even though such interest is not expressly mentioned or described in the conveyance or other instrument. (1963, c. 685, s. 6.)

§ 47A-7. Common areas and facilities not subject to partition or division.

The common areas and facilities shall remain undivided and no unit owner or any other person shall bring any action for partition or division of any part thereof, unless the property has been removed from the provisions of this Article as provided in G.S. 47A-16 and 47A-25. Any covenant to the contrary shall be null and void. This restraint against partition shall not apply to the individual condominium unit. (1963, c. 685, s. 7; 1983, c. 624, s. 2.)

§ 47A-8. Use of common areas and facilities.

Each unit owner may use the common areas and facilities in accordance with the purpose for which they are intended, without hindering or encroaching upon the lawful rights of the other unit owners. (1963, c. 685, s. 8.)

§ 47A-9. Maintenance, repair and improvements to common areas and facilities; access to units for repairs.

The necessary work of maintenance, repair, and replacement of the common areas and facilities and the making of any additions or improvements thereto shall be carried out only as provided herein and in the bylaws. The association of unit owners shall have the irrevocable right, to be exercised by the manager or board of directors, or other managing body as provided in the bylaws, to have access to each unit from time to time during reasonable hours as may be necessary for the maintenance, repair or replacement of any of the common areas and facilities therein or accessible therefrom, or for making emergency repairs therein necessary to prevent damage to the common areas and facilities or to another unit or units. (1963, c. 685, s. 9.)

§ 47A-10. Compliance with bylaws, regulations and covenants; damages; injunctions.

Each unit owner shall comply strictly with the bylaws and with the administrative rules and regulations adopted pursuant thereto, as either of the same may be lawfully amended from time to time, and with the covenants, conditions and restrictions set forth in the declaration or in the deed to his unit. Failure to comply with any of the same shall be grounds for an action to recover sums due, for damages or injunctive relief, or both, maintainable by the manager or board of directors on behalf of the association of unit owners or, in a proper case, by an aggrieved unit owner. (1963, c. 685, s. 10.)

§ 47A-11. Unit owners not to jeopardize safety of property or impair easements.

No unit owner shall do any work which would jeopardize the soundness or safety of the property or impair any easement or hereditament without in every such case the unanimous consent of all the other unit owners affected being first obtained. (1963, c. 685, s. 11.)

§ 47A-12. Unit owners to contribute to common expenses; distribution of common profits.

The unit owners are bound to contribute pro rata, in the percentages computed according to G.S. 47A-6 of this Article, toward the expenses of administration and of maintenance and repair of the general common areas and facilities and, in proper cases of the limited common areas and facilities, of the building and toward any other expense lawfully agreed upon. No unit owner may exempt himself from contributing toward such expense by waiver of the use or enjoyment of the common areas and facilities or by abandonment of the unit belonging to him.

Provided, however, that the common profits of the property, if any, shall be distributed among the unit owners according to the percentage of the undivided interest in the common areas and facilities. (1963, c. 685, s. 12; 1983, c. 624, s. 2.)

§ 47A-13. Declaration creating unit ownership; contents; recordation.

The declaration creating and establishing unit ownership as provided in G.S. 47A-3 of this Article, shall be recorded in the office of the county register of deeds and shall contain the following particulars:

(1)   Description of the land on which the building and improvements are or are to be located.

(2)   Description of the building, stating the number of stories and basements, the number of units, and the principal materials of which it is constructed.

(3)   The unit designation of each unit, and a statement of its location, approximate area, number of rooms, and immediate common area to which it has access, and any other data necessary for its proper identification.

(4)   Description of the general common areas and facilities and the proportionate interest of each unit owner therein.

(5)   Description of the limited common areas and facilities, if any, stating what units shall share the same and in what proportion.

(6)   Statement of the purpose for which the building and each of the units are intended and restricted as to use.

(7)   The name of a person to receive service of process in the cases hereinafter provided, together with the residence or the place of business of such person which shall be within the city and county in which the building is located.

(8)   Any further details in connection with the property which the person executing the declaration may deem desirable to set forth consistent with this Article.

(9)   The method by which the declaration may be amended, consistent with the provisions of this Article. (1963, c. 685, s. 13; 1983, c. 624, s. 2.)

§ 47A-14. Repealed by Session Laws 1981, c. 527, s. 1, effective October 1, 1981.

§ 47A-14.1. Deeds conveying units.

(a) Any conveyance of a condominium unit executed on or after October 1, 1981, which complies with the general requirements of the laws of this State concerning conveyances of real property shall be valid.

(b) All conveyances of condominium units executed before October 1, 1981, which comply with the general requirements of the laws of this State concerning conveyances of real property shall be valid even though such conveyances failed to comply with one or more of the particulars set out in former G.S. 47A-14. (1981, c. 527, ss. 2, 3.)

§ 47A-15. Plans of building to be attached to declaration; recordation; certificate of architect or engineer.

(a) There shall be attached to the declaration, at the time it is filed for record, a full and exact copy of the plans of the building, which copy of plans shall be entered of record along with the declaration. Said plans shall show graphically all particulars of the building, including, but not limited to, the layout, location, ceiling and floor elevations, unit numbers and dimensions of the units, stating the name of the building or that it has no name, area and location of the common areas and facilities affording access to each unit, and such plans shall bear the verified statement of a registered architect or licensed professional engineer certifying that it is an accurate copy of portions of the plans of the building as filed with and approved by the municipal or other governmental subdivision having jurisdiction over the issuance of permits for the construction of buildings. If such plans do not include a verified statement by such architect or engineer that such plans fully and accurately depict the layout, location, ceiling and floor elevations, unit numbers and dimensions of the units, as built, there shall be recorded prior to the first conveyance of any unit an amendment to the declaration to which shall be attached a verified statement of a registered architect or licensed professional engineer certifying that the plans theretofore filed, or being filed simultaneously with such amendment, fully depict the layout, ceiling and floor elevations, unit numbers and dimensions of the units as built. Such plans shall be kept by the register of deeds in a separate file, indexed in the same manner as a conveyance entitled to record, numbered serially in the order of receipt, each designated "Unit Ownership," with the name of the building, if any, and each containing a reference to the book and page numbers and date of the recording of the declaration.

(b)   In order to be recorded, plans filed for recording pursuant to subsection (a) shall:

(1)   Be reproducible plans on cloth, linen, film or other permanent material and be submitted in that form; and

(2)   Have an outside marginal size of not more than 21 inches by 30 inches nor less than eight and one-half inches by 11 inches, including one and one-half inches for binding on the left margin and a one-half inch border on each of the other sides. Where size of the buildings, or suitable scale to assure legibility require, plans may be placed on two or more sheets with appropriate match lines.

(c)   The fee for recording each plan sheet submitted pursuant to subsection (a) shall be as prescribed by G.S. 161-10(a)(3). (1963, c. 685, s. 15; 1981, c. 587.)

§ 47A-16. Termination of unit ownership; consent of lienholders; recordation of instruments.

(a)   All of the unit owners may remove a property from the provisions of this Article by an instrument to that effect, duly recorded, provided that the holders of all liens, affecting any of the units consent thereto or agree, in either case by instruments duly recorded, that their liens be transferred to the percentage of the undivided interest of the unit owner in the property as hereinafter provided.

(b)   Upon removal of the property from the provisions of this Article, the property shall be deemed to be owned as tenants in common by the unit owners. The undivided interest in the property owned as tenants in common which shall appertain to each unit owner shall be the percentage of the undivided interest previously owned by such unit owner in the common areas and facilities. (1963, c. 685, s. 16; 1983, c. 624, s. 2.)

§ 47A-17. Termination of unit ownership; no bar to reestablishment.

The removal provided for in G.S. 47A-16 shall in no way bar the subsequent resubmission of the property to the provisions of this Article. (1963, c. 685, s. 17; 1983, c. 624, s. 2; 2002-159, s. 10.)

§ 47A-18. Bylaws; annexed to declaration; amendments.

The administration of every property shall be governed by bylaws, a true copy of which shall be annexed to the declaration. No modification of or amendment to the bylaws shall be valid, unless set forth in an amendment to the declaration and such amendment is duly recorded. (1963, c. 685, s. 18; 1973, c. 734.)

§ 47A-19. Bylaws; contents.

The bylaws shall provide for the following:

(1)   Form of administration, indicating whether this shall be in charge of an administrator, manager, or of a board of directors or board of administration, independent corporate body, or otherwise, and specifying the powers, manner of removal, and, where proper, the compensation thereof.

(2)   Method of calling or summoning the unit owners to assemble; what percentage, if other than a majority of unit owners, shall constitute a quorum; who is to preside over the meeting and who will keep the minute book wherein the resolutions shall be recorded.

(3)   Maintenance, repair and replacement of the common areas and facilities and payments therefor, including the method of approving payment vouchers.

(4)   Manner of collecting from the unit owners their share of the common expenses.

(5)   Designation and removal of personnel necessary for the maintenance, repair and replacement of the common areas and facilities.

(6)   Method of adopting and of amending administrative rules and regulations governing the details of the operation and use of the common areas and facilities.

(7)   Such restrictions on and requirements respecting the use and maintenance of the units and the use of the common areas and facilities, not set forth in the declaration, as are designed to prevent unreasonable interference with the use of their respective units and of the common areas and facilities by the several unit owners.

(8)   The percentage of votes required to amend the bylaws, and a provision that such amendment shall not become operative unless set forth in an amended declaration and duly recorded.

(9)   A provision that all unit owners shall be bound to abide by any amendment upon the same being passed and duly set forth in an amended declaration, duly recorded.

(10)   Other provisions as may be deemed necessary for the administration of the property consistent with this Article. (1963, c. 685, s. 19; 1983, c. 624, s. 2.)

§ 47A-20. Records of receipts and expenditures; availability for examination; annual audit.

The manager or board of directors, or other form of administration provided in the bylaws, as the case may be, shall keep detailed, accurate records in chronological order of the receipts and expenditures affecting the common areas and facilities, specifying and identifying the maintenance and repair expenses of the common areas and facilities and any other expense incurred. Both said book and the vouchers accrediting the entries thereupon shall be available for examination by all the unit owners, their duly authorized agents or attorneys, at convenient hours on working days that shall be set and announced for general knowledge. All books and records shall be kept in accordance with good and accepted accounting practices and an outside audit shall be made at least once a year. (1963, c. 685, s. 20.)

§ 47A-21. Units taxed separately.

Each condominium unit and its percentage of undivided interest in the common areas and facilities shall be deemed to be a parcel and shall be separately assessed and taxed by each assessing unit and special district for all types of taxes authorized by law including but not limited to special ad valorem levies and special assessments. Each unit holder shall be liable solely for the amount of taxes against his individual unit and shall not be affected by the consequences resulting from the tax delinquency of other unit holders. Neither the building, the property nor any of the common areas and facilities shall be deemed to be a parcel. (1963, c. 685, s. 21.)

§ 47A-22. Liens for unpaid common expenses; recordation; priorities; foreclosure.

(a) Any sum assessed by the association of unit owners for the share of the common expenses chargeable to any unit, and remaining unpaid for a period of 30 days or longer, shall constitute a lien on such unit when filed of record in the office of the clerk of superior court of the county in which the property is located in the manner provided therefor by Article 8 of Chapter 44 of the General Statutes. Upon the same being duly filed, such lien shall be prior to all other liens except the following:

(1) Assessments, liens and charges for real estate taxes due and unpaid on the unit;

(2) All sums unpaid on deeds of trust, mortgages and other encumbrances duly of record against the unit prior to the docketing of the aforesaid lien.

(3) Materialmen's and mechanics' liens.

(b) Provided the same is duly filed in accordance with the provisions contained in subsection (a) of this section, a lien created by nonpayment of a unit owner's pro rata share of the common expenses may be foreclosed by suit by the manager or board of directors, acting on behalf of the unit owners, in like manner as a deed of trust or mortgage of real property. In any such foreclosure the unit owner shall be required to pay a reasonable rental for the unit, if so provided in the bylaws, and the plaintiff in such foreclosure shall be entitled to the appointment of a receiver to collect the same. The manager or board of directors, acting on behalf of the unit owners shall have power, unless prohibited by the declaration, to bid in the unit at foreclosure sale, and to acquire and hold, lease, mortgage and convey the same. A suit to recover a money judgment for unpaid common expenses shall be maintainable without foreclosing or waiving the lien securing the same.

(c)   Where the mortgagee of a first mortgage of record or other purchaser of a unit obtains title to the unit as a result of foreclosure of the first mortgage, such purchaser, his successors and assigns, shall not be liable for the share of the common expenses or assessments by the association of unit owners chargeable to such unit which became due prior to the acquisition of title to such unit by such purchaser. Such unpaid share of common expenses or assessments shall be deemed to be common expenses collectible from all of the unit owners including such purchaser, his successors and assigns. (1963, c. 685, s. 22.)

§ 47A-23. Liability of grantor and grantee of unit for unpaid common expenses.

The grantee of a unit shall be jointly and severally liable with the grantor for all unpaid assessments against the latter for his proportionate share of the common expenses up to the time of the grant or conveyance, without prejudice to the grantee's right to recover from the grantor the amounts paid by the grantee therefor. However, any such grantee shall be entitled to a statement from the manager or board of directors, as the case may be, setting forth the amount of the unpaid assessments against the grantor and such grantee shall not be liable for, nor shall the unit conveyed be subject to a lien for, any unpaid assessments in excess of the amount therein set forth. (1963, c. 685, s. 23.)

§ 47A-24. Insurance on property; right to insure units.

The manager of the board of directors, or other managing body, if required by the declaration, bylaws or by a majority of the unit owners, shall have the authority to, and shall, obtain insurance for the property against loss or damage by fire and such other hazards under such terms and for such amounts as shall be required or requested. Such insurance coverage shall be written on the property in the name of such manager or of the board of directors of the association of unit owners, as trustee for each of the unit owners in the percentages established in the declaration. The trustee so named shall have the authority on behalf of the unit owners to deal with the insurer in the settlement of claims. The premiums for such insurance on the building shall be deemed common expenses. Provision for such insurance shall be without prejudice to the right of each unit owner to insure his own unit for his benefit. (1963, c. 685, s. 24.)

§ 47A-25. Damage to or destruction of property; repair or restoration; partition sale on resolution not to restore.

Except as hereinafter provided, damage to or destruction of the building shall be promptly repaired and restored by the manager or board of directors, or other managing body, using the proceeds of insurance on the building for that purpose, and unit owners shall be liable for assessment for any deficiency; provided, however, if the building shall be more than two-thirds destroyed by fire or other disaster and the owners of three-fourths of the building duly resolve not to proceed with repair or restoration, then and in that event:

(1)   The property shall be deemed to be owned as tenants in common by the unit owners;

(2)   The undivided interest in the property owned by the unit owners as tenants in common which shall appertain to each unit owner shall be the percentage of undivided interest previously owned by such owner in the common areas and facilities;

(3)   Any liens affecting any of the units shall be deemed to be transferred in accordance with the existing priorities to the percentage of the undivided interest of the unit owner in the property as provided herein; and

(4)   The property shall be subject to an action for sale for partition at the suit of any unit owner, in which event the net proceeds of sale, together with the net proceeds of insurance policies, if any, shall be considered as one fund and shall be divided among all the unit owners in proportion to their respective undivided ownership of the common areas and facilities, after first paying off, out of the respective shares of unit owners, to the extent sufficient for that purpose, all liens on the unit of each unit owner. (1963, c. 685, s. 25.)

§ 47A-26. Actions as to common interests; service of process on designated agent; exhaustion of remedies against association.

Without limiting the rights of any unit owner, actions may be brought by the manager or board of directors, in either case in the discretion of the board of directors, on behalf of two or more of the unit owners, as their respective interests may appear, with respect to any course of action relating to the common areas and facilities or more than one unit. Service of process on two or more unit owners in any action relating to the common areas and facilities or more than one unit may be made on the person designated in the declaration to receive service of process. Any individual, corporation, partnership, association, trustee, or other legal entity claiming damages for injuries without any participation by a unit owner shall first exhaust all available remedies against the association of unit owners prior to proceeding against any unit owner individually. (1963, c. 685, s. 26.)

§ 47A-27. Zoning regulations governing condominium projects.

Whenever they deem it proper, the planning and zoning commission of any county or municipality may adopt supplemental rules and regulations governing a condominium project established under this Article in order to implement this program. (1963, c. 685, s. 27; 1983, c. 624, s. 2.)

§ 47A-28. Persons subject to Article, declaration and bylaws; effect of decisions of association of unit owners.

(a) All unit owners, tenants of such owners, employees of owners and tenants, or any other persons that may in any manner use the property or any part thereof submitted to the provisions of this Article, shall be subject to this Article and to the declaration and bylaws of the association of unit owners adopted pursuant to the provisions of this Article.

(b) All agreements, decisions and determinations lawfully made by the association of unit owners in accordance with the voting percentages established in the Article, declaration or bylaws, shall be deemed to be binding on all unit owners. (1963, c. 685, s. 28; 1983, c. 624, s. 2.)

§§ 47A-29 through 47A-33. Reserved for future codification purposes.

Article 2.

Renters in Conversion Buildings Protected.

§ 47A-34. Definitions.

The definitions set out in G.S. 47A-3 also apply to this Article. As used in this Article, unless the context requires otherwise, the term:

(1) "Conversion building" means a building that at any time before creation of the condominium was occupied wholly or partially by persons other than purchasers and persons who occupy with the consent of purchasers.

(2) "Declarant" means any person or group of persons acting in concert who, as part of a common promotional plan, offers to dispose of his or its interest in a unit not previously disposed of.

(3) "Dispose" or "disposition" means a voluntary transfer to a purchaser of any legal or equitable interest in a unit, but does not include the transfer or release of a security interest.

(4) "Offering" means any advertisement, inducement, solicitation, or attempt to encourage any person to acquire any interest in a unit, other than as security for an obligation.

(5) "Residential purposes" means use for dwelling or recreational purposes, or both. (1983, c. 624, s. 1.)

§ 47A-35. Offering statement.

An offering statement must contain or fully and accurately disclose:

(1) The name and principal address of the declarant;

(2)   A general description of the condominium including, to the extent possible, a listing of any improvements and amenities that declarant anticipates including in the condominium, and declarant's schedule of completion of construction on buildings;

(3)   The terms and significant limitations of any warranties provided by the declarant; and

(4)   Any other information made available to the general public in connection with the offering. (1983, c. 624, s. 1.)

§ 47A-36. Time to vacate; right of first refusal to purchase.

(a)   A declarant of a condominium containing conversion buildings, and any person in the business of selling real estate for his own account who intends to offer units in such a condominium, shall provide each of the residential tenants and any residential subtenant in possession of a portion of a conversion building notice of the conversion as well as an offering statement as provided in G.S. 47A-35 no later than 90 days before the tenant or subtenant are required to vacate. The notice shall set forth generally the rights of tenants and subtenants under this section and section (b) of G.S. 47A-36. This notice shall be hand-delivered to the unit or mailed by prepaid United States mail to the tenant and subtenant at the address of the unit or any other mailing address provided by a tenant. No tenant or subtenant may be required to vacate upon less than 90 days' notice, except by reason of nonpayment of rent, waste, conduct that disturbs other tenants' peaceful enjoyment of the premises or breach of lease giving rise to the right of repossession of the unit by the declarant, and the terms of the tenancy may not be altered during that period. Failure to give notice as required by this section is a defense to an action for possession.

(b)   For 30 days after the delivery of the notice described in subsection (a), the person required to give the notice shall offer to convey each unit or proposed unit occupied for residential use to the tenant who leases that unit. The tenant can accept an offer under this section by entering into an agreement to purchase within the 30-day period. The tenant shall be allowed a 30-day period after acceptance in which to complete a purchase transaction. This subsection does not apply to any unit in a conversion building if that unit will be restricted exclusively to nonresidential use or the boundaries of the converted unit do not substantially conform to the dimensions of the residential unit before conversion.

(c) If a declarant, in violation of subsection (b), conveys a unit to a purchaser, recordation of the deed conveying the unit extinguishes any right a tenant may have under subsection (b) to purchase that unit, but does not affect any other right of a tenant. (1983, c. 624, s. 1.)

§ 47A-37. Applicability.

This Article applies to condominiums of five or more units created on or after January 1, 1984. (1983

Chapter 47B.

Real Property Marketable Title Act.

§ 47B-1. Declaration of policy and statement of purpose.

It is hereby declared as a matter of public policy by the General Assembly of the State of North Carolina that:

(1) Land is a basic resource of the people of the State of North Carolina and should be made freely alienable and marketable so far as is practicable.

(2) Nonpossessory interests in real property, obsolete restrictions and technical defects in titles which have been placed on the real property records at remote times in the past often constitute unreasonable restraints on the alienation and marketability of real property.

(3) Such interests and defects are prolific producers of litigation to clear and quiet titles which cause delays in real property transactions and fetter the marketability of real property.

(4) Real property transfers should be possible with economy and expediency. The status and security of recorded real property titles should be determinable from an examination of recent records only.

It is the purpose of the General Assembly of the State of North Carolina to provide that if a person claims title to real property under a chain of record title for 30 years, and no other person has filed a notice of any claim of interest in the real property during the 30-year period, then all conflicting claims based upon any title transaction prior to the 30-year period shall be extinguished. (1973, c. 255, s. 1.)

§ 47B-2. Marketable record title to estate in real property; 30-year unbroken chain of title of record; effect of marketable title.

(a) Any person having the legal capacity to own real property in this State, who, alone or together with his predecessors in title, shall have been vested with any estate in real property of record for 30 years or more, shall have a marketable record title to such estate in real property.

(b) A person has an estate in real property of record for 30 years or more when the public records disclose a title transaction affecting the title to the real property which has been of record for not less than 30 years purporting to create such estate either in:

(1) The person claiming such estate; or

(2) Some other person from whom, by one or more title transactions, such estate has passed to the person claiming such estate;

with nothing appearing of record, in either case, purporting to divest such claimant of the estate claimed.

(c) Subject to the matters stated in G.S. 47B-3, such marketable record title shall be free and clear of all rights, estates, interests, claims or charges whatsoever, the existence of which depends upon any act, title transaction, event or omission that occurred prior to such 30-year period. All such rights, estates, interests, claims or charges, however denominated, whether such rights, estates, interests, claims or charges are or appear to be held or asserted by a person sui juris or under a disability, whether such person is natural or corporate, or is private or governmental, are hereby declared to be null and void.

(d) In every action for the recovery of real property, to quiet title, or to recover damages for trespass, the establishment of a marketable record title in any person pursuant to this statute shall be prima facie evidence that such person owns title to the real property described in his record chain of title. (1973, c. 255, s. 1; c. 881; 1981, c. 682, s. 11.)

§ 47B-3. Exceptions.

Such marketable record title shall not affect or extinguish the following rights:

(1) Rights, estates, interests, claims or charges disclosed by and defects inherent in the muniments of title of which such 30-year chain of record title is formed, provided, however, that a general reference in any of such muniments to rights, estates, interests, claims or charges created prior to such 30-year period shall not be sufficient to preserve them unless specific identification by reference to book and page or record be made therein to a recorded title transaction which imposed, transferred or continued such rights, estates, interests, claims or charges.

(2) Rights, estates, interests, claims or charges preserved by the filing of a proper notice in accordance with the provisions of G.S. 47B-4.

(3) Rights, estates, interests, claims or charges of any person who is in present, actual and open possession of the real property so long as such person is in such possession.

(4) Rights of any person who likewise has a marketable record title as defined in G.S. 47B-2 and who is listed as the owner of such real property on the tax books of the county in which the real property is located at the time that marketability is to be established.

(5) Rights of any owners of mineral rights.

(6) Rights-of-way of any railroad company (irrespective of nature of its title or interest therein whether fee, easement, or other quality) and all real estate other than right-of-way property of a railroad company in actual use for railroad purposes or being held or retained for prospective future use for railroad operational purposes. The use by any railroad company or the holding for future use of any part of a particular tract or parcel of right-of-way or non-right-of-way property shall preserve the interest of the railway company in the whole of such particular tract or parcel. Operational use is defined as railroad use requiring

proximity and access to railroad tracts. Nothing in this section shall be construed as repealing G.S. 1-44.1.

(7)   Rights, interests, or servitudes in the nature of easements, rights-of-way or terminal facilities of any railroad (company or corporation) obtained by the terms of its charter or through any other congressional or legislative grant not otherwise extinguished.

(8)   Rights of any person who has an easement or interest in the nature of an easement, whether recorded or unrecorded and whether possessory or nonpossessory, when such easement or interest in the nature of an easement is for any one of the following purposes:

a.   Flowage, flooding or impounding of water, provided that the watercourse or body of water, which such easement or interest in the nature of an easement serves, continues to exist.

b.   Placing and maintaining lines, pipes, cables, conduits or other appurtenances which are either aboveground, underground or on the surface and which are useful in the operation of any water, gas, natural gas, petroleum products, or electric generation, transmission or distribution system, or any sewage collection or disposal system, or any telephone, telegraph or other communications system, or any surface water drainage or disposal system whether or not the existence of the same is clearly observable by physical evidence of its use.

c.   Conserving land or water areas pursuant to a conservation agreement or preserving a structure or site pursuant to a preservation agreement under Article 4 of Chapter 121 of the General Statutes.

(9)   Rights, titles or interests of the United States to the extent that the extinguishment of such rights, titles or interest is prohibited by the laws of the United States.

(10)   Rights, estates, interests, claims or charges created subsequent to the beginning of such 30-year period.

(11)   Deeds of trust, mortgages and security instruments or security agreements duly recorded and not otherwise unenforceable.

(12) Rights, estates, interests, claims or charges with respect to any real property registered under the Torrens Law as provided by Chapter 43 of the General Statutes of North Carolina.

(13) Covenants applicable to a general or uniform scheme of development which restrict the property to residential use only, provided said covenants are otherwise enforceable. The excepted covenant may restrict the property to multi-family or single-family residential use or simply to residential use. Restrictive covenants other than those mentioned herein which limit the property to residential use only are not excepted from the provisions of Chapter 47B. (1973, c. 255, s. 1; 1995, c. 443, s. 3.)

§ 47B-4. Preservation by notice; contents; recording; indexing.

(a) Any person claiming a right, estate, interest or charge which would be extinguished by this Chapter may preserve the same by registering within such 30-year period a notice in writing, duly acknowledged, in the office of the register of deeds for the county in which the real property is situated, setting forth the nature of such claim, which notice shall have the effect of preserving such claim for a period of not longer than 30 years after registering the same unless again registered as required herein. No disability or lack of knowledge of any kind on the part of any person shall delay the commencement of or suspend the running of said 30-year period. Such notice may be registered by the claimant or by any other person acting on behalf of any claimant who is

(1) Under a disability;

(2) Unable to assert a claim on his behalf; or

(3) One of a class, but whose identity cannot be established or is uncertain at the time of filing such notice of claim for record.

(b) To be effective and to be entitled to registration, such notice shall contain an accurate and full description of all real property affected by such notice, which description shall be set forth in particular terms and not be by general reference; but if such claim is founded upon a recorded instrument, then the description in such notice may be the same as that contained in the recorded instrument. Such notice shall also contain the name of any record owner of the real property at the time the notice is registered and a statement of the claim showing the nature, description and extent of such claim. The register of deeds of each county shall accept all such notices presented to him which are duly acknowledged and certified for recordation and shall enter and record full copies thereof in the same way that deeds and other instruments are recorded, and each register of deeds shall be entitled to charge the same fees for the recording thereof as are charged for the recording of deeds. In indexing such notices in his office each register of deeds shall enter such notices under the grantee indexes of deeds under the names of persons on whose behalf such notices are executed and registered and under the grantor indexes of deeds under the names of the record owners of the possessory estates in the real property to be affected against whom the claim is to be preserved at the time of the registration. (1973, c. 255, s. 1.)

§ 47B-5. Extension of time for registering notice of claims which Chapter would otherwise bar.

If the 30-year period specified in this Chapter shall have expired prior to October 1, 1973, no right, estate, interest, claim or charge shall be barred by G.S. 47B-2 until October 1, 1976, and any right, estate, interest, claim or charge that would otherwise be barred by G.S. 47B-2 may be preserved and kept effective by the registration of a notice of claim as set forth in G.S. 47B-4 of this Chapter prior to October 1, 1976. (1973, c. 255, s. 1.)

§ 47B-6. Registering false claim.

No person shall use the privilege of registering notices hereunder for the purpose of asserting false or fictitious claims to real property; and in any action relating thereto if the court shall find that any person has intentionally registered a false or fictitious claim, the court may award to the prevailing party all costs incurred by him in such action, including a reasonable attorney's fee, and in addition thereto may award to the prevailing party treble the damages that he may have sustained as a result of the registration of such notice of claim. (1973, c. 255, s. 1.)

§ 47B-7. Limitations of actions and recording acts.

Nothing contained in this Chapter shall be construed to extend the period for the bringing of an action or for the doing of any other required act under the statutes of limitations, nor, except as herein specifically provided, to affect the operation of any statutes governing the effect of the registering or the failure to register any instrument affecting real property. (1973, c. 255, s. 1.)

§ 47B-8. Definitions.

As used in this Chapter:

(1)   The term "person" denotes singular or plural, natural or corporate, private or governmental, including the State and any political subdivision or agency thereof, and a partnership, unincorporated association, or other entity capable of owning an interest in real property.

(2)   The term "title transaction" means any transaction affecting title to any interest in real property, including but not limited to title by will or descent, title by tax deed, or by trustee's, referee's, commissioner's, guardian's, executor's, administrator's, or sheriff's deed, contract, lease or reservation, or judgment or order of any court, as well as warranty deed, quitclaim deed, or mortgage. (1973, c. 255, s. 1.)

§ 47B-9. Chapter to be liberally construed.

This Chapter shall be liberally construed to effect the legislative purpose of simplifying and facilitating real property title transactions by allowing persons to rely on a record chain of title of 30 years as described in G.S. 47B-2, subject only to such limitations as appear in G.S. 47B-3. (1973, c. 255, s. 1.)

Chapter 47C.

North Carolina Condominium Act.

Article 1.

General Provisions.

§ 47C-1-101. Short title.

This chapter shall be known and may be cited as the North Carolina Condominium Act. (1985 (Reg. Sess., 1986), c. 877, s. 1.)

§ 47C-1-102. Applicability.

(a) This Chapter applies to all condominiums created within this State after October 1, 1986. G.S. 47C-1-105 (Separate Titles and Taxation), 47C-1-106 (Applicability of Local Ordinances, Regulations, and Building Codes), 47C-1-107 (Eminent Domain), 47C-2-103 (Construction and Validity of Declaration and Bylaws), 47C-2-104 (Description of Units), 47C-2-121 (Merger or Consolidation of Condominiums), 47C-3-102(a)(1) through (6) and (11) through (16)(Powers of Unit Owners' Association), 47C-3-103 (Executive board members and officers), 47C-3-107.1 (Procedures for fines and suspension of condominium privileges or services), 47C-3-108 (Meetings), 47C-3-111 (Tort and Contract Liability), 47C-3-112 (Conveyance or Encumbrance of Common Elements), 47C-3-116 (Lien for Assessments), 47C-3-118 (Association Records), 47C-3-121 (American and State flags and political sign displays), and 47C-4-117 (Effect of Violation on Rights of Action; Attorney's Fees), and G.S. 47C-1-103 (Definitions), to the extent necessary in construing any of those sections, apply to all condominiums created in this State on or before October 1, 1986, unless the declaration expressly provides to the contrary. Those sections apply only with respect to events and circumstances occurring after October 1, 1986, and do not invalidate existing provisions of the declarations, bylaws, or plats or plans of those condominiums.

(b) The provisions of Chapter 47A, the Unit Ownership Act, do not apply to condominiums created after October 1, 1986 and do not invalidate any amendment to the declaration, bylaws, and plats and plans of any condominium created on or before October 1, 1986 if the amendment would be permitted by this chapter. The amendment must be adopted in conformity with the procedures and requirements specified by those instruments and by Chapter 47A, the Unit Ownership Act. If the amendment grants to any person any rights, powers, or privileges permitted by this chapter, all correlative obligations, liabilities, and restrictions in this chapter also apply to that person.

(c)   This chapter does not apply to condominiums or units located outside this State, but the public offering statement provisions (G.S. 47C-4-102 through 47C-4-108) apply to all contracts for the dispositions thereof signed in this State by any party unless exempt under G.S. 47C-4-101(b). (1985 (Reg. Sess., 1986), c. 877, s. 1; 1995, c. 509, s. 135.1(h); 2002-112, s. 1; 2004-109, s. 1; 2005-422, s. 19.)

§ 47C-1-103. Definitions.

In the declaration and bylaws, unless specifically provided otherwise or the context otherwise requires, and in this chapter:

(1)   "Affiliate of a declarant" means any person who controls, is controlled by, or is under common control with a declarant. A person "controls" a declarant if the person (i) is a general partner, officer, director, or employer of the declarant, (ii) directly or indirectly or acting in concert with one or more other persons, or through one or more subsidiaries, owns, controls, holds with power to vote, or holds proxies representing, more than twenty percent (20%) of the voting interests in the declarant, (iii) controls in any manner the election of a majority of the directors of the declarant, or (iv) has contributed more than twenty percent (20%) of the capital of the declarant. A person "is controlled by" a declarant if the declarant (i) is a general partner, officer, director, or employer of the person, (ii) directly or indirectly or acting in concert with one or more other persons, or through one or more subsidiaries, owns, controls, holds with power to vote, or holds proxies representing, more than twenty percent (20%) of the voting interests in the person, (iii) controls in any manner the election of a majority of the directors of the person, or (iv) has contributed more than twenty percent (20%) of the capital of the person. Control does not exist if the powers described in this paragraph are held solely as security for an obligation and are not exercised.

(2)   "Allocated interests" means the undivided interests in the common elements, the common expense liability, and votes in the association allocated to each unit.

(3)   "Association" or "unit owners' associations" means the unit owners' associations organized under G.S. 47C-3-101.

(4) "Common elements" means all portions of a condominium other than the units.

(5) "Common expenses" means expenditures made by or financial liabilities of the association, together with any allocations to reserves.

(6) "Common expense liability" means the liability for common expenses allocated to each unit pursuant to G.S. 47C-2-107.

(7) "Condominium" means real estate, portions of which are designated for separate ownership and the remainder of which is designated for common ownership solely by the owners of those portions. Real estate is not a condominium unless the undivided interests in the common elements are vested in the unit owners.

(8) "Conversion building" means a building that at any time before creation of the condominium was occupied wholly or partially by persons other than purchasers or by persons who occupy with the consent of purchasers.

(9) "Declarant" means any person or group of persons acting in concert who (i) as part of a common promotional plan offers to dispose of his or its interest in a unit not previously disposed of or (ii) reserves or succeeds to any special declarant right.

(10) "Declaration" means any instruments, however denominated, which create a condominium, and any amendments to those instruments.

(11) "Development rights" means any right or combination of rights reserved by a declarant in the declaration to add real estate to a condominium; to create units, common elements, or limited common elements within a condominium; to subdivide units or convert units into common elements; or to withdraw real estate from a condominium.

(12) "Dispose" or "disposition" means a voluntary transfer to a purchaser of any legal or equitable interest in a unit, but does not include the transfer or release of a security interest.

(13) "Executive board" means the body, regardless of name, designated in the declaration to act on behalf of the association.

(14) "Identifying number" means a symbol or address that identifies only one unit in a condominium.

(15) "Leasehold condominium" means a condominium in which all or a portion of the real estate is subject to a lease the expiration or termination of which will terminate the condominium or reduce its size.

(16) "Limited common element" means a portion of the common elements allocated by the declaration or by operation of G.S. 47C-2-102(2) or (4) for the exclusive use of one or more but fewer than all of the units.

(17) "Master association" means an organization described in G.S. 47C-2-120, whether or not it is also an association described in G.S. 47C-3-101.

(18) "Offering" means any advertisement, inducement, solicitation, or attempt to encourage any person to acquire any interest in a unit, other than as security for an obligation. An advertisement in a newspaper or other periodical of general circulation, or in any broadcast medium to the general public, of a condominium not located in this State, is not an offering if the advertisement states that an offering may be made only in compliance with the law of the jurisdiction in which the condominium is located.

(19) "Person" means a natural person, corporation, business trust, estate, trust, partnership, association, joint venture, government, governmental subdivision or agency, or other legal or commercial entity.

(20) "Purchaser" means any person, other than a declarant or a person in the business of selling real estate for his own account, who by means of a voluntary transfer acquires a legal or equitable interest in a unit other than (i) a leasehold interest (including renewal options) of less than five years, or (ii) as security for an obligation.

(21) "Real estate" means any leasehold or other estate or interest in, over, or under land, including structures, fixtures, and other improvements and interests which by custom, usage, or law, pass with a conveyance of land though not described in the contract of sale or instrument of conveyance. "Real estate" includes parcels, with or without upper or lower boundaries, and spaces that may be filled with air or water.

(22) "Residential purposes" means use for dwelling or recreational purposes, or both.

(23) "Special declarant rights" means rights reserved for the benefit of a declarant to complete improvements indicated on plats and plans filed with the declaration (G.S. 47C-2-109); to exercise any development right (G.S. 47C-2-110); to maintain sales offices, management offices, signs advertising the condominium, and models (G.S. 47C-2-115); to use easements through the common elements for the purpose of making improvements within the condominium or within real estate which may be added to the condominium (G.S. 47C-2-116); to make the condominium part of a larger condominium (G.S. 47C-2-121); or to appoint or remove any officer of the association or any executive board member during any period of declarant control (G.S. 47C-3-103(d)).

(24) "Time share" means a "time share" as defined in G.S. 93A-41(9).

(25) "Unit" means a physical portion of the condominium designated for separate ownership or occupancy, the boundaries of which are described pursuant to (G.S. 47C-2-105(a)(5).

(26) "Unit owner" means a declarant or other person who owns a unit, or a lessee of a unit in a leasehold condominium whose lease expires simultaneously with any lease the expiration or termination of which will remove the unit from the condominium, but does not include a person having an interest in a unit solely as security for an obligation.

(27) "Lessee" means the party entitled to present possession of a leased unit whether lessee, sublessee or assignee. (1985 (Reg. Sess., 1986), c. 877, s. 1.)

§ 47C-1-104. Variation; power of attorney or proxy to declarant.

(a) Except as specifically provided in specific sections of this chapter, the provisions of this chapter may not be varied by the declaration or bylaws.

(b) The provisions of this chapter may not be varied by agreement; however, after breach of a provision of this chapter, rights created hereunder may be knowingly waived in writing.

(c) If a declarant, in good faith, has attempted to comply with the requirements of this chapter and has substantially complied with the chapter, nonmaterial errors or omissions shall not be actionable.

(d) Notwithstanding any other provision of this chapter, a declarant may not act under a power of attorney or proxy or use any other device to evade the limitations or prohibitions of this chapter, the declaration, or the bylaws. (1985 (Reg. Sess., 1986), c. 877, s. 1.)

§ 47C-1-105. Separate titles and taxation.

(a) If there is any unit owner other than a declarant, each unit that has been created, together with its interest in the common elements, constitutes for all purposes a separate parcel of real estate.

(b) If there is any unit owner other than a declarant, each unit must be separately taxed and assessed, and no separate tax or assessment may be rendered against any common elements for which a declarant has reserved no developmental rights.

(c) Any portion of the common elements for which the declarant has reserved any developmental right must be separately taxed and assessed against the declarant, and the declarant alone is liable for payment of those taxes.

(d) If there is no unit owner other than a declarant, the real estate comprising the condominium may be taxed and assessed in any manner provided by law.

(e) Except as provided in subsection (c) of this section, extraterritorial common property taxed pursuant to G.S. 105-277.8 shall be assessed, pro rata, among the unit owners based on the number of the units in the association. (1985 (Reg. Sess., 1986), c. 877, s. 1; 2012-157, s. 2.)

§ 47C-1-106. Applicability of local ordinances, regulations, and building codes.

A zoning, subdivision, or building code or other real estate use law, ordinance, or regulation may not prohibit the condominium form of ownership or impose any requirement upon a condominium which it would not impose upon a substantially similar development under a different form of ownership. Otherwise, no provision of this chapter invalidates or modifies any provision of any zoning, subdivision, or building code or other real estate use law, ordinance, or regulation. No local ordinance or regulation may require the recordation of a declaration prior to the date required by this chapter. (1985 (Reg. Sess., 1986), c. 877, s. 1.)

§ 47C-1-107. Eminent domain.

(a) If a unit is acquired by eminent domain, or if part of a unit is acquired by eminent domain leaving the unit owner with a remnant which may not practically or lawfully be used for any purpose permitted by the declaration, the award must compensate the unit owner for his unit and its interest in the common elements, whether or not any common elements are acquired. Unless the condemnor acquires the right to use the unit's interest in common elements, that unit's allocated interests are automatically reallocated to the remaining units in proportion to the respective allocated interests of those units before the taking exclusive of the unit taken, and the association shall promptly prepare, execute, and record an amendment to the declaration reflecting the reallocations. Any remnant of a unit remaining after part of a unit is taken under this subsection is thereafter a common element.

(b) Except as provided in subsection (a), if part of a unit is acquired by eminent domain, the award must compensate the unit owner for the reduction in value of the unit and of its interest in the common elements, whether or not any common elements are acquired. Upon acquisition, unless the decree otherwise provides, (1) that unit's allocated interests are reduced in proportion to the reduction in the size of the unit, or on any other basis specified in the declaration, and (2) the portion of the allocated interests divested from the partially acquired unit is automatically reallocated to that unit and the remaining units in proportion to the respective allocated interests of those units before the taking, with the partially acquired unit participating in the reallocation on the basis of its reduced allocated interests.

(c) If part of the common elements is acquired by eminent domain, the portion of the award not payable to unit owners under subsection (a) must be paid to the association. Unless the declaration provides otherwise, any portion of the award attributable to the acquisition of a limited common element must be apportioned among the owners of the units to which that limited common element was allocated at the time of acquisition.

(d)   The court decree shall be recorded in every county in which any portion of the condominium is located. (1985 (Reg. Sess., 1986), c. 877, s. 1.)

§ 47C-1-108. Supplemental general principles of law applicable.

The principles of law and equity supplement the provisions of this chapter, except to the extent inconsistent with this chapter. (1985 (Reg. Sess., 1986), c. 877, s. 1.)

§ 47C-1-109. Inconsistent time share provisions.

The provisions of this Chapter shall apply, so far as appropriate, to every time share program or project created within this State after October 1, 1986, except to the extent that specific statutory provisions in Chapter 93A are inconsistent with this Chapter, in which case the provisions of Chapter 93A shall prevail. (1985 (Reg. Sess., 1986), c. 877, s. 1.)

Article 2.

Creation, Alteration, and Termination of Condominiums.

§ 47C-2-101. Execution and recordation of declaration.

(a)   A declaration creating a condominium shall be executed in the same manner as a deed, shall be recorded in every county in which any portion of the condominium is located.

(b) A declaration or an amendment to a declaration adding units to a condominium, may not be recorded unless all structural components and mechanical systems of all buildings containing or comprising any units thereby created are substantially completed in accordance with the plans, as evidenced by a recorded certificate of completion executed by an architect licensed under the provisions of Chapter 83 [83A] of the General Statutes or an engineer registered under the provisions of Chapter 89C of the General Statutes. (1985 (Reg. Sess., 1986), c. 877, s. 1; 2012-18, s. 1.5.)

§ 47C-2-102. Unit boundaries.

Except as provided by the declaration:

(1) If walls, floors or ceilings are designated as boundaries of a unit, then all lath, furring, wallboard, plasterboard, plaster, paneling, tiles, wallpaper, paint, finished flooring and any other materials constituting any part of the finished flooring, and any other materials constituting any part of the finished surfaces thereof are a part of the unit; and all other portions of such walls, floors, or ceilings are a part of the common elements.

(2) If any chute, flue, duct, wire, conduit, bearing wall, bearing column, or any other fixture lies partially within and partially outside the designated boundaries of a unit, any portion thereof serving only that unit is a limited common element allocated exclusively to that unit, and any portion thereof serving more than one unit or any portion of the common elements is a part of the common elements.

(3) Subject to the provisions of paragraph (2), all spaces, interior partitions, and other fixtures and improvements within the boundaries of a unit are a part of the unit.

(4) Any shutters, awnings, window boxes, doorsteps, stoops, decks, porches, balconies, patios, and all exterior doors and windows or other fixtures designed to serve a single unit but located outside the unit's boundaries are limited common elements allocated exclusively to that unit. (1985 (Reg. Sess., 1986), c. 877, s. 1.)

§ 47C-2-103. Construction and validity of declaration and bylaws.

(a) All provisions of the declaration and bylaws are severable.

(b) The rule against perpetuities may not be applied to defeat any provision of the declaration, bylaws, or rules and regulations adopted pursuant to G.S. 47C-3-102(a)(1).

(c) In the event of a conflict between the provisions of the declaration and the bylaws, the declaration prevails except to the extent the declaration is inconsistent with this chapter.

(d) Title to a unit and common elements is not rendered unmarketable or otherwise affected by reason of an insubstantial failure of the declaration to comply with this chapter. Whether a substantial failure to comply with this chapter impairs marketability shall be determined by the law of this State relating to marketability. (1985 (Reg. Sess., 1986), c. 877, s. 1.)

§ 47C-2-104. Description of units.

A description of a condominium unit which sets forth the name of the condominium, the recording data for the declaration, and the identifying number of the unit or which otherwise complies with the general requirements of the laws of this State concerning description of real property is sufficient legal description of that unit and all rights, obligations, and interests appurtenant to that unit which were created by the declaration or bylaws. (1985 (Reg. Sess., 1986), c. 877, s. 1.)

§ 47C-2-105. Contents of declaration.

(a) The declaration for a condominium must contain:

(1) The name of the condominium, which must include the word "condominium" or be followed by the words "a condominium", and the name of the association;

(2) The name of every county in which any part of the condominium is situated;

(3) A legally sufficient description of the real estate included in the condominium;

(4) A statement of the maximum number of units which the declarant reserves the right to create;

(5) A description (by reference to the plats or plans described in G.S. 47C-2-109) of the boundaries of each unit created by the declaration, including the unit's identifying number;

(6) A description of any limited common elements, other than those specified in subsections 47C-2-102(2) and (4), as provided in G.S. 47C-2-109(b)(7);

(7) A description of any real estate (except real estate subject to development rights) which may be allocated subsequently as limited common elements, other than limited common elements specified in subsections 47C-2-102(2) and (4), together with a statement that they may be so allocated;

(8) A description of any development rights and other special declarant rights reserved by the declarant, together with a legally sufficient description of the real estate to which each of those rights applies, and a time limit within which each of those rights must be exercised;

(9) If any development right may be exercised with respect to different parcels of real estate at different times, a statement to that effect, together with (i) either a statement fixing the boundaries of those portions and regulating the order in which those portions may be subjected to the exercise of each development right or a statement that no assurances are made in those regards, and (ii) a statement as to whether, if any development right is exercised in any portion of the real estate subject to that development right, that development right must be exercised in all or in any other portion of the remainder of that real estate;

(10) Any other conditions or limitations under which the rights described in paragraph (8) may be exercised or will lapse;

(11) An allocation to each unit of the allocated interests in the manner described in G.S. 47C-2-107;

(12) Any restrictions on use, occupancy, or alienation of the units;

(13) The recording data for recorded easements and licenses appurtenant to or included in the condominium or to which any portion of the condominium is or may become subject by virtue of a reservation in the declaration; and

(14) All matters required by G.S. 47C-2-106, 47C-2-107, 47C-2-108, 47C-2-109, 47C-2-115, 47C-2-116, and 47C-3-103(d).

(b) The declaration may contain any other matters the declarant deems appropriate. (1985 (Reg. Sess., 1986), c. 877, s. 1.)

§ 47C-2-106. Leasehold condominiums.

(a) Any lease, or a memorandum thereof, the expiration or termination of which may terminate the condominium or reduce its size shall be recorded. Every lessor of those leases must sign the declaration, and the declaration shall state:

(1) Where the complete lease may be inspected;

(2) The date on which the lease is scheduled to expire;

(3) A legally sufficient description of the real estate subject to the lease;

(4) Any right of the unit owners to redeem the reversion and the manner whereby those rights may be exercised or a statement that they do not have those rights;

(5) Any right of the unit owners to remove any improvements after the expiration or termination of the lease or a statement that they do not have those rights; and

(6) Any rights of the unit owners to renew the lease and the conditions of any renewal or a statement that they do not have those rights.

(b) After the declaration for a leasehold condominium is recorded, neither the lessor nor his successor in interest may terminate the leasehold interest of a unit owner who, after demand, makes timely payment of his share of the rent determined in proportion to his common element interest and otherwise complies with all covenants which, if violated, would entitle the lessor to terminate the lease. A unit owner's leasehold interest is not affected by failure of any other person to pay rent or fulfill any other covenant under the lease.

(c) Acquisition of the leasehold interest of any unit owner by the owner of the reversion or remainder does not merge the leasehold and fee simple interests unless the leasehold interests of all unit owners subject to that reversion or remainder are acquired.

(d) If the expiration or termination of a lease decreases the number of units in a condominium, the allocated interests shall be reallocated in accordance with G.S. 47C-1-107(a) as though those units had been taken by eminent domain. Reallocations shall be confirmed by an amendment to the declaration prepared, executed, and recorded by the association. (1985 (Reg. Sess., 1986), c. 877, s. 1.)

§ 47C-2-107. Allocation of common element, interests, votes, and common expense liabilities.

(a) The declaration shall allocate a fraction or percentage of undivided interests in the common elements and in the common expenses of the association and a portion of the votes in the association to each unit and state the formulas used to establish those allocations. Those allocations may not discriminate in favor of units owned by the declarant.

(b) If units may be added to or withdrawn from the condominium, the declaration must state the formulas to be used to reallocate the allocated interests among all units included in the condominium after the addition or withdrawal.

(c) The declaration may provide: (i) that different allocations of votes shall be made to the units on particular matters specified in the declaration; (ii) for cumulative voting only for the purpose of electing members of the executive board; and (iii) for class voting on specified issues affecting the class if necessary to protect valid interests of the class. A declarant may not utilize cumulative or class voting for the purpose of evading any limitation imposed on declarants by this chapter nor may units constitute a class because they are owned by a declarant.

(d)   Except for minor variations due to rounding, the sum of the undivided interests in the common elements and common expense liabilities allocated at any time to all the units must each equal one if stated as fractions or one hundred percent (100%) if stated as percentages. If the declaration allocates to each of the units a fraction or percentage of ownership of the common elements that results in an actual total of such fractions or percentages that is greater or less than the actual whole of such ownership, each unit's ownership of the common elements shall be automatically reallocated so that each unit is allocated the same fraction or percentage of ownership of the actual whole as that unit had of the actual total that was greater or less than the actual whole. The declarant or the association shall file an amendment to the declaration reflecting such reallocation which amendment need not be executed by any other party.

(e)   The common elements are not subject to partition, and any purported conveyance, encumbrance, judicial sale, or other voluntary or involuntary transfer of an undivided interest in the common elements made without the unit to which that interest is allocated is void. (1985 (Reg. Sess., 1986), c. 877, s. 1.)

§ 47C-2-108. Limited common elements.

(a)   Except for the limited common elements described in subsections 47C-2-102(2) and (4), the declaration shall specify to which unit or units each limited common element is allocated. That allocation may not be altered without the unanimous consent of the unit owners whose units are affected.

(b)   Except as the declaration otherwise provides, a limited common element may be reallocated by an amendment to the declaration executed by all the unit owners between or among whose units the reallocations is made. The persons executing the amendment shall provide a copy thereof to the association, which shall record it. The amendment shall be recorded in the same manner as a deed in the names of the parties and the condominium.

(c)   A common element not previously allocated as a limited common element may not be so allocated except by unanimous consent or pursuant to provisions in the declaration made in accordance with G.S. 47C-2-105(a)(7). All such allocations shall be made by amendments to the declaration and shall become effective in accordance with G.S. 47C-2-117(c). (1985 (Reg. Sess., 1986), c. 877, s. 1.)

§ 47C-2-109. Plats and plans.

(a)   The declarant shall file with the register of deeds in each county where the condominium is located the condominium's plat or plan prepared in accordance with this section. The plat or plan shall be considered a part of the declaration but shall be recorded separately, and the declaration shall refer by number to the file where such plat or plan is recorded. Each plat or plan must contain a certification by an architect licensed under the provisions of Chapter 83A of the General Statutes or an engineer registered under the provisions of Chapter 89C of the General Statutes that it contains all of the information required by this section.

(b)   Each plat or plan or combination thereof must show:

(1)   The name and a survey or general schematic map of the entire condominium;

(2)   The location and dimensions of all real estate not subject to development rights or subject only to the development right to withdraw and the location and dimensions of all existing improvements within that real estate;

(3)   The location and dimensions of any real estate subject to development rights, labeled to identify the rights applicable to each parcel;

(4)   The extent of any encroachments by or upon any portion of the condominium;

(5)   The location and dimensions of all easements having specific location and dimensions and serving or burdening any portion of the condominium;

(6)   The verified statement of an architect licensed under the provisions of Chapter 83A of the General Statutes or an engineer registered under the provisions of Chapter 89C of the General Statutes certifying that such plats or

plans fully and accurately depict the layout, location, ceiling and floor elevations, unit numbers and dimensions of the units, as built;

(6a) The certificate by a registered land surveyor licensed under the provisions of Chapter 89C of the General Statutes stating that the plats or plans accurately depict the legal boundaries and the physical location of the units and other improvements relative to those boundaries;

(7) The locations and dimensions of limited common elements; however, parking spaces and the limited common elements described in subsections 47C-2-102(2) and (4) need not be shown, except for decks, stoops, porches, balconies, and patios;

(8) A legally sufficient description of any real estate in which the unit owners will own only an estate for years, labeled as "leasehold real estate";

(9) The distance between noncontiguous parcels of real estate comprising the condominium;

(10) Any unit in which the declarant has reserved the right to create additional units or common elements.

(c) A plat may also show the intended location and dimensions of any contemplated improvement to be constructed anywhere within the condominium. Any contemplated improvement shown must be labeled either "MUST BE BUILT" or "NEED NOT BE BUILT".

(d) Upon exercising any development right, the declarant shall record either new plats and plans necessary to conform to the requirements of subsections (a), (b), and (c) or new certifications of plats and plans previously recorded if those plats and plans otherwise conform to the requirements of those subsections.

(e) In order to be recorded, plats or plans filed shall:

(1) Be reproducible plats or plans on cloth, linen, film, or other permanent material and be submitted in that form; and

(2) Have an outside marginal size of not more than 21 inches by 30 inches nor less than eight and one-half inches by 11 inches, including one and one-half inches for binding on the left margin and a one-half inch border on each of the

other sides. Where size of the buildings or suitable scale to assure legibility require, plats or plans may be placed on two or more sheets with appropriate match lines.

(f) The fee for recording each plat or plan sheet submitted shall be as prescribed by G.S. 161-10(a)(3). (1985 (Reg. Sess., 1986), c. 877, s. 1; 1987, c. 282, s. 8; 1989, c. 571; 2012-18, s. 1.6.)

§ 47C-2-110. Exercise of development rights.

(a) To exercise any development right reserved under G.S. 47C-2-105(a)(8), the declarant shall record an amendment to the declaration (G.S. 47C-2-117) and comply with G.S. 47C-2-109. The declarant is the unit owner of any units thereby created. The amendment to the declaration must assign an identifying number to each new unit created and, except in the case of subdivision or conversion of units described in subsection (c), reallocate the allocated interests among all units. The amendment must describe any common elements and any limited common elements thereby created and, in the case of limited common elements, designate the unit to which each is allocated to the extent required by G.S. 47C-2-108 (Limited Common Elements).

(b) Development rights may be reserved within any real estate added to the condominium if the amendment adding that real estate includes all matters required by, and is in compliance with, G.S. 47C-2-105 and, if a leasehold condominium, G.S. 47C-2-106 and also if the plats and plans include all matters required by G.S. 47C-2-109. This provision does not extend the limit on the exercise of developmental rights imposed by the declaration pursuant to G.S. 47C-2-105(a)(8).

(c) When a declarant exercises a development right to subdivide or convert a unit previously created into additional units, common elements, or both:

(1) If the declarant converts the unit entirely to common elements, the amendment to the declaration must reallocate all the allocated interests of that unit among the other units as if that unit had been taken by eminent domain; or

(2) If the declarant subdivides the unit into two or more units, whether or not any part of the unit is converted into common elements, the amendment to the declaration must reallocate all the allocated interests of the unit among the

units created by the subdivision in any reasonable manner prescribed by the declarant.

(d) If the declaration provides pursuant to G.S. 47C-2-105(a)(8) that all or a portion of the real estate is subject to the development right of withdrawal:

(1) If all the real estate is subject to withdrawal, and the declaration does not describe separate portions of real estate subject to that right, no part of the real estate may be withdrawn after a unit has been conveyed to a purchaser; and

(2) If a portion or portions are subject to withdrawal, no part of a portion may be withdrawn after a unit in that portion has been conveyed to a purchaser. (1985 (Reg. Sess., 1986), c. 877, s. 1.)

§ 47C-2-111. Alterations of units.

Subject to the provisions of the declaration and other provisions of law, a unit owner:

(1) May make any improvements or alterations to his unit that do not impair the structural integrity or mechanical systems or lessen the support of any portion of the condominium;

(2) May not change the appearance of the common elements or the exterior appearance of a unit or any other portion of the condominium without permission of the association; and

(3) May, after acquiring an adjoining unit, remove or alter any intervening partition or create apertures therein, even if the partition is a common element, if those acts do not impair the structural integrity or mechanical systems or lessen the support of any portion of the condominium. Removal of partitions or creation of apertures under this paragraph is not an alteration of boundaries. (1985 (Reg. Sess., 1986), c. 877, s. 1.)

§ 47C-2-112. Relocation of boundaries between adjoining units.

(a) Subject to the provisions of the declaration and other provisions of law, the boundaries between adjoining units may be relocated upon application to the association by the owners of those units. Any such application to the association must be in such form and contain such data as may be reasonably required by the association and be accompanied by a plat prepared by an architect licensed under the provisions of Chapter 83 [83A] of the General Statutes or an engineer registered under the provisions of Chapter 89C of the General Statutes detailing the relocation of the boundaries between the affected units. If the owners of the adjoining units have specified a reallocation between their units of their allocated interests, the application must state the proposed reallocations. Unless the executive board determines within 30 days that the reallocations are unreasonable, the association, at the expense of the owners filing the application, shall prepare and record an amendment to the declaration that identifies the units involved, states the reallocations, is executed by those unit owners and the association, contains words of conveyance, and is indexed in the name of the grantor and the grantee by the register of deeds.

(b) The association, at the expense of the unit owners filing the application, shall prepare and record plats or plans necessary to show the altered boundaries between adjoining units and their dimensions and identifying numbers. (1985 (Reg. Sess., 1986), c. 877, s. 1.)

§ 47C-2-113. Subdivision of units.

(a) If the declaration expressly so permits, a unit may be subdivided into two or more units. Subject to the provisions of the declaration and other provisions of law, upon application of a unit owner to subdivide a unit, the association, at the expense of the unit owner, shall prepare, execute, and record an amendment to the declaration, including the plats and plans, subdividing that unit.

(b) The amendment to the declaration must be executed by the owner of the unit to be subdivided, assign an identifying number to each unit created, and reallocate the allocated interests formerly allocated to the subdivided unit to the new units in any reasonable manner prescribed by the owner of the subdivided unit. (1985 (Reg. Sess., 1986), c. 877, s. 1.)

§ 47C-2-114. Easement for encroachments.

(a) To the extent that any unit or common element encroaches on any other unit or common element, a valid easement for the encroachment exists. The easement does not relieve a unit owner of liability in case of his willful misconduct nor relieve a declarant or any other person of liability for failure to adhere to the plats and plans.

(b) With respect to all condominiums created prior to October 1, 1986, the provisions of subsection (a) of this section shall be deemed to apply to such condominiums, unless an action asserting otherwise shall have been brought within six months from October 1, 1986. (1985 (Reg. Sess., 1986), c. 877, s. 1.)

§ 47C-2-115. Use for sales purposes.

A declarant may maintain sales offices, management offices, and models in units or on common elements in the condominium only if the declaration so provides and specifies the rights of a declarant with regard to the number, size, location, and relocation thereof. Any sales office, management office, or model not designated a unit by the declaration is a common element, and if a declarant ceases to be a unit owner, he ceases to have any rights with regard thereto unless it is removed promptly from the condominium in accordance with a right to remove reserved in the declaration. Subject to any limitations in the declaration, a declarant may maintain signs on the common elements advertising the condominium. The provisions of this section are subject to the provisions of other State law and to local ordinances. (1985 (Reg. Sess., 1986), c. 877, s. 1.)

§ 47C-2-116. Easement to facilitate exercise of special declarant rights.

Subject to the provisions of the declaration, a declarant has such easements through the common elements as may be reasonably necessary for the purpose of discharging a declarant's obligations or exercising special declarant rights whether arising under this Chapter or reserved in the declaration. (1985 (Reg. Sess., 1986), c. 877, s. 1.)

§ 47C-2-117. Amendment of declaration.

(a)   Except in cases of amendments that may be executed by a declarant under G.S. 47C-2-109(d) or 47C-2-110, the association under G.S. 47C-1-107, 47C-1-106(d), 47C-2-112(a), or 47C-2-113, or certain unit owners under G.S. 47C-2-108(b), 47C-2-112(a), 47C-2-113(b), or 47C-2-118(b), and except as limited by subsection (d), the declaration may be amended only by affirmative vote of or a written agreement signed by, unit owners of units to which at least sixty-seven percent (67%) of the votes in the association are allocated or any larger majority the declaration specifies. The declaration may specify a smaller number only if all of the units are restricted exclusively to nonresidential use.

(b)   No action to challenge the validity of an amendment adopted by the association pursuant to this section may be brought more than one year after the amendment is recorded.

(c)   Every amendment to the declaration must be recorded in every county in which any portion of the condominium is located and is effective only upon recordation. An amendment shall be indexed in the Grantee's index in the name of the condominium and the association and in the Grantor's index in the name of the parties executing the amendment.

(d)   Except to the extent expressly permitted or required by other provisions of this Chapter, no amendment may create or increase special declarant rights, increase the number of units, or change the boundaries of any unit, the allocated interest of a unit, or the uses to which any unit is restricted, in the absence of unanimous consent of the unit owners.

(e)   Amendments to the declaration required by this Chapter to be recorded by the association shall be prepared, executed, recorded, and certified on behalf of the association by any officer of the association designated for that purpose or, in the absence of designation, by the president of the association. (1985 (Reg. Sess., 1986), c. 877, s. 1.)

§ 47C-2-118. Termination of condominium.

(a)   Except in the case of a taking of all the units by eminent domain (G.S. 47C-1-107), a condominium may be terminated only by agreement of unit owners of units to which at least eighty percent (80%) of the votes in the association are allocated, or any larger percentage the declaration specifies. The declaration may specify a smaller percentage only if all of the units in the condominium are restricted exclusively to nonresidential uses.

(b)   An agreement to terminate must be evidenced by the execution of a termination agreement, or ratifications thereof, in the same manner as a deed, by the requisite number of unit owners. The termination agreement must specify a date after which the agreement will be void unless recorded before that date. A termination agreement and all ratifications thereof must be recorded in every county in which a portion of the condominium is situated, and is effective only upon recordation.

(c)   In the case of a condominium containing only units having horizontal boundaries described in the declaration, a termination agreement may provide that all the common elements and units of the condominium shall be sold following termination. If, pursuant to the agreement, any real estate in the condominium is to be sold following termination, the termination agreement must set forth the minimum terms of the sale.

(d)   In the case of a condominium containing any units not having horizontal boundaries described in the declaration, a termination agreement may provide for sale of the common elements, but may not require that the units be sold following termination, unless the declaration as originally recorded provided otherwise or unless all the unit owners consent to the sale.

(e)   The association, on behalf of the unit owners, may contract for the sale of real estate in the condominium, but the contract is not binding on the unit owners until approved pursuant to subsections (a) and (b). If any real estate in the condominium is to be sold following termination, title to that real estate, upon termination, vests in the association as trustee for the holders of all interests in the units. Thereafter, the association has all powers necessary and appropriate to effect the sale. Until the sale has been concluded and the proceeds thereof distributed, the association continues in existence with all powers it had before termination. Proceeds of the sale must be distributed to unit owners and lienholders as their interests may appear, in proportion to the respective interests of unit owners as provided in subsection (h). Unless otherwise specified in the termination agreement, as long as the association holds title to the real estate, each unit owner and his successors in interest have an exclusive right to occupancy of the portion of the real estate that formerly constituted his unit. During the period of that occupancy, each unit owner and his successors in interest remain liable for all assessments and other obligations imposed on unit owners by this Chapter or the declaration.

(f) If the real estate constituting the condominium is not to be sold following termination, title to the common elements and, in a condominium containing only units having horizontal boundaries described in the declaration, title to all the real estate in the condominium, vests in the unit owners upon termination as tenants in common in proportion to their respective interests as provided in subsection (h), and liens on the units shift accordingly. While the tenancy in common exists, each unit owner and his successors in interest have an exclusive right to occupancy of the portion of the real estate that formerly constituted his unit.

(g) Following termination of the condominium, the proceeds of any sale of real estate, together with the assets of the association, are held by the association as trustee for unit owners and holders of liens on the units as their interests may appear. Following termination, creditors of the association holding liens on the units, which were recorded before termination, may enforce those liens in the same manner as any lienholder. All other creditors of the association are to be treated as if they had perfected liens on the units immediately before termination.

(h) The respective interests of unit owners referred to in subsections (e), (f) and (g) are as follows:

(1) Except as provided in paragraph (2), the respective interests of unit owners are the fair market value of their units, limited common elements, and common element interests immediately before the termination, as determined by one or more independent appraisers selected by the association. The decision of the independent appraisers shall be distributed to the unit owners and becomes final unless disapproved within 30 days after distribution by unit owners of units to which twenty-five percent (25%) of the votes in the association are allocated. The proportion of any unit owner's interest to that of all unit owners is determined by dividing the fair market value of that unit owner's unit and common element interest by the total fair market values of all the units and common elements.

(2) If any unit or any limited common element is destroyed to the extent that an appraisal of the fair market value thereof prior to destruction cannot be made, the interests of all unit owners are their respective common element interests immediately before the termination.

(i)   Except as provided in subsection (j), foreclosure or enforcement of a lien or encumbrance against the entire condominium does not of itself terminate the condominium, and foreclosure or enforcement of a lien or encumbrance against a portion of the condominium, other than withdrawable real estate, does not withdraw that portion from the condominium. Foreclosure or enforcement of a lien or encumbrance against withdrawable real estate does not of itself withdraw that real estate from the condominium, but the person taking title thereto has the right to require from the association, upon request, an amendment excluding the real estate from the condominium.

(j)   If a lien or encumbrance against a portion of the real estate comprising the condominium has priority over the declaration, and the lien or encumbrance has not been released, the parties foreclosing the lien or encumbrance may upon foreclosure, record an instrument excluding the real estate subject to that lien or encumbrance from the condominium. (1985 (Reg. Sess., 1986), c. 877, s. 1.)

§ 47C-2-119. Reserved for future codification purposes.

§ 47C-2-120. Master associations.

(a)   If the declaration for a condominium provides that any of the powers described in G.S. 47C-3-102 are to be exercised by or may be delegated to a profit or nonprofit corporation (or unincorporated association) which exercises those or other powers on behalf of one or more condominiums or for the benefit of the unit owners of one or more condominiums, all provisions of this chapter applicable to unit owners' associations apply to any such corporation (or unincorporated association), except as modified by this section.

(b)   Unless a master association is acting in the capacity of an association described in G.S. 47C-3-101, it may exercise the powers set forth in G.S. 47C-3-102(a)(2) only to the extent expressly permitted in the declarations of condominiums which are part of the master association or expressly described in the delegations of power from those condominiums to the master association.

(c)   If the declaration of any condominium provides that the executive board may delegate certain powers to a master association, the members of the executive board have no liability for the acts or omissions of the master association with respect to those powers following delegation.

(d)   The rights and responsibilities of unit owners with respect to the unit owners' association set forth in G.S. 47C-3-103, 47C-3-108, 47C-3-109, and 47C-3-110 apply in the conduct of the affairs of a master association only to those persons who elect the board of a master association, whether or not those persons are otherwise unit owners within the meaning of this Chapter.

(e)   Notwithstanding the provisions of G.S. 47C-3-103(f) with respect to the election of the executive board of an association by all unit owners after the period of declarant control ends and even if a master association is also an association described in G.S. 47C-3-101, the certificate of incorporation or other instrument creating the master association and the declaration of each condominium, the powers of which are assigned by the declaration or delegated to the master association, may provide that the executive board of the master association must be elected after the period of declarant control in any of the following ways:

(1)   All unit owners of all condominiums subject to the master association may elect all members of that executive board.

(2)   All members of the executive boards of all condominiums subject to the master association may elect all members of that executive board.

(3)   All unit owners of each condominium subject to the master association may elect specified members of that executive board.

(4)   All members of the executive board of each condominium subject to the master association may elect specified members of that executive board. (1985 (Reg. Sess., 1986), c. 877, s. 1.)

§ 47C-2-121. Merger or consolidation of condominiums.

(a)   Any two or more condominiums may, by agreement of the unit owners as provided in subsection (b), be merged or consolidated into a single condominium. In the event of a merger or consolidation, unless the agreement otherwise provides, the resultant condominium shall be, for all purposes, the legal successor of all of the pre-existing condominiums, and the operations and activities of all associations of the pre-existing condominiums shall be merged or consolidated into a single association which shall hold all powers, rights, obligations, assets and liabilities of all pre-existing associations.

(b) An agreement of two or more condominiums to merge or consolidate pursuant to subsection (a) must be evidenced by an agreement prepared, executed, recorded and certified by the president of the association of each of the pre-existing condominiums following approval by owners of units to which are allocated the percentage of votes in each condominium required to terminate that condominium. Any such agreement must be executed in the same manner as a deed and recorded in every county in which a portion of the condominium is located and is not effective until recorded.

(c) Every merger or consolidation agreement must provide for the reallocation of the allocated interests in the new association among the units of the resultant condominium either (i) by stating such reallocations or the formulas upon which they are based or (ii) by stating the percentage of overall allocated interests of the new condominium which are allocated to all of the units comprising each of the pre-existing condominiums and providing that the portion of such percentages allocated to each unit formerly comprising a part of such pre-existing condominium shall be equal to the percentages of allocated interests allocated to such unit by the declaration of the pre-existing condominiums. (1985 (Reg. Sess., 1986), c. 877, s. 1.)

Article 3.

Management of the Condominium.

§ 47C-3-101. Organization of unit owners' association.

A unit owners' association shall be organized no later than the date the first unit in the condominium is conveyed. The membership of the association at all times shall consist exclusively of all the unit owners, or following termination of the condominium, of all persons entitled to distributions of proceeds under G.S. 47C-2-118. The association shall be organized as a profit or nonprofit corporation or as an unincorporated nonprofit association. (1985 (Reg. Sess., 1986), c. 877, s. 1; 2006-226, s. 4.)

§ 47C-3-102. Powers of unit owners' association.

(a)　Unless the declaration expressly provides to the contrary, the association, even if unincorporated, may:

(1)　Adopt and amend bylaws and rules and regulations;

(2)　Adopt and amend budgets for revenues, expenditures, and reserves and collect assessments for common expenses from unit owners;

(3)　Hire and terminate managing agents and other employees, agents, and independent contractors;

(4)　Institute, defend, or intervene in its own name in litigation or administrative proceedings on matters affecting the condominium;

(5)　Make contracts and incur liabilities;

(6)　Regulate the use, maintenance, repair, replacement, and modification of common elements;

(7)　Cause additional improvements to be made as a part of the common elements;

(8)　Acquire, hold, encumber, and convey in its own name any right, title, or interest to real or personal property, provided that common elements may be conveyed or subjected to a security interest only pursuant to G.S. 47C-3-112;

(9)　Grant easements, leases, licenses, and concessions through or over the common elements;

(10)　Impose and receive any payments, fees, or charges for the use, rental, or operation of the common elements other than limited common elements described in subsections 47C-2-102(2) and (4) and for services provided to unit owners;

(11) Impose charges for late payment of assessments, not to exceed the greater of twenty dollars ($20.00) per month or ten percent (10%) of any assessment installment unpaid and, after notice and an opportunity to be heard, suspend privileges or services provided by the association (except rights of access to lots) during any period that assessments or other amounts due and owing to the association remain unpaid for a period of 30 days or longer, and levy reasonable fines not to exceed one hundred dollars ($100.00) (G.S. 47C-3-107.1) for violations of the declaration, bylaws, and rules and regulations of the association.

(12) Impose reasonable charges for the preparation and recordation of amendments to the declaration, resale certificates required by G.S. 47C-4-109, or statements of unpaid assessments;

(13) Provide for the indemnification of and maintain liability insurance for its officers, executive board, directors, employees and agents;

(14) Assign its right to future income, including the right to receive common expense assessments.

(15) Exercise all other powers that may be exercised in this State by legal entities of the same types as the association; and

(16) Exercise any other powers necessary and proper for the governance and operation of the association.

(b) Notwithstanding subsection (a), the declaration may not impose limitations on the power of the association to deal with the declarant that are more restrictive than the limitations imposed on the power of the association to deal with other persons. (1985 (Reg. Sess., 1986), c. 877, s. 1; 2004-109, s. 2; 2005-422, ss. 10, 11.)

§ 47C-3-103. Executive board members and officers.

(a) Except as provided in the declaration, the bylaws, or subsection (b) or other provisions of this chapter, the executive board may act in all instances on behalf of the association. In the performance of their duties, the officers and members of the executive board shall be deemed to stand in a fiduciary relationship to the association and the unit owners and shall discharge their duties in good faith, and with that diligence and care which ordinarily prudent men would exercise under similar circumstances in like positions.

(b) The executive board may not act on behalf of the association to amend the declaration (G.S. 47C-2-117), to terminate the condominium (G.S. 47C-2-118), or to elect members of the executive board or determine the qualifications, powers and duties, or terms of office of executive board members (G.S. 47C-3-103(e) and (f)), but the executive board may fill vacancies in its membership for the unexpired portion of any term. Notwithstanding any provision of the declaration or bylaws to the contrary, the unit owners, by at least sixty-seven percent (67%) vote of all persons present and entitled to vote at any meeting of the unit owners at which a quorum is present, may remove any member of the executive board with or without cause, other than members appointed by the declarant.

(c) Within 30 days after adoption of any proposed budget for the condominium, the executive board shall provide a summary of the budget to all the unit owners, and shall set a date for a meeting of the unit owners to consider ratification of the budget not less than 14 nor more than 30 days after mailing of the summary. There shall be no requirement that a quorum be present at the meeting. The budget is ratified unless at that meeting a majority of all the unit owners or any larger vote specified in the declaration rejects the budget. In the event the proposed budget is rejected, the periodic budget last ratified shall be continued until such time as the unit owners ratify a subsequent budget proposed by the executive board.

(d) Subject to subsection (e), the declaration may provide for a period of declarant control of the association, during which period a declarant, or persons designated by him, may appoint and remove the officers and members of the executive board. Regardless of the period provided in the declaration, a period of declarant control terminates no later than the earlier of: (i) 120 days after conveyance of seventy-five percent (75%) of the units (including units which may be created pursuant to special declarant rights) to unit owners other than a declarant; (ii) two years after all declarants have ceased to offer units for sale in the ordinary course of business; or (iii) two years after any development right to add new units was last exercised. A declarant may voluntarily surrender the right to appoint and remove officers and members of the executive board before termination of that period, but in that event he may require, for the duration of the period of declarant control, that specified actions of the association or executive board, as described in a recorded instrument executed by the declarant, be approved by the declarant before they become effective.

(e) Not later than 60 days after conveyance of twenty-five percent (25%) of the units (including units which may be created pursuant to special rights) to unit owners other than a declarant, at least one member and not less than twenty-five percent (25%) of the members of the executive board shall be elected by unit owners other than the declarant. Not later than 60 days after conveyance of fifty percent (50%) of the units (including units which may be created pursuant to special declarant rights) to unit owners other than a declarant, not less than thirty-three percent (33%) of the members of the executive board shall be elected by unit owners other than the declarant.

(f) Not later than the termination of any period of declarant control, the unit owners shall elect an executive board of at least three members, at least a majority of whom must be unit owners. The executive board shall elect the officers. The executive board members and officers shall take office upon election.

(g) The association shall publish the names and addresses of all officers and board members of the association within 30 days of the election. (1985 (Reg. Sess., 1986), c. 877, s. 1; 2005-422, ss. 12, 13.)

§ 47C-3-104. Transfer of special declarant rights.

(a) No special declarant right (G.S. 47C-1-103(23)) created or reserved under this chapter may be transferred except by an instrument evidencing the transfer recorded in every county in which any portion of the condominium is located. The instrument is not effective unless executed by the transferee.

(b) Upon transfer of any special declarant right, the liability of a transferor declarant is as follows:

(1) A transferor is not relieved of any obligation or liability arising before the transfer, including, but not limited to, liability or obligations relating to warranties. Lack of privity does not deprive any unit owner of standing to bring an action to enforce any obligation of the transferor.

(2) If the successor to any special declarant right is an affiliate of a declarant (G.S. 47C-1-103(1)), the transferor is jointly and severally liable with

the successor for any obligation or liability of the successor which relates to the condominium.

(3)   If a transferor retains any special declarant right, but transfers other special declarant rights to a successor who is not an affiliate of the declarant, the transferor is liable for any obligations or liabilities imposed on a declarant by this chapter or by the declaration relating to the retained special declarant rights and arising after the transfer.

(4)   A transferor has no liability for any act or omission or any breach of a contractual or warranty obligation arising from the exercise of a special declarant right by a successor declarant who is not an affiliate of the transferor.

(c)   Unless otherwise provided in a mortgage instrument or deed of trust, in case of foreclosure of a mortgage, tax sale, judicial sale, sale by a trustee under a deed of trust, or sale under Bankruptcy Code or receivership proceedings, of any units owned by a declarant, or real estate in a condominium subject to development rights, a person acquiring title to all the real estate being foreclosed or sold, but only upon his request, succeeds to all special declarant rights related to that real estate held by that declarant, or only to any rights reserved in the declaration and held by that declarant to maintain models, sales offices and signs. The judgment or instrument conveying title shall provide for transfer of only the special declarant rights requested.

(d)   Upon foreclosure, tax sale, judicial sale, sale by a trustee under a deed of trust, or sale under Bankruptcy Code or receivership proceedings, of all units and other real estate in a condominium owned by a declarant the declarant ceases to have any special declarant rights.

(e)   The liabilities and obligations of persons who succeed to special declarant rights are as follows:

(1)   A successor to any special declarant right who is an affiliate of a declarant is subject to all obligations and liabilities imposed on the transferor related to the condominium.

(2)   A successor to any special declarant right, other than a successor described in paragraphs (3) and (4) who is not an affiliate of a declarant, is subject to all obligations and liabilities:

a. On a declarant which relate to his exercise or nonexercise of special declarant rights; or

b. On his transferor, other than:

(i) Misrepresentations by any prior declarant;

(ii) Warranty obligations on improvements made by any previous declarant, or made before the condominium was created;

(iii) Breach of any fiduciary obligation by any previous declarant or his appointees to the executive board; or

(iv) Any liability or obligation imposed on the transferor as a result of the transferor's acts or omissions after the transfer.

(3) A successor to only a right reserved in the declaration to maintain models, sales offices, and signs (G.S. 47C-2-115), if he is not an affiliate of a declarant, may not exercise any other special declarant right, and is not subject to any liability or obligation as a declarant, except the obligation to provide a public offering statement, and any liability arising as a result thereof.

(4) A successor to all special declarant rights held by his transferor who is not an affiliate of that declarant and who succeeded to those rights pursuant to a deed in lieu of foreclosure or a judgment or instrument conveying title to units under subsection (c), may declare his intention in a recorded instrument to hold those rights solely for transfer to another person. Thereafter, until transferring all special declarant rights to any person acquiring title to any unit owned by the successor, or until recording an instrument permitting exercise of all those rights other than the right held by his transferor to control the executive board in accordance with the provisions of G.S. 47C-3-103(d) for the duration of any period of declarant control, and any attempted exercise of those rights is void. So long as a successor declarant may not exercise special declarant rights under this subsection, he is not subject to any liability or obligation as a declarant other than liability for his acts and omissions under G.S. 47C-3-103(d). (1985 (Reg. Sess., 1986), c. 877, s. 1.)

§ 47C-3-105. Termination of contracts and leases of declarant.

If entered into by or on behalf of the association before the executive board elected by the unit owners pursuant to G.S. 47C-3-103(f) takes office, (1) any management contract, employment contract, or lease of recreational or parking areas or facilities, (2) any other contract or lease between the association and a declarant or an affiliate of a declarant, or (3) any contract or lease that is not bona fide or was unconscionable to the unit owners at the time entered into under the circumstances then prevailing may be terminated without penalty by the association at any time after the executive board elected by the unit owners pursuant to G.S. 47C-3-103(f) takes office upon not less than 90 days' notice to the other party. Notice of the substance of the provisions of this section shall be set out in each contract entered into by or on behalf of the association before the executive board elected by the unit owners pursuant to G.S. 47C-3-103(f) takes office. Failure of the contract to contain such a provision shall not effect the rights of the association under this section. This section does not apply to any lease the termination of which would terminate the condominium or reduce its size, unless the real estate subject to that lease was included in the condominium for the purpose of avoiding the right of the association to terminate a lease under this section. (1985 (Reg. Sess., 1986), c. 877, s. 1.)

§ 47C-3-106. Bylaws.

(a)   The bylaws of the association shall provide for:

(1)   The number of members of the executive board and the titles of the officers of the association;

(2)   Election by the executive board of the officers of the association;

(3)   The qualifications, powers and duties, terms of office, and manner of electing and removing executive board members and officers and filling vacancies;

(4)   Which, if any, of its powers the executive board or officers may delegate to other persons or to a managing agent;

(5)   Which of its officers may prepare, execute, certify, and record amendments to the declaration on behalf of the association; and

(6)   The method of amending the bylaws.

(b) Any other matters the association deems necessary or appropriate. (1985 (Reg. Sess., 1986), c. 877, s. 1.)

§ 47C-3-107. Upkeep; damages; assessments for damages, fines.

(a) Except as provided in G.S. 47C-3-113(h), the association is responsible for causing the common elements to be maintained, repaired, and replaced when necessary and to assess the unit owners as necessary to recover the costs of such maintenance, repair, or replacement except that the cost of maintenance, repair or replacement of a limited common element shall be assessed as provided in G.S. 47C-3-115(b). Each unit owner is responsible for maintenance, repair and replacement of his unit. Each unit owner shall afford to the association and when necessary to another unit owner access through his unit or the limited common element assigned to his unit reasonably necessary for any such maintenance, repair or replacement activity.

(b) If damage, for which a unit owner is legally responsible and which is not covered by insurance provided by the association pursuant to G.S. 47C-3-113 is inflicted on any common element or limited common element, the association may direct such unit owner to repair such damage or the association may itself cause the repairs to be made and recover the costs thereof from the responsible unit owner.

(c) If damage is inflicted on any unit by an agent of the association in the scope of his activities as such agent, the association is liable to repair such damage or to reimburse the unit owner for the cost of repairing such damages. The association shall also be liable for any losses to the unit owner.

(d) The bylaws of the association may in cases when the claim under subsection (b) or (c) is five hundred dollars ($500.00) or less provide for hearings before an adjudicatory panel to determine if a unit owner is responsible for damages to any common element or whether the association is responsible for damages to any unit. Such panel shall accord to the party charged with causing damages notice of the charge, opportunity to be heard and to present evidence, and notice of the decision. This panel may assess a liability for each damage incident not in excess of five hundred dollars ($500.00) against each unit owner charged or against the association. Liabilities of unit owners so assessed shall be assessments secured by lien under G.S. 47C-3-116.

Liabilities of the association may be offset by the unit owner against sums owing the association and if so offset shall reduce the amount of any lien of the association against the unit at issue.

(e) The declarant alone is liable for maintenance, repair and all other expenses in connection with real estate subject to development rights. (1985 (Reg. Sess., 1986), c. 877, s. 1; 2013-34, s. 1.)

§ 47C-3-107.1. Procedures for fines and suspension of condominium privileges or services.

Unless a specific procedure for the imposition of fines or suspension of condominium privileges or services is provided for in the declaration, a hearing shall be held before the executive board or an adjudicatory panel appointed by the executive board to determine if any unit owner should be fined or if condominium privileges or services should be suspended pursuant to the powers granted to the association in G.S. 47C-3-102(11). Any adjudicatory panel appointed by the executive board shall be composed of members of the association who are not officers of the association or members of the executive board. The unit owner charged shall be given notice of the charge, opportunity to be heard and to present evidence, and notice of the decision. If it is decided that a fine should be imposed, a fine not to exceed one hundred dollars ($100.00) may be imposed for the violation and without further hearing, for each day more than five days after the decision that the violation occurs. Such fines shall be assessments secured by liens under G.S. 47C-3-116. If it is decided that a suspension of condominium privileges or services should be imposed, the suspension may be continued without further hearing until the violation or delinquency is cured. A unit owner may appeal a decision of an adjudicatory panel to the full executive board by delivering written notice of appeal to the executive board within 15 days after the date of the decision. The executive board may affirm, vacate, or modify the prior decision of the adjudicatory body. (1985 (Reg. Sess., 1986), c. 877, s. 1; 1997-456, s. 27; 2005-422, s. 14.)

§ 47C-3-108. Meetings.

(a) A meeting of the association shall be held at least once each year. Special meetings of the association may be called by the president, a majority of the executive board, or by unit owners having twenty percent (20%) or any lower percentage specified in the bylaws of the votes in the association. Not less than 10 nor more than 50 days in advance of any meeting, the secretary or other officer specified in the bylaws shall cause notice to be hand-delivered or sent prepaid by United States mail to the mailing address of each unit or to any other mailing address designated in writing by the unit owner, or sent by electronic means, including by electronic mail over the Internet, to an electronic mailing address designated in writing by the unit owner. The notice of any meeting must state the time and place of the meeting and the items on the agenda, including the general nature of any proposed amendment to the declaration or bylaws, any budget changes, and any proposal to remove a director or officer.

(b)   Meetings of the executive board shall be held as provided in the bylaws. At regular intervals, the executive board meeting shall provide unit owners an opportunity to attend a portion of an executive board meeting and to speak to the executive board about their issues and concerns. The executive board may place reasonable restrictions on the number of persons who speak on each side of an issue and may place reasonable time restrictions on persons who speak.

(c)   Except as otherwise provided for in the bylaws, meetings of the association and executive board shall be conducted in accordance with the most recent edition of Robert's Rules of Order Newly Revised. (1985 (Reg. Sess., 1986), c. 877, s. 1; 2004-109, s. 5; 2005-422, s. 15.)

§ 47C-3-109. Quorums.

(a)   Unless the bylaws provide otherwise, a quorum is deemed present throughout any meeting of the association if persons entitled to cast twenty percent (20%) of the votes which may be cast for election of the executive board are present in person or by proxy at the beginning of the meeting.

(b)   Unless the bylaws specify a larger percentage, a quorum is deemed present throughout any meeting of the executive board of persons entitled to cast fifty percent (50%) of the votes on that board are present at the beginning of the meeting. (1985 (Reg. Sess., 1986), c. 877, s. 1.)

§ 47C-3-110. Voting; proxies.

(a) If only one of the multiple owners of a unit is present at a meeting of the association, he is entitled to cast all the votes allocated to that unit. If more than one of the multiple owners are present, the votes allocated to that unit may be cast only in accordance with the agreement of a majority in interest of the multiple owners, unless the declaration or bylaws expressly provides otherwise. Majority agreement is conclusively presumed if any one of the multiple owners casts the votes allocated to that unit without protest being made promptly to the person presiding over the meeting by any of the other owners of the unit.

(b) Votes allocated to a unit may be cast pursuant to a proxy duly executed by a unit owner. If a unit is owned by more than one person, each owner of the unit may vote or register protest to the casting of votes by the other owners of the unit through a duly executed proxy. A unit owner may not revoke a proxy given pursuant to this section except by written notice of revocation delivered to the person presiding over a meeting of the association. A proxy is void if it is not dated. A proxy terminates one year after its date, unless it specifies a shorter term.

(c) If the declaration requires that votes on specified matters affecting the condominium be cast by lessees rather than unit owners of leased units: (i) the provisions of subsection (a) and (b) apply to lessees as if they were unit owners; (ii) unit owners who have leased their units to other persons may not cast votes on those specified matters; and (iii) lessees are entitled to notice of meetings, access to records, and other rights respecting those matters as if they were unit owners. Unit owners must also be given notice, in the manner provided in G.S. 47C-3-108, of all meetings at which lessees may be entitled to vote.

(d) No votes allocated to a unit owned by the association may be cast.

(e) The declaration may provide that on specified issues only a defined subgroup of unit owners may vote provided:

(1) The issue being voted on is of special interest solely to members of the subgroup; and

(2) All except de minimis costs that will be incurred based on the vote taken will be assessed solely against those unit owners entitled to vote.

(f) For purposes of subdivision (e)(1) above an issue to be voted on is not of special interest solely to a subgroup if it substantially affects the overall appearance of the condominium or substantially affects living conditions of unit owners not included in the voting subgroup. (1985 (Reg. Sess., 1986), c. 877, s. 1.)

§ 47C-3-111. Tort and contract liability.

(a) Neither the association nor any unit owner except the declarant is liable for that declarant's torts in connection with any part of the condominium which that declarant has the responsibility to maintain.

(b) An action alleging a wrong done by the association must be brought against the association and not against a unit owner.

(c) If an action is brought against the association for a wrong which occurred during any period of declarant control, and if the association gives the declarant who then controlled the association reasonable notice of and an opportunity to defend against the action, such declarant is liable to the association:

(1) for all tort losses not covered by insurance carried by the association suffered by the association or that unit owner, and

(2) for all losses which the association would not have incurred but for a breach of contract. Nothing in this subsection shall be construed to impose strict or absolute liability upon the declarant for wrongs or actions which occurred during the period of declarant control.

(d) In any case where the declarant is liable to the association under this section, the declarant is also liable for all litigation expenses, including reasonable attorneys' fees, incurred by the association. Any statute of limitation affecting the association's right of action under this section is tolled until the period of declarant control terminates. A unit owner is not precluded from bringing an action contemplated by this section because he is a unit owner or a member or officer of the association. Liens resulting from judgments against the association are governed by G.S. 47C-3-117 (Other Liens Affecting the Condominium). (1985 (Reg. Sess., 1986), c. 877, s. 1.)

§ 47C-3-112. Conveyance or encumbrance of common elements.

(a) Portions of the common elements may be conveyed or subjected to a security interest by the association if persons entitled to cast at least eighty percent (80%) of the votes in the association, including eighty percent (80%) of the votes allocated to units not owned by a declarant, or any larger percentage the declaration specifies, agree to that action; provided, that all the owners of units to which any limited common element is allocated must agree in order to convey that limited common element or subject it to a security interest. The declaration may specify a smaller percentage only if all of the units are restricted exclusively to nonresidential uses. Distribution of the proceeds of the sale of a limited common element shall be as provided by agreement between the unit owners to which it is allocated and the association. Proceeds of the sale or financing of a common element (other than a limited common element) shall be an asset of the association.

(b) An agreement to convey common elements or subject them to a security interest must be evidenced by the execution of an agreement, or ratifications thereof, in the same manner as a deed, by the requisite number of unit owners. The agreement must specify a date after which the agreement will be void unless recorded before that date. The agreement and all ratifications thereof must be recorded in every county in which a portion of the condominium is situated, and is effective only upon recordation.

(c) The association, on behalf of the unit owners, may contract to convey common elements, or subject them to a security interest, but the contract is not enforceable against the association until approved pursuant to subsections (a) and (b). Thereafter, the association has all powers necessary and appropriate to effect the conveyance or encumbrance, including the power to execute deeds or other instruments.

(d) Any purported conveyance, encumbrance, judicial sale or other voluntary transfer of common elements, unless made pursuant to this section, is void.

(e) A conveyance or encumbrance of common elements pursuant to this section shall not deprive any unit of its rights of access and support. (1985 (Reg. Sess., 1986), c. 877, s. 1.)

§ 47C-3-113. Insurance.

(a) Commencing not later than the time of the first conveyance of a unit to a person other than a declarant, the association shall maintain, to the extent available:

(1) Property insurance on the common elements insuring against all risks of direct physical loss commonly insured against including fire and extended coverage perils. The total amount of insurance after application of any deductibles shall be not less than eighty percent (80%) of the replacement cost of the insured property at the time the insurance is purchased and at each renewal date, exclusive of land, excavations, foundations and other items normally excluded from property policies; and

(2) Liability insurance in reasonable amounts, covering all occurrences commonly insured against death, bodily injury and property damage arising out of or in connection with the use, ownership, or maintenance of the common elements.

(b) In the case of a building containing units having horizontal boundaries described in the declaration, the insurance maintained under subdivision (a)(1), to the extent reasonably available, shall include the units, but need not include improvements and betterments installed by unit owners.

(c) If the insurance described in subsection (a) or (b) of this section is not reasonably available, the association promptly shall cause notice of that fact to be hand-delivered or sent prepaid by United States mail to all unit owners. The declaration may require the association to carry any other insurance, and the association in any event may carry any other insurance it deems appropriate to protect the association or the unit owners.

(d) Insurance policies carried pursuant to subsection (a) must provide that:

(1) Each unit owner is an insured person under the policy with respect to liability arising out of his interest in the common elements or membership in the association;

(2) The insurer waives its right to subrogation under the policy against any unit owner or members of his household;

(3) No act or omission by any unit owner, unless acting within the scope of his authority on behalf of the association, will preclude recovery under the policy; and

(4) If, at the time of a loss under the policy, there is other insurance in the name of a unit owner covering the same risk covered by the policy, the association's policy provides primary insurance.

(e) Any loss covered by the property policy under subsections (a)(1) and (b) shall be adjusted with the association, but the insurance proceeds for that loss shall be payable to any insurance trustee designated for that purpose, or otherwise to the association, and not to any mortgagee or beneficiary under a deed of trust. The insurance trustee or the association shall hold any insurance proceeds in trust for unit owners and lienholders as their interests may appear. Subject to the provisions of subsection (h), the proceeds shall be disbursed first for the repair or restoration of the damaged property, and unit owners and lienholders are not entitled to receive payment of any portion of the proceeds unless there is a surplus of proceeds after the property has been completely repaired or restored, or the condominium is terminated.

(f) An insurance policy issued to the association does not prevent a unit owner from obtaining insurance for his own benefit.

(g) An insurer that has issued an insurance policy under this section shall issue certificates or memoranda of insurance to the association and, upon written request, to any unit owner, mortgagee, or beneficiary under a deed of trust. The insurer issuing the policy may not cancel or refuse to renew it until 30 days after notice of the proposed cancellation or nonrenewal has been mailed to the association, each unit owner and each mortgagee or beneficiary under a deed of trust to whom certificates or memoranda of insurance have been issued at their respective last known addresses.

(h) Any portion of the condominium for which insurance is required under this section which is damaged or destroyed shall be repaired or replaced promptly by the association unless (1) the condominium is terminated, (2) repair or replacement would be illegal under any State or local health or safety statute or ordinance, or (3) the unit owners decide not to rebuild by an eighty percent (80%) vote, including one hundred percent (100%) approval of owners of units not to be rebuilt or owners assigned to limited common elements not to be rebuilt. The cost of repair or replacement in excess of insurance proceeds and reserves is a common expense. If the entire condominium is not repaired or replaced, (1) the insurance proceeds attributable to the damaged common elements shall be used to restore the damaged area to a condition compatible with the remainder of the condominium, (2) the insurance proceeds attributable to units and limited common elements which are not rebuilt shall be distributed to the owners of those units and the owners of the units to which those limited common elements were allocated or to lienholders, as their interest may appear, and (3) the remainder of the proceeds shall be distributed to all the unit owners or lienholders, as their interest may appear, in proportion to their common element interest. If the unit owners vote not to rebuild any unit, that unit's allocated interests are automatically reallocated upon the vote as if the unit had been condemned under G.S. 47C-1-107(a), and the association promptly shall prepare, execute, and record an amendment to the declaration reflecting the reallocations. Notwithstanding the provisions of this subsection, G.S. 47C-2-118 governs the distribution of insurance proceeds if the condominium is terminated.

(i) The provisions of this section may be varied or waived in the case of a condominium all of whose units are restricted to nonresidential use. (1985 (Reg. Sess., 1986), c. 877, s. 1; 1998-211, s. 8(a)-(c).)

§ 47C-3-114. Surplus funds.

Unless otherwise provided in the declaration, any surplus funds of the association remaining after payment of or provisions for common expenses and any prepayment of reserves must be paid to the unit owners in proportion to their common expense liabilities or credited to them to reduce their future common expense assessments. (1985 (Reg. Sess., 1986), c. 877, s. 1.)

§ 47C-3-115. Assessments for common expense.

(a) Until the association makes a common expense assessment, the declarant shall pay all the common expenses. After any assessment has been made by the association, assessments thereafter must be made at least annually by the association.

(b) Except for assessments under subsections (c), (d), and (e), all common expenses must be assessed against all the units in accordance with the allocations set forth in the declaration pursuant to G.S. 47C-2-107(a). Any past due common expense assessment or installment thereof bears interest at the rate established by the association not exceeding eighteen percent (18%) per year.

(c) To the extent required by the declaration:

(1) Any common expense associated with the maintenance, repair, or replacement of a limited common element must be assessed against the units to which that limited common element is assigned, equally, or in any other proportion that the declaration provides;

(2) Any common expense or portion thereof benefiting fewer than all of the units must be assessed exclusively against the units benefited; and

(3) The costs of insurance must be assessed in proportion to risk and the costs of utilities must be assessed in proportion to usage.

(d) Assessments to pay a judgment against the association (G.S. 47C-3-117(a)) may be made only against the units in the condominium at the time the judgment was entered, in proportion to their common expense liabilities.

(e) If any common expense is caused by the misconduct of any unit owner, the association may assess that expense exclusively against his unit.

(f) If common expense liabilities are reallocated, common expense assessments and any installment thereof not yet due shall be recalculated in accordance with the reallocated common expense liabilities. (1985 (Reg. Sess., 1986), c. 877, s. 1.)

§ 47C-3-116. Lien for sums due the association; enforcement.

(a) Any assessment attributable to a unit which remains unpaid for a period of 30 days or longer shall constitute a lien on that unit when a claim of lien is filed of record in the office of the clerk of superior court of the county in which the unit is located in the manner provided in this section. Once filed, a claim of lien secures all sums due the association through the date filed and any sums due to the association thereafter. Unless the declaration provides otherwise, fees, charges, late charges and other charges imposed pursuant to G.S. 47C-3-102, 47C-3-107, 47C-3-107.1, and 47C-3-115 are subject to the claim of lien under this section as well as any other sums due and payable to the association under the declaration, the provisions of this Chapter, or as the result of an arbitration, mediation, or judicial decision.

(b) The association must make reasonable and diligent efforts to ensure that its records contain the unit owner's current mailing address. No fewer than 15 days prior to filing the lien, the association shall mail a statement of the assessment amount due by first-class mail to the physical address of the unit and the unit owner's address of record with the association and, if different, to the address for the unit owner shown on the county tax records for the unit. If the unit owner is a corporation or limited liability company, the statement shall also be sent by first-class mail to the mailing address of the registered agent for the corporation or limited liability company. Notwithstanding anything to the contrary in this Chapter, the association is not required to mail a statement to an address known to be a vacant unit or to a unit for which there is no United States postal address.

(c) A claim of lien shall set forth the name and address of the association, the name of the record owner of the unit at the time the claim of lien is filed, a description of the unit, and the amount of the lien claimed. A claim of lien may also appoint a trustee to conduct a foreclosure as provided in subsection (f) of this section. The first page of the claim of lien shall contain the following statement in print that is in boldface, capital letters, and no smaller than the largest print used elsewhere in the document:

"THIS DOCUMENT CONSTITUTES A LIEN AGAINST YOUR PROPERTY, AND IF THE LIEN IS NOT PAID, THE HOMEOWNERS ASSOCIATION MAY PROCEED WITH FORECLOSURE AGAINST YOUR PROPERTY IN LIKE MANNER AS A MORTGAGE UNDER NORTH CAROLINA LAW."

The person signing the claim of lien on behalf of the association shall attach to and file with the claim of lien a certificate of service attesting to the attempt of service on the record owner, which service shall be attempted in accordance with G.S. 1A-1, Rule 4(j), for service of a copy of a summons and a complaint. If the actual service is not achieved, the person signing the claim of lien on behalf of the association shall be deemed to have met the requirements of this subsection if service has been attempted pursuant to both of the following: (i) G.S. 1A-1, Rule 4(j)(1)c, d, or e and (ii) by mailing a copy of the lien by regular, first-class mail, postage prepaid to the physical address of the unit and the unit owner's address of record with the association, and, if different, to the address for the unit owner shown on the county tax records and the county real property records for the unit. In the event that the owner of record is not a natural person, and actual service is not achieved, the person signing the claim of lien on behalf of the association shall be deemed to have met the requirements of this subsection if service has been attempted once pursuant to the applicable provisions of G.S. 1A-1, Rule 4(j)(3) through G.S. 1A-1, Rule 4(j)(9). Notwithstanding anything to the contrary in this Chapter, the association is not required to mail a claim of lien to an address which is known to be a vacant unit or to a unit for which there is no United States postal address. A lien for unpaid assessments is extinguished unless proceedings to enforce the lien are instituted within three years after the filing of the claim of lien in the office of the clerk of superior court.

(d) A claim of lien filed under this section is prior to all liens and encumbrances on a unit except (i) liens and encumbrances, specifically including, but not limited to, a mortgage or deed of trust on the unit, recorded before the filing of the claim of lien in the office of the clerk of superior court and (ii) liens for real estate taxes and other governmental assessments and charges against the unit. This subsection does not affect the priority of mechanics' or materialmen's liens.

(e) The association shall be entitled to recover the reasonable attorneys' fees and costs it incurs in connection with the collection of any sums due. A unit owner may not be required to pay attorneys' fees and court costs until the unit owner is notified in writing of the association's intent to seek payment of attorneys' fees, costs, and expenses. The notice must be sent by first-class mail to the physical address of the unit and the unit owner's address of record with the association and, if different, to the address for the unit owner shown on the county tax records for the unit. The association must make reasonable and diligent efforts to ensure that its records contain the unit owner's current mailing address. Notwithstanding anything to the contrary in this Chapter, there shall be no requirement that notice under this subsection be mailed to an address which is known to be a vacant unit or a unit for which there is no United States postal address. The notice shall set out the outstanding balance due as of the date of the notice and state that the unit owner has 15 days from the mailing of the notice by first-class mail to pay the outstanding balance without the attorneys' fees and court costs. If the unit owner pays the outstanding balance within this period, then the unit owner shall have no obligation to pay attorneys' fees, costs, or expenses. The notice shall also inform the unit owner of the opportunity to contact a representative of the association to discuss a payment schedule for the outstanding balance as provided in subsection (i) of this section and shall provide the name and telephone number of the representative.

(f) Except as provided in subsection (h) of this section, the association, acting through the executive board, may foreclose a claim of lien in like manner as a mortgage or deed of trust on real estate under power of sale, as provided in Article 2A of Chapter 45 of the General Statutes, if the assessment remains unpaid for 90 days or more. The association shall not foreclose the claim of lien unless the executive board votes to commence the proceeding against the specific unit. The following provisions and procedures shall be applicable to and complied with in every nonjudicial power of sale foreclosure of a claim of lien, and these provisions and procedures shall control to the extent they are inconsistent or in conflict with the provisions of Article 2A of Chapter 45 of the General Statutes:

(1) The association shall be deemed to have a power of sale for purposes of enforcement of its claim of lien.

(2) The terms "mortgagee" and "holder" as used in Article 2A of Chapter 45 of the General Statutes shall mean the association, except as provided otherwise in this Chapter.

(3) The term "security instrument" as used in Article 2A of Chapter 45 of the General Statutes shall mean the claim of lien.

(4) The term "trustee" as used in Article 2A of Chapter 45 of the General Statutes shall mean the person or entity appointed by the association under subdivision (6) of this subsection.

(5) After the association has filed a claim of lien and prior to the commencement of a nonjudicial foreclosure, the association shall give to the unit owner notice of the association's intention to commence a nonjudicial foreclosure to enforce its claim of lien. The notice shall contain the information required in G.S. 45-21.16(c)(5a).

(6) The association shall appoint a trustee to conduct the nonjudicial foreclosure proceeding and sale. The appointment of the trustee shall be included in the claim of lien or in a separate instrument filed with the office of the clerk of court in the county in which the unit is located as an exhibit to the notice of hearing. The association, at its option, may from time to time remove a trustee previously appointed and appoint a successor trustee by filing a Substitution of Trustee with the clerk of court in the foreclosure proceeding. Counsel for the association may be appointed by the association to serve as the

trustee and may serve in that capacity as long as the unit owner does not contest the obligation to pay the amount of any sums due the association, or the validity, enforcement, or foreclosure of the claim of lien as provided in subdivision (12) of this subsection. Any trustee appointed pursuant to this subsection shall have the same fiduciary duties and obligations as a trustee in the foreclosure of a deed of trust.

(7) If a valid debt, default, and notice to those entitled to receive notice under G.S. 45-21.16(b) are found to exist, then the clerk of court shall authorize the sale of the property described in the claim of lien by the trustee.

(8) If, prior to the expiration of the upset bid period provided in G.S. 45-21.27, the unit owner satisfies the debt secured by the claim of lien and pays all expenses and costs incurred in filing and enforcing the association assessment lien, including, but not limited to, advertising costs, attorneys' fees, and the trustee's commission, then the trustee shall dismiss the foreclosure action and the association shall cancel the claim of lien of record in accordance with the provisions of G.S. 45-36.3. The unit owner shall have all rights granted under Article 4 of Chapter 45 of the General Statutes to ensure the association's satisfaction of the claim of lien.

(9) Any person, other than the trustee, may bid at the foreclosure sale. Unless prohibited in the declaration or bylaws, the association may bid on the unit at a foreclosure sale directly or through an agent. If the association or its agent is the high bidder at the sale, the trustee shall allow the association to pay the costs and expenses of the sale and apply a credit against the sums due by the unit owner to the association in lieu of paying the bid price in full.

(10) Upon the expiration of the upset bid period provided in G.S. 45-21.27, the trustee shall have full power and authority to execute a deed for the unit to the high bidder.

(11) The trustee shall be entitled to a commission for services rendered which shall include fees, costs, and expenses reasonably incurred by the trustee in connection with the foreclosure whether or not a sale is held. Except as provided in subdivision (12) of this subsection, the trustee's commission shall be paid without regard to any limitations on compensation otherwise provided by law, including, without limitation, the provisions of G.S. 45-21.15.

(12) If the unit owner does not contest the obligation to pay or the amount of any sums due the association or the validity, enforcement, or foreclosure of the

claim of lien at any time after the expiration of the 15-day period following notice as required in subsection (b) of this section, then attorneys' fees and the trustee's commission collectively charged to the unit owner shall not exceed one thousand two hundred dollars ($1,200), not including costs or expenses incurred. The obligation to pay and the amount of any sums due the association and the validity, enforcement, or foreclosure of the claim of lien remain uncontested as long as the unit owner does not dispute, contest, or raise any objection, defense, offset, or counterclaim as to the amount or validity of any portion of the sums claimed due by the association or the validity, enforcement, or foreclosure of the claim of lien. Any judgment, decree, or order in any action brought under this section shall include costs and reasonable attorneys' fees for the prevailing party.

(13) Unit owners shall be deemed to have the rights and remedies available to mortgagors under G.S. 45-21.34.

(g) The provisions of subsection (f) of this section do not prohibit or prevent an association from pursuing judicial foreclosure of a claim of lien, from taking other actions to recover the sums due the association, or from accepting a deed in lieu of foreclosure. Any judgment, decree, or order in any judicial foreclosure or civil action relating to the collection of assessments shall include an award of costs and reasonable attorneys' fees for the prevailing party, which shall not be subject to the limitation provided in subdivision (f)(12) of this section.

(h) A claim of lien securing a debt consisting solely of fines imposed by the association, interest on unpaid fines, or attorneys' fees incurred by the association solely associated with fines imposed by the association may only be enforced by judicial foreclosure, as provided in Article 29A of Chapter 1 of the General Statutes. In addition, an association shall not levy, charge, or attempt to collect a service, collection, consulting, or administration fee from any unit owner unless the fee is expressly allowed in the declaration, and any claim of lien securing a debt consisting solely of these fees may only be enforced by judicial foreclosure, as provided in Article 29A of Chapter 1 of the General Statutes.

(i) The association, acting through its executive board and in the board's sole discretion, may agree to allow payment of an outstanding balance in installments. Neither the association nor the unit owner is obligated to offer or accept any proposed installment schedule. Reasonable administrative fees and costs for accepting and processing installments may be added to the outstanding balance and included in an installment payment schedule.

Reasonable attorneys' fees may be added to the outstanding balance and included in an installment schedule after the unit owner has been given notice, as required in subsection (e) of this section. Attorneys' fees incurred in connection with any request that the association agrees to accept payment of all or any part of sums due in installments shall not be included or considered in the calculation of fees chargeable under subdivision (f)(12) of this section.

(j) Where the holder of a first mortgage or first deed of trust of record or other purchaser of a unit obtains title to the unit as a result of foreclosure of a first mortgage or first deed of trust, the purchaser and its heirs, successors, and assigns shall not be liable for the assessments against the unit which became due prior to the acquisition of title to the unit by the purchaser. The unpaid assessments shall be deemed to be common expenses collectible from all the unit owners, including the purchaser, its heirs, successors, and assigns. For purposes of this subsection, the term "acquisition of title" means and refers to the recording of a deed conveying title or the time at which the rights of the parties are fixed following the foreclosure of a mortgage or deed of trust, whichever occurs first. (1985 (Reg. Sess., 1986), c. 877, s. 1; 2005-422, s. 16; 2006-226, s. 14(a); 2009-515, s. 2; 2011-362, s. 2; 2013-202, s. 1.)

§ 47C-3-116.1. Validation of certain nonjudicial foreclosure proceedings and sales.

All nonjudicial foreclosure proceedings commenced by an association before October 1, 2013, and all sales and transfers of real property as part of those proceedings pursuant to the provisions of this Chapter, Chapter 47A of the General Statutes, or provisions contained in the declaration of the condominium, are declared to be valid unless an action to set aside the foreclosure is commenced on or before October 1, 2013, or within one year after the date of the sale, whichever occurs last. (2013-202, s. 2.)

§ 47C-3-117. Other liens affecting the condominium.

(a) A judgment for money against the association is not a lien on the common elements, but if docketed is a lien in favor of the judgment lienholder against all of the units in the condominium at the time the judgment was entered. No other property of a unit owner is subject to the claims of creditors of the association.

(b) Notwithstanding the provisions of subsection (a), if the association has granted a security interest in the common elements to a creditor of the association pursuant to G.S. 47C-3-112, the holder of that security interest must exercise its right against the common elements before its judgment lien on any unit may be enforced.

(c) Whether perfected before or after the creation of the condominium, if a lien other than a deed of trust or mortgage, including a judgment lien or lien attributable to work performed or materials supplied before creation of the condominium, becomes effective against two or more units, the unit owner of an affected unit may pay the lienholder the amount of the lien attributable to his unit, and the lienholder, upon receipt of payment, promptly shall deliver a release of the lien covering that unit. The amount of the payment must be proportionate to the ratio which that unit owner's common expense liability bears to the common expense liabilities of all unit owners whose units are subject to the lien. After payment, the association may not assess or have a lien against that unit owner's unit for any portion of the common expenses incurred in connection with that lien.

(d) A judgment against the association shall be indexed in the name of the condominium and the association and, if so indexed, is notice of the lien against the units. (1985 (Reg. Sess., 1986), c. 877, s. 1.)

§ 47C-3-118. Association records.

(a) The association shall keep financial records sufficiently detailed to enable the association to comply with this chapter. All financial and other records, including records of meetings of the association and executive board, shall be made reasonably available for examination by any unit owner and the unit owner's authorized agents as required by the bylaws and by Chapter 55A of the General Statutes if the association is a nonprofit corporation. If the bylaws do not specify particular records to be maintained, the association shall keep accurate records of all cash receipts and expenditures and all assets and liabilities. In addition to any specific information that is required by the bylaws to be assembled and reported to the unit owners at specified times, the association shall make an annual income and expense statement and balance sheet available to all unit owners at no charge and within 75 days after the close of the fiscal year to which the information relates. Notwithstanding the bylaws, a more extensive compilation, review, or audit of the association's books and records for the current or immediately preceding fiscal year may be required by a vote of the majority of the executive board or by the affirmative vote of a majority of the unit owners present and voting in person or by proxy at any annual meeting or any special meeting duly called for that purpose.

(b) The association, upon written request, shall furnish a unit owner or the unit owner's authorized agents a statement setting forth the amount of unpaid assessments and other charges against a unit. The statement shall be furnished within 10 business days after receipt of the request and is binding on the association, the executive board, and every unit owner.

(c) In addition to the limitations of Article 8 of Chapter 55A of the General Statutes, no financial payments, including payments made in the form of goods and services, may be made to any officer or member of the association's executive board or to a business, business associate, or relative of an officer or member of the executive board, except as expressly provided for in the bylaws or in payments for services or expenses paid on behalf of the association which are approved in advance by the executive board. (1985 (Reg. Sess., 1986), c. 877, s. 1; 2005-422, s. 17.)

§ 47C-3-119. Association as trustee.

With respect to a third person dealing with the association in the association's capacity as a trustee under G.S. 47C-2-118 following termination or G.S. 47C-3-113 for insurance proceeds, the existence of trust powers and their proper exercise by the association may be assumed without inquiry. A third person is not bound to inquire whether the association has power to act as trustee or is properly exercising trust powers and a third person, without actual knowledge that the association is exceeding or improperly exercising its powers, is fully protected in dealing with the association as if it possessed and properly exercised the powers it purports to exercise. A third person is not bound to assure the proper application of trust assets paid or delivered to the association in its capacity as such trustee. (1985 (Reg. Sess., 1986), c. 877, s. 1.)

§ 47C-3-120. Reserved for future codification purposes.

§ 47C-3-121. American and State flags and political sign displays.

Notwithstanding any provision in any declaration of covenants, no restriction on the use of land shall be construed to:

(1) Regulate or prohibit the display of the flag of the United States or North Carolina, of a size no greater than four feet by six feet, which is displayed in accordance with or in a manner consistent with the patriotic customs set forth in 4 U.S.C. §§ 5-10, as amended, governing the display and use of the flag of the United States unless:

a. For restrictions registered prior to October 1, 2005, the restriction specifically uses the following terms:

1. Flag of the United States of America;

2. American flag;

3. United States flag; or

4. North Carolina flag.

b. For restrictions registered on or after October 1, 2005, the restriction shall be written on the first page of the instrument or conveyance in print that is in boldface type, capital letters, and no smaller than the largest print used elsewhere in the instrument or conveyance. The restriction shall be construed to regulate or prohibit the display of the United States or North Carolina flag only if the restriction specifically states: "THIS DOCUMENT REGULATES OR PROHIBITS THE DISPLAY OF THE FLAG OF THE UNITED STATES OF AMERICA OR STATE OF NORTH CAROLINA".

This subdivision shall apply to owners of property who display the flag of the United States or North Carolina on property owned exclusively by them and does not apply to common areas, easements, rights-of-way, or other areas owned by others.

(2) Regulate or prohibit the indoor or outdoor display of a political sign by an association member on that member's property owned exclusively by the member, unless:

a. For restrictions registered prior to October 1, 2005, the restriction specifically uses the term "political signs".

b. For restrictions registered on or after October 1, 2005, the restriction shall be written on the first page of the instrument or conveyance in print that is in boldface type, capital letters, and no smaller than the largest print used elsewhere in the instrument or conveyance. The restriction shall be construed to regulate or prohibit the display of political signs only if the restriction specifically states: "THIS DOCUMENT REGULATES OR PROHIBITS THE DISPLAY OF POLITICAL SIGNS".

Even when display of a political sign is permitted under this subdivision, an association (i) may prohibit the display of political signs earlier than 45 days before the day of the election and later than seven days after an election day, and (ii) may regulate the size and number of political signs that may be placed on a member's property if the association's regulation is no more restrictive than any applicable city, town, or county ordinance that regulates the size and number of political signs on residential property. If the local government in which the property is located does not regulate the size and number of political signs on residential property, the association shall permit at least one political sign with the maximum dimensions of 24 inches by 24 inches on a member's property. For the purposes of this subdivision, "political sign" means a sign that attempts to influence the outcome of an election, including supporting or opposing an issue on the election ballot. This subdivision shall apply to owners of property who display political signs on property owned exclusively by them and does not apply to common areas, easements, rights-of-way, or other areas owned by others. (2005-422, s. 18; 2006-226, s. 14(b).)

§ 47C-3-122. Irrigation of landscaping.

Notwithstanding any provision in any declaration of covenants, no requirement to irrigate landscaping shall be construed to:

(1) Require the irrigation of landscaping, during any period in which the U.S. Drought Monitor, as defined in G.S. 143-350, or the Secretary of Environment

and Natural Resources has designated an area in which the association is located as an area of severe, extreme, or exceptional drought and the Governor, a State agency, or unit of local government has imposed water conservation measures applicable to the area unless:

a. For covenants registered prior to October 1, 2008, the covenant specifically requires the irrigation of landscaping notwithstanding water conservation measures imposed by the Governor, a State agency, or unit of local government. The association may not fine or otherwise penalize an owner of land for violation of an irrigation requirement during a period of drought as designated under this subdivision, unless the covenant specifically authorizes fines or other penalties.

b. For covenants registered on or after October 1, 2008, the covenant must specifically state that any requirement to irrigate landscaping is suspended to the extent the requirement would otherwise be prohibited during any period in which the Governor, a State agency, or unit of local government has imposed water conservation measures. The association may not fine or otherwise penalize an owner of land for violation of an irrigation requirement during a drought designated under this subdivision, unless the covenant authorizes the fines or other penalties. This authorization must be written on the first page of the covenant in print that is in boldface type, capital letters, and no smaller than the largest print used elsewhere in the declarations of covenants.

(2) For purposes of this section, the term "landscaping" includes lawns, trees, shrubbery, and other ornamental or decorative plants. (2008-143, s. 19(a).)

Article 4.

Protection of Purchasers.

§ 47C-4-101. Applicability; waiver.

(a) This Article applies to all units subject to this chapter, except as provided in subsection (b) or as modified or waived by agreement of purchasers of units in a condominium in which all units are restricted to nonresidential use.

(b) Neither a public offering statement nor a resale certificate need be prepared or delivered in the case of a disposition which is:

(1) Gratuitous;

(2) Pursuant to court order;

(3) By a government or governmental agency;

(4) By foreclosure or deed in lieu of foreclosure;

(5) To a person in the business of selling real estate who intends to offer those units to purchasers; or

(6) Subject to cancellation at any time for any reason by the purchasers without penalty. (1985 (Reg. Sess., 1986), c. 877, s. 1.)

§ 47C-4-102. Liability for public offering statement requirements.

(a) Except as provided in subsection (b), a declarant must, prior to the offering of any interest in a unit to the public, prepare a public offering statement conforming to the requirements of G.S. 47C-4-103, 47C-4-104, 47C-4-105, and 47C-4-106.

(b) A declarant may transfer responsibility for preparation of all or a part of the public offering statement to a successor declarant or to a person in the business of selling real estate who intends to offer units in the condominium for his own account. In the event of any such transfer, the transferor must provide the transferee with any information necessary to enable the transferee to fulfill the requirements of subsection (a).

(c) Any declarant or other person in the business of selling real estate who offers a unit for his own account to a purchaser shall deliver a public offering statement in the manner prescribed in G.S. 47C-4-108(a). The person who prepared all or a part of or delivered the public offering statement is subject to G.S. 47C-4-117 for any false or misleading statement set forth therein or for any omission of material fact therefrom with respect to that portion of the public offering statement which he prepared. If a declarant did not prepare any part of or deliver a public offering statement, he is not liable for any false or misleading statement set forth therein or for any omission of material fact therefrom unless he had actual knowledge of the statement or omission. A declarant, who has transferred responsibility for preparation of all or a part of the public offering statement under subsection (b), shall be liable when a false or misleading statement in the public offering statement prepared by another results from the declarant's failure to provide the information required in subsection (b).

(d)   If a unit is a part of a condominium and is part of any other real estate regime in connection with the sale of which the delivery of a public offering statement is required under the laws of this State, a single public offering statement conforming to the requirements of G.S. 47C-4-103, 47C-4-104, 47C-4-105, and 47C-4-106 as those requirements relate to all real estate regimes in which the unit is located, and to any other requirements imposed under the laws of this State, may be prepared and delivered in lieu of providing two or more public offering statements. (1985 (Reg. Sess., 1986), c. 877, s. 1.)

§ 47C-4-103. Public offering statement; general provisions.

(a)   A public offering statement must contain or fully and accurately disclose:

(1)   The name and principal address of the declarant and of the condominium;

(2)   A general description of the condominium, including to the extent possible, the types, number, and declarant's schedule of commencement and completion of construction of buildings and amenities which declarant anticipates including as part of the condominium;

(3)   The number of units in the condominium;

(4)   Copies of the recorded or proposed declaration (other than the plats and plans) and any other recorded covenants, conditions, restrictions and reservations affecting the condominium; the bylaws, and any rules or regulations of the association; copies of any contracts and leases to be signed by purchasers at closing, and copies of or a brief narrative description of any contracts or leases that will or may be subject to cancellation by the association under G.S. 47C-3-105;

(5) Any current balance sheet and a projected budget for the association, either within or as an exhibit to the public offering statement, for one year after the date of the first conveyance to a purchaser, and thereafter the current budget of the association, a statement of who prepared the budget, and a statement of the budget's assumptions concerning occupancy and inflation factors. The budget must include, without limitation:

a. A statement of the amount, or a statement that there is no amount, included in the budget as a reserve for repairs and replacement;

b. A statement of any other reserves;

c. The projected common expense assessment by category of expenditures for the association; and

d. The projected monthly common expense assessment for each type of unit;

(6) Any services that the declarant provides or expenses that he pays which are not reflected in the budget and that he expects may become at any subsequent time a common expense of the association and the projected common expense assessment attributable to each of those services or expenses for the association and for each type of unit;

(7) Any initial or special fee due from the purchaser at closing, together with a description of the purpose and method of calculating the fee;

(8) A description of any known or recorded liens, encumbrances or defects affecting the title to the condominium;

(9) The terms and limitations of any warranties provided by the declarant;

(10) A statement that the purchaser must receive a public offering statement before signing a contract for purchase and that no conveyance can occur until seven calendar days following the signing of a contract for purchase; and that the purchaser has the absolute right to cancel the contract during the seven calendar days period;

(11) A statement of any known or recorded unsatisfied judgments or pending suits against the association, and the status of any pending suits material to the condominium of which a declarant has actual knowledge;

(12) A statement that any deposit made in connection with the purchase of a unit will be held in an escrow account pursuant to G.S. 47C-4-108, together with the name and address of the escrow agent;

(13) Any restraints on alienation of any portion of the condominium;

(14) A description of the insurance coverage provided for the benefit of unit owners;

(15) Any current or known future fees or charges to be paid by unit owners for the use of the common elements and other facilities related to the condominium;

(16) The extent to which financial arrangements have been provided for completion of all improvements labeled "MUST BE BUILT" pursuant to G.S. 47C-4-119;

(17) A brief narrative description of any existing zoning and other land use requirements governing the condominium; and

(18) A statement that any common element may be alienated or conveyed in accordance with G.S. 47C-3-112.

(b) A declarant promptly shall amend the public offering statement to report any material change in the information required by this section and provide a copy of any such material changes to any purchaser who has executed a contract. If any material change is made in a proposed declaration after a contract for purchase of a unit has been signed but before conveyance, the purchaser may rescind the contract within seven days after receipt of the notice of the change. (1985 (Reg. Sess., 1986), c. 877, s. 1; 1997-456, s. 27.)

§ 47C-4-104. Same; condominiums subject to developmental rights.

If the declaration provides that a condominium is subject to any development rights reserved by the declarant, the public offering statement shall disclose, in addition to the information required by G.S. 47C-4-103:

(1) The maximum number of units, and the maximum number of units per acre, that may be created;

(2) How many or what percentage of the units which may be created will be restricted exclusively to residential use, or a statement that no representations are made regarding use restrictions;

(3) If any of the units that may be built within real estate subject to development rights are not to be restricted exclusively to residential use, a statement, with respect to each portion of that real estate, of the maximum percentage of the real estate areas and the maximum percentage of the floor areas of all units that may be created therein that are not restricted exclusively to residential use;

(4) A brief narrative description of any development rights and of any conditions relating to or limitations upon the exercise of development rights;

(5) The maximum extent to which each unit's allocated interests may be changed by the exercise of any development right;

(6) The extent to which any buildings or other improvements that may be erected pursuant to any development right in any part of the condominium will be compatible with existing buildings and improvements in the condominium in terms of architectural style, quality of construction, and size, or a statement that no assurances are made in those regards;

(7) General descriptions of all other improvements that may be made and limited common elements that may be created within any part of the condominium pursuant to any development right, or a statement that no assurances are made in that regard;

(8) Any limitations as to the locations of any building or other improvement that may be made within any part of the condominium pursuant to any development right, or a statement that no assurances are made in that regard;

(9) A statement that any limited common elements created pursuant to any development right will be of the same general types and sizes as the limited common elements within other parts of the condominium, or a statement of the types and sizes planned, or a statement that no assurances are made in that regard;

(10) A statement that the proportion of limited common elements to units created pursuant to any development right will be approximately equal to the proportion existing within other parts of the condominium, or a statement of any other assurances in that regard, or a statement that no assurances are made in that regard;

(11) A statement that all restrictions in the declaration affecting use, occupancy, and alienation of units will apply to any units created pursuant to any development right, or a statement of any differentiations that may be made as to those units, or a statement that no assurances are made in that regard; and

(12) A statement of the extent to which any assurances made pursuant to this section apply or do not apply in the event that any development right is not exercised by the declarant. (1985 (Reg. Sess., 1986), c. 877, s. 1.)

§ 47C-4-105. Same; time share.

(a) If the declaration provides that ownership or occupancy of any units are or may be owned in time shares, the public offering statement shall disclose, in addition to the information required by G.S. 47C-4-103:

(1) The number and identity of units in which time shares may be created;

(2) The total number of time shares that may be created;

(3) The minimum duration of any time shares which may be created; and

(4) The extent to which the creation of time shares will or may affect the enforceability of the association's lien for assessments provided in G.S. 47C-3-116.

(b) The provisions of subsection (a) apply to all purchasers of units in the condominium. In addition, the purchaser of time shares shall receive the information required by G.S. 93A-44. (1985 (Reg. Sess., 1986), c. 877, s. 1.)

§ 47C-4-106. Conversion buildings.

Condominiums containing conversion buildings shall be subject to the provisions of Article 2 of Chapter 47A. (1985 (Reg. Sess., 1986), c. 877, s. 1.)

§ 47C-4-107. Same; condominium securities.

(a) If an interest in a condominium is registered with the Securities and Exchange Commission of the United States, a declarant satisfies the requirements relating to the preparation of a public offering statement of this chapter if he delivers to the purchaser a copy of the public offering statement filed with the Securities and Exchange Commission to the extent such statement provides the information required by G.S. 47C-4-103, 47C-4-104, 47C-4-105 and 47C-4-106.

(b) The North Carolina Securities Act, Chapter 78A, shall apply to condominiums deemed to be investment contracts or to other securities offered with or incident to a condominium. In the event of such applicability of the North Carolina Securities Act, any real estate broker or salesman registered under Article 1 of Chapter 93A shall not be subject to the provisions of G.S. 78A-36. The exemption provided by the preceding sentence shall not apply to any person who is required to register with the Securities Exchange Commission as a broker or dealer under the Securities and Exchange Act of 1934. (1985 (Reg. Sess., 1986), c. 877, s. 1.)

§ 47C-4-108. Purchaser's right to cancel.

(a) A person required to deliver a public offering statement pursuant to G.S. 47C-4-102(c) shall provide a purchaser of a unit or the spouse of such purchaser with a copy of the public offering statement and all amendments thereto before a contract to purchase the unit is executed. No conveyance pursuant to the contract to purchase may occur until seven calendar days following the execution of the contract and a purchaser has the absolute right to cancel the contract at any time during this seven calendar period. Cancellation is without penalty, and all payments made by the purchaser before cancellation shall be refunded promptly.

(b) If a purchaser elects to cancel a contract pursuant to subsection (a), he may do so by hand-delivering notice thereof to the offeror or by mailing notice thereof by prepaid United States mail to the offeror or to his agent for service of process. (1985 (Reg. Sess., 1986), c. 877, s. 1.)

§ 47C-4-109. Resales of units.

Except in the case of a sale where delivery of a public offering statement is required, or unless exempt under G.S. 47C-4-101(b), a unit owner shall furnish to a prospective purchaser before conveyance a statement setting forth the monthly common expense assessment and any other fees payable by unit owners. (1985 (Reg. Sess., 1986), c. 877, s. 1.)

§ 47C-4-110. Escrow of deposits.

(a) Any deposit made in connection with the purchase or reservation of a unit from a person required to deliver a public offering statement pursuant to G.S. 47C-4-102(c) shall be immediately deposited in a trust or escrow account in an insured bank or savings and loan association in North Carolina and shall remain in such account for such period of time as a purchaser is entitled to cancel pursuant to G.S. 47C-4-108 or cancellation by the purchaser thereunder whichever occurs first. Payments held in such trust or escrow accounts shall be deemed to belong to the purchaser and not the seller.

(b) Except as provided in G.S. 47C-4-108, nothing in subsection (a) is intended to preclude the parties to a contract from providing for the use of progress payments by the declarant during construction. (1985 (Reg. Sess., 1986), c. 877, s. 1.)

§ 47C-4-111. Release of liens or encumbrances.

(a) In the case of a sale of a unit where delivery of a public offering statement is required pursuant to G.S. 47C-4-102(c), a seller shall, at or before conveying a unit, record or furnish to the purchaser, releases of all liens or encumbrances affecting that unit and its common element interest which the purchaser does not expressly agree to take subject to or assume, or shall provide a surety bond or substitute collateral for or insurance against the lien or encumbrance as provided for liens or encumbrances on real estate in G.S. 44A-16(5) and (6) or insurance against the lien or encumbrance acceptable to the purchaser. This subsection does not apply to any real estate which a declarant has the right to withdraw.

(b) Before conveying real estate to the association the declarant shall have that real estate released from: (1) all liens or encumbrances the foreclosure of which would deprive unit owners of any right of access to or easement of support of their units, and (2) all other liens or encumbrances on that real estate unless the public offering statement describes certain real estate which may be conveyed subject to liens or encumbrances in specified amounts. (1985 (Reg. Sess., 1986), c. 877, s. 1.)

§ 47C-4-112. Reserved for future codification purposes.

§ 47C-4-113. Express warranties of quality.

The law relating to express warranties is applicable to the sale of a condominium unit and supplements the provisions of this chapter; provided, however, that the existence of express warranties shall not constitute a disclaimer of implied warranties. (1985 (Reg. Sess., 1986), c. 877, s. 1.)

§ 47C-4-114. Implied warranties of quality.

The law relating to implied warranties, including but not limited to, implied warranties that the premises are free from defective materials, constructed in a workmanlike manner, constructed according to sound engineering and construction standards and that the premises may be used for a particular purpose, is applicable to the sale of a condominium unit and supplements the provisions of this chapter. (1985 (Reg. Sess., 1986), c. 877, s. 1.)

§ 47C-4-115. Exclusion of modification of implied warranties of quality.

(a) Except as limited by subsection (b) with respect to a purchaser of a unit that may be used for residential use, implied warranties of quality:

(1) May be excluded or modified by agreement of the parties; and

(2) Are excluded by expression of disclaimer, such as "as is," "with all faults," or other language which in common understanding calls the buyer's attention to the exclusion of warranties.

(b) With respect to a purchaser of a unit that may be occupied for residential use, no general disclaimer of implied warranties of quality is effective, but a declarant and any person in the business of selling real estate for his own account may disclaim liability in an instrument signed by the purchaser for a specified defect or specified failure to comply with applicable law, if the defect or failure entered into and became a part of the basis of the bargain. (1985 (Reg. Sess., 1986), c. 877, s. 1.)

§ 47C-4-116. Statute of limitations for warranties.

(a) A judicial proceeding for breach of any obligation arising under G.S. 47C-4-113 or 47C-4-114 must be commenced within the applicable period of limitations set out in Chapter 1 of the North Carolina General Statutes.

(b) If a warranty of quality explicitly extends to future performance or duration of any improvement or component of the condominium, the cause of action accrues at the time the breach is discovered or at the end of the period for which the warranty explicitly extends, whichever is earlier. (1985 (Reg. Sess., 1986), c. 877, s. 1.)

§ 47C-4-117. Effect of violations on rights of action; attorney's fees.

If a declarant or any other person subject to this chapter fails to comply with any provision hereof or any provision of the declaration or bylaws, any person or class of person adversely affected by that failure has a claim for appropriate relief. The court may award reasonable attorney's fees to the prevailing party. (1985 (Reg. Sess., 1986), c. 877, s. 1.)

§ 47C-4-118. Labeling of promotional material.

If any improvement contemplated in a condominium is labeled "NEED NOT BE BUILT" on a plat or plan, or is to be located within a portion of the condominium with respect to which the declarant has reserved a development right, no promotional material may be displayed or delivered to prospective purchasers which describes or portrays that improvement unless the description or portrayal of the improvement in the promotional material is conspicuously labeled or identified as "NEED NOT BE BUILT". (1985 (Reg. Sess., 1986), c. 877, s. 1.)

§ 47C-4-119. Declarant's obligation to complete.

(a)   The declarant shall complete all improvements labeled "MUST BE BUILT" on plats or plans prepared pursuant to G.S. 47C-2-109.

(b)   The declarant is subject to liability for the prompt repair and restoration, to a condition compatible with the remainder of the condominium, of any portion of the condominium affected by the exercise of rights reserved pursuant to or created by G.S. 47C-2-110, 47C-2-111, 47C-2-112, 47C-2-113, 47C-2-115, and 47C-2-116. (1985 (Reg. Sess., 1986), c. 877, s. 1.)

§ 47C-4-120. Substantial completion of units.

In the case of a sale of a unit where delivery of a public offering statement is required, a contract of sale may be executed, but no interest in that unit may be conveyed until the declaration is recorded and the unit is substantially completed, as evidenced by a recorded certificate of substantial completion executed by an architect licensed under the provisions of Chapter 83 [83A] of the General Statutes or an engineer registered under the provisions of Chapter 89C of the General Statutes, or by issuance of a certificate of occupancy authorized by law. (1985 (Reg. Sess., 1986), c. 877, s. 1.)

Chapter 47D.

Notice of Settlement Act.

§§ 47D-1 through 47D-10: Expired.

Chapter 47E.

Residential Property Disclosure Act.

§ 47E-1. Applicability.

This Chapter applies to the following transfers of residential real property consisting of not less than one nor more than four dwelling units, whether or not the transaction is with the assistance of a licensed real estate broker or salesman:

(1)   Sale or exchange,

(2)   Installment land sales contract,

(3)   Option, or

(4)   Lease with option to purchase, except as provided in G.S. 47E-2(10). (1995, c. 476, s. 1; 1997-472, s. 5.)

§ 47E-2. Exemptions.

The following transfers are exempt from the provisions of this Chapter:

(1)   Transfers pursuant to court order, including transfers ordered by a court in administration of an estate, transfers pursuant to a writ of execution, transfers by foreclosure sale, transfers by a trustee in bankruptcy, transfers by eminent domain, and transfers resulting from a decree for specific performance.

(2)   Transfers to a beneficiary from the grantor or his successor in interest in a deed of trust, or to a mortgagee from the mortgagor or his successor in interest in a mortgage, if the indebtedness is in default; transfers by a trustee under a deed of trust or a mortgagee under a mortgage, if the indebtedness is in

default; transfers by a trustee under a deed of trust or a mortgagee under a mortgage pursuant to a foreclosure sale, or transfers by a beneficiary under a deed of trust, who has acquired the real property at a sale conducted pursuant to a foreclosure sale under a deed of trust.

(3) Transfers by a fiduciary in the course of the administration of a decedent's estate, guardianship, conservatorship, or trust.

(4) Transfers from one or more co-owners solely to one or more other co-owners.

(5) Transfers made solely to a spouse or a person or persons in the lineal line of consanguinity of one or more transferors.

(6) Transfers between spouses resulting from a decree of divorce or a distribution pursuant to Chapter 50 of the General Statutes or comparable provision of another state.

(7) Transfers made by virtue of the record owner's failure to pay any federal, State, or local taxes.

(8) Transfers to or from the State or any political subdivision of the State.

(9) Transfers involving the first sale of a dwelling never inhabited.

(10) Lease with option to purchase contracts where the lessee occupies or intends to occupy the dwelling.

(11) Transfers between parties when both parties agree not to complete a residential property disclosure statement or an owners' association and mandatory covenants disclosure statement. (1995, c. 476, s. 1; 2011-362, s. 3(a).)

§ 47E-3. Definitions.

When used in this Chapter, unless the context requires otherwise, the term:

(1) "Owner" means each person having a recorded present or future interest in real estate that is identified in a real estate contract subject to this

Chapter; but shall not mean or include the trustee in a deed of trust, or the owner or holder of a mortgage, deed of trust, mechanic's or materialman's lien, or other lien or security interest in the real property, or the owner of any easement or license encumbering the real property.

(2)   "Purchaser" means each person or entity named as "buyer" or "purchaser" in a real estate contract subject to this Chapter.

(3)   "Real estate contract" means a contract for the transfer of ownership of real property by the means described in G.S. 47E-1.

(4)   "Real property" means the lot or parcel, and the dwelling unit(s) thereon, described in a real estate contract subject to this Chapter. (1995, c. 476, s. 1.)

§ 47E-4. Required disclosures.

(a)   With regard to transfers described in G.S. 47E-1, the owner of the real property shall furnish to a purchaser a residential property disclosure statement. The disclosure statement shall:

(1)   Disclose those items which are required to be disclosed relative to the characteristics and condition of the property and of which the owner has actual knowledge; or

(2)   State that the owner makes no representations as to the characteristics and condition of the real property or any improvements to the real property except as otherwise provided in the real estate contract.

(b)   The North Carolina Real Estate Commission shall develop and require the use of a standard disclosure statement to comply with the requirements of this section. The disclosure statement shall specify that certain transfers of residential property are excluded from this requirement by G.S. 47E-2, including transfers of residential property made pursuant to a lease with an option to purchase where the lessee occupies or intends to occupy the dwelling, and shall include at least the following characteristics and conditions of the property:

(1)   The water supply and sanitary sewage disposal system;

(2) The roof, chimneys, floors, foundation, basement, and other structural components and any modifications of these structural components;

(3) The plumbing, electrical, heating, cooling, and other mechanical systems;

(4) Present infestation of wood-destroying insects or organisms or past infestation the damage for which has not been repaired;

(5) The zoning laws, restrictive covenants, building codes, and other land-use restrictions affecting the real property, any encroachment of the real property from or to adjacent real property, and notice from any governmental agency affecting this real property; and

(6) Presence of lead-based paint, asbestos, radon gas, methane gas, underground storage tank, hazardous material or toxic material (whether buried or covered), and other environmental contamination.

The disclosure statement shall provide the owner with the option to indicate whether the owner has actual knowledge of the specified characteristics or conditions, or the owner is making no representations as to any characteristic or condition.

(b1) With regard to transfers described in G.S. 47E-1, the owner of the real property shall furnish to a purchaser an owners' association and mandatory covenants disclosure statement.

(1) The North Carolina Real Estate Commission shall develop and require the use of a standard disclosure statement to comply with the requirements of this subsection. The disclosure statement shall specify that certain transfers of residential property are excluded from this requirement by G.S. 47E-2, including transfers of residential property made pursuant to a lease with an option to purchase where the lessee occupies or intends to occupy the dwelling. The standard disclosure statement shall require disclosure of whether or not the property to be conveyed is subject to regulation by one or more owners' association(s) and governing documents which impose various mandatory covenants, conditions, and restrictions upon the property, including, but not limited to, obligations to pay regular assessments or dues and special assessments. The statement required by this subsection shall include information on all of the following:

a. The name, address, telephone number, or e-mail address for the president or manager of the association to which the lot is subject.

b. The amount of any regular assessments or dues to which the lot is subject.

c. Whether there are any services that are paid for by regular assessments or dues to which the lot is subject.

d. Whether, as of the date the disclosure is signed, there are any assessments, dues, fees, or special assessments which have been duly approved as required by the applicable declaration or bylaws, payable to an association to which the lot is subject.

e. Whether, as of the date the disclosure is signed, there are any unsatisfied judgments against or pending lawsuits involving the lot, the planned community or the association to which the lot is subject, with the exception of any action filed by the association for the collection of delinquent assessments on lots other than the lot to be sold.

f. Any fees charged by an association or management company to which the lot is subject in connection with the conveyance or transfer of the lot to a new owner.

(2) The owners' association and mandatory covenants disclosure statement shall provide the owner with the option to indicate whether the owner has actual knowledge of the specified characteristics, or conditions or the owner is making no representations as to any characteristic or condition contained in the statement.

(b2) With regard to transfers described in G.S. 47E-1, the owner of the real property shall include in any real estate contract, an oil and gas rights mandatory disclosure as provided in this subsection:

(1) Transfers of residential property set forth in G.S. 47E-2 are excluded from this requirement, except that the exemptions provided under subdivisions (9) and (11) of G.S. 47E-2 specifically are not excluded from this requirement.

(2) The disclosure shall be conspicuous, shall be in boldface type, and shall be as follows:

OIL AND GAS RIGHTS DISCLOSURE

Oil and gas rights can be severed from the title to real property by conveyance (deed) of the oil and gas rights from the owner or by reservation of the oil and gas rights by the owner. If oil and gas rights are or will be severed from the property, the owner of those rights may have the perpetual right to drill, mine, explore, and remove any of the subsurface oil or gas resources on or from the property either directly from the surface of the property or from a nearby location. With regard to the severance of oil and gas rights, Seller makes the following disclosures:

		Yes	No	No Representation
_____ Buyer Initials	1. Oil and gas rights were severed from the property by a previous owner.	__	__	__

		Yes	No
_____ Buyer Initials	2. Seller has severed the oil and gas rights from the property.	__	__
_____ Buyer Initials	3. Seller intends to sever the oil and gas rights from the property prior to transfer of title to Buyer.	__	__

(c) The rights of the parties to a real estate contract as to conditions of the property of which the owner had no actual knowledge are not affected by this Article unless the residential disclosure statement or the owners' association and mandatory covenants disclosure statement, as applicable, states that the owner makes no representations as to those conditions. If the statement states that an owner makes no representations as to the conditions of the property, then the owner has no duty to disclose those conditions, whether or not the owner should have known of them. (1995, c. 476, s. 1.; 1997-472, s. 1; 2011-362, s. 3(b); 2012-143, s. 5.)

§ 47E-5. Time for disclosure; cancellation of contract.

(a)   The owner of real property subject to this Chapter shall deliver to the purchaser the disclosure statements required by this Chapter no later than the time the purchaser makes an offer to purchase, exchange, or option the property, or exercises the option to purchase the property pursuant to a lease with an option to purchase. The residential property disclosure statement or the owners' association and mandatory covenants disclosure statement may be included in the real estate contract, in an addendum, or in a separate document.

(b)   If the disclosure statements required by this Chapter are not delivered to the purchaser prior to or at the time the purchaser makes an offer, the purchaser may cancel any resulting real estate contract. The purchaser's right to cancel shall expire if not exercised prior to the following, whichever occurs first:

(1)   The end of the third calendar day following the purchaser's receipt of the disclosure statement;

(2)   The end of the third calendar day following the date the contract was made;

(3)   Settlement or occupancy by the purchaser in the case of a sale or exchange; or

(4)   Settlement in the case of a purchase pursuant to a lease with option to purchase.

Any right of the purchaser to cancel the contract provided by this subsection is waived conclusively if not exercised in the manner required by this subsection.

In order to cancel a real estate contract when permitted by this section, the purchaser shall, within the time required above, give written notice to the owner or the owner's agent either by hand delivery or by depositing into the United States mail, postage prepaid, and properly addressed to the owner or the owner's agent. If the purchaser cancels a real estate contract in compliance with this subsection, the cancellation shall be without penalty to the purchaser, and the purchaser shall be entitled to a refund of any deposit the purchaser may have paid. Any rights of the purchaser to cancel or terminate the contract for reasons other than those set forth in this subsection are not affected by this subsection. (1995, c. 476, s. 1; 1997-472, s. 2; 2011-362, s. 3(c).)

§ 47E-6. Owner liability for disclosure of information provided by others.

The owner may discharge the duty to disclose imposed by this Chapter by providing a written report attached to the residential property disclosure statement and the owners' association and mandatory covenants disclosure statement by a public agency or by an attorney, engineer, land surveyor, geologist, pest control operator, contractor, home inspector or other expert, dealing with matters within the scope of the public agency's functions or the expert's license or expertise. The owner shall not be liable for any error, inaccuracy, or omission of any information delivered pursuant to this section if the error, inaccuracy, or omission was made in reasonable reliance upon the information provided by the public agency or expert and the owner was not grossly negligent in obtaining the information or transmitting it. (1995, c. 476, s. 1; 1997-472, s. 3; 2011-362, s. 3(d).)

§ 47E-7. Change in circumstances.

If, subsequent to the owner's delivery of a residential property disclosure statement and the owners' association and mandatory covenants disclosure statement to a purchaser, the owner discovers a material inaccuracy in a disclosure statement, or a disclosure statement is rendered inaccurate in a material way by the occurrence of some event or circumstance, the owner shall promptly correct the inaccuracy by delivering a corrected disclosure statement or statements to the purchaser. Failure to deliver a corrected disclosure statement or to make the repairs made necessary by the event or circumstance shall result in such remedies for the buyer as are provided for by law in the event the sale agreement requires the property to be in substantially the same condition at closing as on the date of the offer to purchase, reasonable wear and tear excepted. (1995, c. 476, s. 1; 2011-362, s. 3(e).)

§ 47E-8. Agent's duty.

A real estate broker or salesman acting as an agent in a residential real estate transaction has the duty to inform each of the clients of the real estate broker or salesman of the client's rights and obligations under this Chapter. Provided the owner's real estate broker or salesman has performed this duty, the broker or salesman shall not be responsible for the owner's willful refusal to provide a prospective purchaser with a residential property disclosure statement or an owners' association and mandatory covenants disclosure statement. Nothing in this Chapter shall be construed to conflict with, or alter, the broker or salesman's duties under Chapter 93A of the General Statutes. (1995, c. 476, s. 1; 1997-472, s. 4; 2011-362, s. 3(f).)

§ 47E-9. Rights and duties under Chapter 42, landlord and tenant, not affected during lease.

This Chapter shall not affect the landlord-tenant relationship between the parties to a lease with option to purchase contract during the term of the lease, and the rights and duties of landlords and tenants under Chapter 42 of the General Statutes shall remain in effect until transfer of ownership of the property to the purchaser. (1995, c. 476, s. 1.)

§ 47E-10. Authorization to prepare forms; fees.

The North Carolina Real Estate Commission may prepare, or cause to be prepared, forms for use pursuant to this Chapter. The Commission may charge a fee not to exceed twenty-five cents (25¢) per form plus the costs of postage. (1995, c. 476, s. 1.)

Chapter 47F.

North Carolina Planned Community Act.

Article 1.

General Provisions.

§ 47F-1-101. Short title.

This Chapter shall be known and may be cited as the North Carolina Planned Community Act. (1998-199, s. 1.)

§ 47F-1-102. Applicability.

(a) This Chapter applies to all planned communities created within this State on or after January 1, 1999, except as otherwise provided in this section.

(b) This Chapter does not apply to a planned community created within this State on or after January 1, 1999:

(1) Which contains no more than 20 lots (including all lots which may be added or created by the exercise of development rights) unless the declaration provides or is amended to provide that this Chapter does apply to that planned community; or

(2) In which all lots are restricted exclusively to nonresidential purposes, unless the declaration provides or is amended to provide that this Chapter does apply to that planned community.

(c) Notwithstanding the provisions of subsection (a) of this section, G.S. 47F-1-104 (Variation), G.S. 47F-2-103 (Construction and validity of declaration and bylaws), G.S. 47F-2-117 (Amendment of declaration), G.S. 47F-3-102(1) through (6) and (11) through (17)(Powers of owners' association), G.S. 47F-3-103(f)(Executive board members and officers), G.S. 47F-3-107(a), (b), and (c)(Upkeep of planned community; responsibility and assessments for damages), G.S. 47F-3-107.1 (Procedures for fines and suspension of planned community privileges or services), G.S. 47F-3-108 (Meetings), G.S. 47F-3-115 (Assessments for common expenses), G.S. 47F-3-116 (Lien for assessments), G.S. 47F-3-118 (Association records), and G.S. 47F-3-121 (American and State flags and political sign displays) apply to all planned communities created in this State before January 1, 1999, unless the articles of incorporation or the declaration expressly provides to the contrary, and G.S. 47F-3-120 (Declaration limits on attorneys' fees) applies to all planned communities created in this State before January 1, 1999. These sections apply only with respect to events and circumstances occurring on or after January 1, 1999, and do not invalidate existing provisions of the declaration, bylaws, or plats and plans of those planned communities. G.S. 47F-1-103 (Definitions) also applies to all planned communities created in this State before January 1, 1999, to the extent necessary in construing any of the preceding sections.

(d)   Notwithstanding the provisions of subsections (a) and (c) of this section, any planned community created prior to January 1, 1999, may elect to make the provisions of this Chapter applicable to it by amending its declaration to provide that this Chapter shall apply to that planned community. The amendment may be made by affirmative vote or written agreement signed by lot owners of lots to which at least sixty-seven percent (67%) of the votes in the association are allocated or any smaller majority the declaration specifies. To the extent the procedures and requirements for amendment in the declaration conflict with the provisions of this subsection, this subsection shall control with respect to any amendment to provide that this Chapter applies to that planned community.

(e)   This Chapter does not apply to planned communities or lots located outside this State. (1998-199, s. 1; 2002-112, s. 2; 2004-109, s. 3; 2005-214, s. 1; 2005-422, s. 9; 2006-226, s. 15(a); 2013-34, s. 6.)

§ 47F-1-103. Definitions.

In the declaration and bylaws, unless specifically provided otherwise or the context otherwise requires, and in this Chapter:

(1)   Reserved.

(2)   "Allocated interests" means the common expense liability and votes in the association allocated to each lot.

(3)   "Association" or "owners' association" means the association organized as allowed under North Carolina law, including G.S. 47F-3-101.

(4)   "Common elements" means any real estate within a planned community owned or leased by the association, other than a lot.

(5)   "Common expenses" means expenditures made by or financial liabilities of the association, together with any allocations to reserves.

(6) "Common expense liability" means the liability for common expenses allocated to each lot as permitted by this Chapter, the declaration or otherwise by law.

(7) "Condominium" means real estate, as defined and created under Chapter 47C [of the General Statutes].

(8) "Cooperative" means real estate owned by a corporation, trust, trustee, partnership, or unincorporated association, where the governing instruments of that organization provide that each of the organization's members, partners, stockholders, or beneficiaries is entitled to exclusive occupancy of a designated portion of that real estate.

(9) "Declarant" means any person or group of persons acting in concert who (i) as part of a common promotional plan, offers to dispose of the person's or group's interest in a lot not previously disposed of, or (ii) reserves or succeeds to any special declarant right.

(10) "Declaration" means any instruments, however denominated, that create a planned community and any amendments to those instruments.

(11), (12) Reserved.

(13) "Executive board" means the body, regardless of name, designated in the declaration to act on behalf of the association.

(14), (15) Reserved.

(16) "Leasehold planned community" means a planned community in which all or a portion of the real estate is subject to a lease, the expiration or termination of which will terminate the planned community or reduce its size.

(17) "Lessee" means the party entitled to present possession of a leased lot whether lessee, sublessee, or assignee.

(18) "Limited common element" means a portion of the common elements allocated by the declaration or by operation of law for the exclusive use of one or more but fewer than all of the lots.

(19) "Lot" means a physical portion of the planned community designated for separate ownership or occupancy by a lot owner.

(20) "Lot owner" means a declarant or other person who owns a lot, or a lessee of a lot in a leasehold planned community whose lease expires simultaneously with any lease the expiration or termination of which will remove the lot from the planned community, but does not include a person having an interest in a lot solely as security for an obligation.

(21) "Master association" means an organization described in G.S. 47F-2-120, whether or not it is also an association described in G.S. 47F-3-101.

(22) "Person" means a natural person, corporation, business trust, estate, trust, partnership, association, joint venture, government, governmental subdivision or agency, or other legal or commercial entity.

(23) "Planned community" means real estate with respect to which any person, by virtue of that person's ownership of a lot, is expressly obligated by a declaration to pay real property taxes, insurance premiums, or other expenses to maintain, improve, or benefit other lots or other real estate described in the declaration. For purposes of this act, neither a cooperative nor a condominium is a planned community, but real estate comprising a condominium or cooperative may be part of a planned community. "Ownership of a lot" does not include holding a leasehold interest of less that [than] 20 years in a lot, including renewal options.

(24) "Purchaser" means any person, other than a declarant or a person in the business of selling real estate for the purchaser's own account, who by means of a voluntary transfer acquires a legal or equitable interest in a lot, other than (i) a leasehold interest (including renewal options) of less than 20 years, or (ii) as security for an obligation.

(25) "Real estate" means any leasehold or other estate or interest in, over, or under land, including structures, fixtures, and other improvements and interests which by custom, usage, or law pass with a conveyance of land though not described in the contract of sale or instrument of conveyance. "Real estate" includes parcels with or without upper or lower boundaries, and spaces that may be filled with air or water.

(26) "Reasonable attorneys' fees" means attorneys' fees reasonably incurred without regard to any limitations on attorneys' fees which otherwise may be allowed by law.

(27) Reserved.

(28) "Special declarant rights" means rights reserved for the benefit of a declarant including, without limitation, any right (i) to complete improvements indicated on plats and plans filed with the declaration; (ii) to exercise any development right; (iii) to maintain sales offices, management offices, signs advertising the planned community, and models; (iv) to use easements through the common elements for the purpose of making improvements within the planned community or within real estate which may be added to the planned community; (v) to make the planned community part of a larger planned community or group of planned communities; (vi) to make the planned community subject to a master association; or (vii) to appoint or remove any officer or executive board member of the association or any master association during any period of declarant control.

(29) Reserved. (1998-199, s. 1.)

§ 47F-1-104. Variation.

(a) Except as specifically provided in specific sections of this Chapter, the provisions of this Chapter may not be varied by the declaration or bylaws. To the extent not inconsistent with the provisions of this Chapter, the declaration, bylaws, and articles of incorporation form the basis for the legal authority for the planned community to act as provided in the declaration, bylaws, and articles of incorporation, and the declaration, bylaws, and articles of incorporation are enforceable by their terms.

(b) The provisions of this Chapter may not be varied by agreement; however, after breach of a provision of this Chapter, rights created hereunder may be knowingly waived in writing.

(c) Notwithstanding any of the provisions of this Chapter, a declarant may not act under a power of attorney or proxy or use any other device to evade the limitations or prohibitions of this Chapter, the declaration, or the bylaws. (1998-199, s. 1; 2013-34, s. 3.)

§ 47F-1-105. Taxation.

Extraterritorial common property taxed pursuant to G.S. 105-277.8 shall be assessed, pro rata, among the lot owners based on the number of lots in the association. (2012-157, s. 3.)

§ 47F-1-106. Applicability of local ordinances, regulations, and building codes.

A zoning, subdivision, or building code or other real estate use law, ordinance, or regulation may not prohibit a planned community or impose any requirement upon a planned community which it would not impose upon a substantially similar development under a different form of ownership or administration. Otherwise, no provision of this Chapter invalidates or modifies any provision of any zoning, subdivision, or building code or any other real estate use law, ordinance, or regulation. No local ordinance or regulation may require the recordation of a declaration prior to the date required by this Chapter. (1998-199, s. 1.)

§ 47F-1-107. Eminent domain.

(a) If a lot is acquired by eminent domain, or if part of a lot is acquired by eminent domain leaving the lot owner with a remnant which may not practically or lawfully be used for any purpose permitted by the declaration, the award shall compensate the lot owner for his lot and its interest in the common element. Upon acquisition, unless the decree otherwise provides, the lot's allocated interests are automatically reallocated to the remaining lots in proportion to the respective allocated interests of those lots before the taking, exclusive of the lot taken.

(b) Except as provided in subsection (a) of this section, if part of a lot is acquired by eminent domain, the award shall compensate the lot owner for the reduction in value of the lot. Upon acquisition, unless the decree otherwise provides, (i) that lot's allocated interests are reduced in proportion to the reduction in the size of the lot, or on any other basis specified in the declaration, and (ii) the portion of the allocated interests divested from the partially acquired lot are automatically reallocated to that lot and the remaining lots in proportion to the respective allocated interests of those lots before the taking, with the partially acquired lot participating in the reallocation on the basis of its reduced allocated interests.

(c)   If there is any reallocation under subsection (a) or (b) of this section, the association shall promptly prepare, execute, and record an amendment to the declaration reflecting the reallocations. Any remnant of a lot remaining after part of a lot is taken under this subsection is thereafter a common element.

(d)   If part of the common elements is acquired by eminent domain, the portion of the award attributable to the common elements taken shall be paid to the association. Unless the declaration provides otherwise, any portion of the award attributable to the acquisition of a limited common element shall be apportioned among the owners of the lots to which that limited common element was allocated at the time of acquisition based on their allocated interest in the common elements before the taking.

(e)   The court decree shall be recorded in every county in which any portion of the planned community is located. (1998-199, s. 1.)

§ 47F-1-108. Supplemental general principles of law applicable.

The principles of law and equity as well as other North Carolina statutes (including the provisions of the North Carolina Nonprofit Corporation Act) supplement the provisions of this Chapter, except to the extent inconsistent with this Chapter. When these principles or statutes are inconsistent or conflict with this Chapter, the provisions of this Chapter will control. (1998-199, s. 1.)

§ 47F-1-109. Reserved for future codification purposes.

Article 2.

Creation, Alteration, and Termination of Planned Communities.

§ 47F-2-101. Creation of the planned community.

A declaration creating a planned community shall be executed in the same manner as a deed and shall be recorded in every county in which any portion of the planned community is located. (1998-199, s. 1; 2012-18, s. 1.7.)

§ 47F-2-102. Reserved for future codification purposes.

§ 47F-2-103. Construction and validity of declaration and bylaws.

(a) To the extent not inconsistent with the provisions of this Chapter, the declaration, bylaws, and articles of incorporation form the basis for the legal authority for the planned community to act as provided in the declaration, bylaws, and articles of incorporation, and the declaration, bylaws, and articles of incorporation are enforceable by their terms. All provisions of the declaration and bylaws are severable.

(b) The rule against perpetuities may not be applied to defeat any provision of the declaration, bylaws, rules, or regulations adopted pursuant to G.S. 47F-3-102(1).

(c) In the event of a conflict between the provisions of the declaration and the bylaws, the declaration prevails except to the extent the declaration is inconsistent with this Chapter.

(d) Title to a lot and common elements is not rendered unmarketable or otherwise affected by reason of an insubstantial failure of the declaration to comply with this Chapter. Whether a substantial failure to comply with this Chapter impairs marketability shall be determined by the law of this State relating to marketability. (1998-199, s. 1; 2013-34, s. 4.)

§§ 47F-2-104 through 47F-2-116. Reserved for future codification purposes.

§ 47F-2-117. Amendment of declaration.

(a) Except in cases of amendments that may be executed by a declarant under the terms of the declaration or by certain lot owners under G.S. 47F-2-118(b), the declaration may be amended only by affirmative vote or written agreement signed by lot owners of lots to which at least sixty-seven percent (67%) of the votes in the association are allocated, or any larger majority the declaration specifies or by the declarant if necessary for the exercise of any development right. The declaration may specify a smaller number only if all of the lots are restricted exclusively to nonresidential use.

(b) No action to challenge the validity of an amendment adopted pursuant to this section may be brought more than one year after the amendment is recorded.

(c) Every amendment to the declaration shall be recorded in every county in which any portion of the planned community is located and is effective only upon recordation.

(d) Any amendment passed pursuant to the provisions of this section or the procedures provided for in the declaration are presumed valid and enforceable.

(e) Amendments to the declaration required by this Chapter to be recorded by the association shall be prepared, executed, recorded, and certified in accordance with G.S. 47-41. (1998-199, s. 1; 2012-18, s. 1.8; 2013-34, s. 5.)

§ 47F-2-118. Termination of planned community.

(a) Except in the case of taking of all the lots by eminent domain (G.S. 47F-1-107), a planned community may be terminated only by agreement of lot owners of lots to which at least eighty percent (80%) of the votes in the association are allocated, or any larger percentage the declaration specifies. The declaration may specify a smaller percentage only if all of the lots in the planned community are restricted exclusively to nonresidential uses.

(b) An agreement to terminate shall be evidenced by the execution of a termination agreement, or ratifications thereof, in the same manner as a deed, by the requisite number of lot owners. The termination agreement shall specify a date after which the agreement will be void unless it is recorded before that date. A termination agreement and all ratifications thereof shall be recorded in every county in which a portion of the planned community is situated and is effective only upon recordation.

(c) A termination agreement may provide for sale of the common elements, but may not require that the lots be sold following termination, unless the declaration as originally recorded provided otherwise or unless all the lot owners consent to the sale. If, pursuant to the agreement, any real estate in the planned community is to be sold following termination, the termination agreement shall set forth the minimum terms of the sale.

(d) The association, on behalf of the lot owners, may contract for the sale of real estate in the planned community, but the contract is not binding until approved pursuant to subsections (a) and (b) of this section. Until the sale has been concluded and the proceeds thereof distributed, the association continues in existence with all powers it had before termination. Proceeds of the sale shall be distributed to lot owners and lienholders as their interests may appear, as provided in the termination agreement.

(e) If the real estate constituting the planned community is not to be sold following termination, title to the common elements vests in the lot owners upon termination as tenants in common in proportion to their respective interests as provided in the termination agreement.

(f) Following termination of the planned community, the proceeds of any sale of real estate, together with the assets of the association, are held by the association as trustee for lot owners and holders of liens on the lots as their interests may appear. All other creditors of the association are to be treated as if they had perfected liens on the common elements immediately before termination.

(g) If the termination agreement does not provide for the distribution of sales proceeds pursuant to subsection (d) of this section or the vesting of title pursuant to subsection (e) of this section, sales proceeds shall be distributed and title shall vest in accordance with each lot owner's allocated share of common expense liability.

(h) Except as provided in subsection (i) of this section, foreclosure or enforcement of a lien or encumbrance against the common elements does not of itself terminate the planned community, and foreclosure or enforcement of a lien or encumbrance against a portion of the common elements other than withdrawable real estate does not withdraw that portion from the planned community. Foreclosure or enforcement of a lien or encumbrance against withdrawable real estate does not of itself withdraw that real estate from the planned community, but the person taking title thereto has the right to require from the association, upon request, an amendment excluding the real estate from the planned community.

(i) If a lien or encumbrance against a portion of the real estate comprising the planned community has priority over the declaration and the lien or encumbrance has not been partially released, the parties foreclosing the lien or encumbrance may, upon foreclosure, record an instrument excluding the real estate subject to that lien or encumbrance from the planned community. (1998-199, s. 1.)

§ 47F-2-119. Reserved for future codification purposes.

§ 47F-2-120. Master associations.

If the declaration for a planned community provides that any of the powers described in G.S. 47F-3-102 are to be exercised by or may be delegated to a profit or nonprofit corporation which exercises those or other powers on behalf of one or more other planned communities or for the benefit of the lot owners of one or more other planned communities, all provisions of this act applicable to lot owners' associations apply to any such corporation. (1998-199, s. 1.)

§ 47F-2-121. Merger or consolidation of planned communities.

(a) Any two or more planned communities, by agreement of the lot owners as provided in subsection (b) of this section, may be merged or consolidated into a single planned community. In the event of a merger or consolidation, unless the agreement otherwise provides, the resultant planned community is, for all purposes, the legal successor of all of the preexisting planned communities, and the operations and activities of all associations of the preexisting planned communities shall be merged or consolidated into a single association which shall hold all powers, rights, obligations, assets, and liabilities of all preexisting associations.

(b) An agreement of two or more planned communities to merge or consolidate pursuant to subsection (a) of this section shall be evidenced by an agreement prepared, executed, recorded, and certified by the president of the association of each of the preexisting planned communities following approval by owners of lots to which are allocated the percentage of votes in each planned community required to terminate that planned community. Any such agreement shall be recorded in every county in which a portion of the planned community is located and is not effective until recorded.

(c) Every merger or consolidation agreement shall provide for the reallocation of the allocated interests in the new association among the lots of the resultant planned community either (i) by stating the reallocations or the formulas upon which they are based or (ii) by stating the percentage of overall common expense liabilities and votes in the new association which are allocated to all of the lots comprising each of the preexisting planned communities, and providing that the portion of the percentages allocated to each lot formerly comprising a part of the preexisting planned community shall be equal to the percentages of common expense liabilities and votes in the association allocated to that lot by the declaration of the preexisting planned community. (1998-199, s. 1.)

§ 47F-3-116.1. Validation of certain nonjudicial foreclosure proceedings and sales.

All nonjudicial foreclosure proceedings commenced by an association before October 1, 2013, and all sales and transfers of real property as part of those proceedings pursuant to the provisions of this Chapter or provisions contained in the declaration of the planned community, are declared to be valid, unless an action to set aside the foreclosure is commenced on or before October 1, 2013, or within one year after the date of the sale, whichever occurs last. (2013-202, s. 4.)

Article 3.

Management of Planned Community.

§ 47F-3-101. Organization of owners' association.

A lot owners' association shall be incorporated no later than the date the first lot in the planned community is conveyed. The membership of the association at all times shall consist exclusively of all the lot owners or, following termination of the planned community, of all persons entitled to distributions of proceeds under G.S. 47F-2-118. Every association created after the effective date of this Chapter shall be organized as a nonprofit corporation. (1998-199, s. 1.)

§ 47F-3-102. Powers of owners' association.

Unless the articles of incorporation or the declaration expressly provides to the contrary, the association may:

(1)   Adopt and amend bylaws and rules and regulations;

(2)   Adopt and amend budgets for revenues, expenditures, and reserves and collect assessments for common expenses from lot owners;

(3)   Hire and discharge managing agents and other employees, agents, and independent contractors;

(4)   Institute, defend, or intervene in litigation or administrative proceedings on matters affecting the planned community;

(5)   Make contracts and incur liabilities;

(6)   Regulate the use, maintenance, repair, replacement, and modification of common elements;

(7)   Cause additional improvements to be made as a part of the common elements;

(8) Acquire, hold, encumber, and convey in its own name any right, title, or interest to real or personal property, provided that common elements may be conveyed or subjected to a security interest only pursuant to G.S. 47F-3-112;

(9) Grant easements, leases, licenses, and concessions through or over the common elements;

(10) Impose and receive any payments, fees, or charges for the use, rental, or operation of the common elements other than the limited common elements and for services provided to lot owners;

(11) Impose reasonable charges for late payment of assessments, not to exceed the greater of twenty dollars ($20.00) per month or ten percent (10%) of any assessment installment unpaid and, after notice and an opportunity to be heard, suspend privileges or services provided by the association (except rights of access to lots) during any period that assessments or other amounts due and owing to the association remain unpaid for a period of 30 days or longer;

(12) After notice and an opportunity to be heard, impose reasonable fines or suspend privileges or services provided by the association (except rights of access to lots) for reasonable periods for violations of the declaration, bylaws, and rules and regulations of the association;

(13) Impose reasonable charges in connection with the preparation and recordation of documents, including, without limitation, amendments to the declaration or statements of unpaid assessments;

(14) Provide for the indemnification of and maintain liability insurance for its officers, executive board, directors, employees, and agents;

(15) Assign its right to future income, including the right to receive common expense assessments;

(16) Exercise all other powers that may be exercised in this State by legal entities of the same type as the association; and

(17) Exercise any other powers necessary and proper for the governance and operation of the association. (1998-199, s. 1; 2004-109, s. 4; 2005-422, s. 1.)

§ 47F-3-103. Executive board members and officers.

(a) Except as provided in the declaration, in the bylaws, in subsection (b) of this section, or in other provisions of this Chapter, the executive board may act in all instances on behalf of the association. In the performance of their duties, officers and members of the executive board shall discharge their duties in good faith. Officers shall act according to the standards for officers of a nonprofit corporation set forth in G.S. 55A-8-42, and members shall act according to the standards for directors of a nonprofit corporation set forth in G.S. 55A-8-30.

(b) The executive board may not act unilaterally on behalf of the association to amend the declaration (G.S. 47F-2-117), to terminate the planned community (G.S. 47F-2-118), or to elect members of the executive board or determine the qualifications, powers and duties, or terms of office of executive board members (G.S. 47F-3-103(e)), but the executive board may unilaterally fill vacancies in its membership for the unexpired portion of any term. Notwithstanding any provision of the declaration or bylaws to the contrary, the lot owners, by a majority vote of all persons present and entitled to vote at any meeting of the lot owners at which a quorum is present, may remove any member of the executive board with or without cause, other than a member appointed by the declarant.

(c) Within 30 days after adoption of any proposed budget for the planned community, the executive board shall provide to all the lot owners a summary of the budget and a notice of the meeting to consider ratification of the budget, including a statement that the budget may be ratified without a quorum. The executive board shall set a date for a meeting of the lot owners to consider ratification of the budget, such meeting to be held not less than 10 nor more than 60 days after mailing of the summary and notice. There shall be no requirement that a quorum be present at the meeting. The budget is ratified unless at that meeting a majority of all the lot owners in the association or any larger vote specified in the declaration rejects the budget. In the event the proposed budget is rejected, the periodic budget last ratified by the lot owners shall be continued until such time as the lot owners ratify a subsequent budget proposed by the executive board.

(d) The declaration may provide for a period of declarant control of the association, during which period a declarant, or persons designated by the declarant, may appoint and remove the officers and members of the executive board.

(e) Not later than the termination of any period of declarant control, the lot owners shall elect an executive board of at least three members, at least a majority of whom shall be lot owners. The executive board shall elect the officers. The executive board members and officers shall take office upon election.

(f) The association shall publish the names and addresses of all officers and board members of the association within 30 days of their election. (1998-199, s. 1; 2005-422, ss. 2, 3.)

§ 47F-3-104. Transfer of special declarant rights.

Except for transfer of declarant rights pursuant to foreclosure, no special declarant right (G.S. 47F-1-103(28)) may be transferred except by an instrument evidencing the transfer recorded in every county in which any portion of the planned community is located. The instrument is not effective unless executed by the transferee. (1998-199, s. 1.)

§ 47F-3-105. Termination of contracts and leases of declarant.

If entered into before the executive board elected by the lot owners pursuant to G.S. 47F-3-103(e) takes office, any contract or lease affecting or related to the planned community that is not bona fide or was unconscionable to the lot owners at the time entered into under the circumstances then prevailing, may be terminated without penalty by the association at any time after the executive board elected by the lot owners pursuant to G.S. 47F-3-103(e) takes office upon not less than 90 days' notice to the other party. (1998-199, s. 1.)

§ 47F-3-106. Bylaws.

(a) The bylaws of the association shall provide for:

(1) The number of members of the executive board and the titles of the officers of the association;

(2) Election by the executive board of officers of the association;

(3) The qualifications, powers and duties, terms of office, and manner of electing and removing executive board members and officers and filling vacancies;

(4) Which, if any, of its powers the executive board or officers may delegate to other persons or to a managing agent;

(5) Which of its officers may prepare, execute, certify, and record amendments to the declaration on behalf of the association; and

(6) The method of amending the bylaws.

(b) The bylaws may provide for any other matters the association deems necessary and appropriate. (1998-199, s. 1.)

§ 47F-3-107. Upkeep of planned community; responsibility and assessments for damages.

(a) Except as otherwise provided in the declaration, G.S. 47F-3-113(h) or subsection (b) of this section, the association is responsible for causing the common elements to be maintained, repaired, and replaced when necessary and to assess the lot owners as necessary to recover the costs of such maintenance, repair, or replacement except that the costs of maintenance, repair, or replacement of a limited common element shall be assessed as provided in G.S. 47F-3-115(c)(1). Except as otherwise provided in the declaration, each lot owner is responsible for the maintenance and repair of his lot and any improvements thereon. Each lot owner shall afford to the association and when necessary to another lot owner access through the lot owner's lot or the limited common element allocated to the lot owner's lot reasonably necessary for any such maintenance, repair, or replacement activity.

(b) If a lot owner is legally responsible for damage inflicted on any common element or limited common element, the association may direct such lot owner to repair such damage, or the association may itself cause the repairs to be made and recover damages from the responsible lot owner.

(c)   If damage is inflicted on any lot by an agent of the association in the scope of the agent's activities as such agent, the association is liable to repair such damage or to reimburse the lot owner for the cost of repairing such damages. The association shall also be liable for any losses to the lot owner.

(d)   When the claim under subsection (b) or (c) of this section is less than or equal to the jurisdictional amount established for small claims by G.S. 7A-210, any aggrieved party may request that a hearing be held before an adjudicatory panel appointed by the executive board to determine if a lot owner is responsible for damages to any common element or the association is responsible for damages to any lot. If the executive board fails to appoint an adjudicatory panel to hear such matters, hearings under this section shall be held before the executive board. Such panel shall accord to the party charged with causing damages notice of the charge, opportunity to be heard and to present evidence, and notice of the decision. This panel may assess liability for each damage incident against each lot owner charged or against the association not in excess of the jurisdictional amount established for small claims by G.S. 7A-210. When the claim under subsection (b) or (c) of this section exceeds the jurisdictional amount established for small claims by G.S. 7A-210, liability of any lot owner charged or the association shall be determined as otherwise provided by law. Liabilities of lot owners determined by adjudicatory hearing or as otherwise provided by law shall be assessments secured by lien under G.S. 47F-3-116. Liabilities of the association determined by adjudicatory hearing or as otherwise provided by law may be offset by the lot owner against sums owing to the association and if so offset, shall reduce the amount of any lien of the association against the lot at issue.

(e)   The association shall not be liable for maintenance, repair, and all other expenses in connection with any real estate which has not been incorporated into the planned community. (1998-199, s. 1; 2013-34, s. 2.)

§ 47F-3-107.1. Procedures for fines and suspension of planned community privileges or services.

Unless a specific procedure for the imposition of fines or suspension of planned community privileges or services is provided for in the declaration, a hearing shall be held before the executive board or an adjudicatory panel appointed by the executive board to determine if any lot owner should be fined or if planned community privileges or services should be suspended pursuant to the powers granted to the association in G.S. 47F-3-102(11) and (12). Any adjudicatory panel appointed by the executive board shall be composed of members of the association who are not officers of the association or members of the executive board. The lot owner charged shall be given notice of the charge, opportunity to be heard and to present evidence, and notice of the decision. If it is decided that a fine should be imposed, a fine not to exceed one hundred dollars ($100.00) may be imposed for the violation and without further hearing, for each day more than five days after the decision that the violation occurs. Such fines shall be assessments secured by liens under G.S. 47F-3-116. If it is decided that a suspension of planned community privileges or services should be imposed, the suspension may be continued without further hearing until the violation or delinquency is cured. The lot owner may appeal the decision of an adjudicatory panel to the full executive board by delivering written notice of appeal to the executive board within 15 days after the date of the decision. The executive board may affirm, vacate, or modify the prior decision of the adjudicatory body. (1997-456, s. 27; 1998-199, s. 1; 2005-422, s. 4.)

§ 47F-3-108. Meetings.

(a) A meeting of the association shall be held at least once each year. Special meetings of the association may be called by the president, a majority of the executive board, or by lot owners having ten percent (10%), or any lower percentage specified in the bylaws, of the votes in the association. Not less than 10 nor more than 60 days in advance of any meeting, the secretary or other officer specified in the bylaws shall cause notice to be hand-delivered or sent prepaid by United States mail to the mailing address of each lot or to any other mailing address designated in writing by the lot owner, or sent by electronic means, including by electronic mail over the Internet, to an electronic mailing address designated in writing by the lot owner. The notice of any meeting shall state the time and place of the meeting and the items on the agenda, including the general nature of any proposed amendment to the declaration or bylaws, any budget changes, and any proposal to remove a director or officer.

(b) Meetings of the executive board shall be held as provided in the bylaws. At regular intervals, the executive board meeting shall provide lot owners an opportunity to attend a portion of an executive board meeting and to speak to the executive board about their issues or concerns. The executive board may place reasonable restrictions on the number of persons who speak on each side of an issue and may place reasonable time restrictions on persons who speak.

(c) Except as otherwise provided in the bylaws, meetings of the association and the executive board shall be conducted in accordance with the most recent edition of Robert's Rules of Order Newly Revised. (1998-199, s. 1; 2004-109, s. 6; 2005-422, s. 5.)

§ 47F-3-109. Quorums.

(a) Unless the bylaws provide otherwise, a quorum is present throughout any meeting of the association if persons entitled to cast ten percent (10%) of the votes which may be cast for election of the executive board are present in person or by proxy at the beginning of the meeting.

(b) Unless the bylaws specify a larger percentage, a quorum is deemed present throughout any meeting of the executive board if persons entitled to cast fifty percent (50%) of the votes on that board are present at the beginning of the meeting.

(c) In the event business cannot be conducted at any meeting because a quorum is not present, that meeting may be adjourned to a later date by the affirmative vote of a majority of those present in person or by proxy. Notwithstanding any provision to the contrary in the declaration or the bylaws, the quorum requirement at the next meeting shall be one-half of the quorum requirement applicable to the meeting adjourned for lack of a quorum. This provision shall continue to reduce the quorum by fifty percent (50%) from that required at the previous meeting, as previously reduced, until such time as a quorum is present and business can be conducted. (1998-199, s. 1.)

§ 47F-3-110. Voting; proxies.

(a) If only one of the multiple owners of a lot is present at a meeting of the association, the owner who is present is entitled to cast all the votes allocated to that lot. If more than one of the multiple owners are present, the votes allocated to that lot may be cast only in accordance with the agreement of a majority in interest of the multiple owners, unless the declaration or bylaws expressly provide otherwise. Majority agreement is conclusively presumed if any one of the multiple owners casts the votes allocated to that lot without protest being made promptly to the person presiding over the meeting by any of the other owners of the lot.

(b)   Votes allocated to a lot may be cast pursuant to a proxy duly executed by a lot owner. If a lot is owned by more than one person, each owner of the lot may vote or register protest to the casting of votes by the other owners of the lot through a duly executed proxy. A lot owner may not revoke a proxy given pursuant to this section except by actual notice of revocation to the person presiding over a meeting of the association. A proxy is void if it is not dated. A proxy terminates 11 months after its date, unless it specifies a shorter term.

(c)   If the declaration requires that votes on specified matters affecting the planned community be cast by lessees rather than lot owners of leased lots, (i) the provisions of subsections (a) and (b) of this section apply to lessees as if they were lot owners; (ii) lot owners who have leased their lots to other persons may not cast votes on those specified matters; and (iii) lessees are entitled to notice of meetings, access to records, and other rights respecting those matters as if they were lot owners. Lot owners shall also be given notice, in the manner provided in G.S. 47F-3-108, of all meetings at which lessees may be entitled to vote.

(d)   No votes allocated to a lot owned by the association may be cast.

(e)   The declaration may provide that on specified issues only a defined subgroup of lot owners may vote provided:

(1)   The issue being voted is of special interest solely to the members of the subgroup; and

(2)   All except de minimis cost that will be incurred based on the vote taken will be assessed solely against those lot owners entitled to vote.

(f)   For purposes of subdivision (e)(1) above, an issue to be voted on is not a special interest solely to a subgroup if it substantially affects the overall appearance of the planned community or substantially affects living conditions of lot owners not included in the voting subgroup. (1998-199, s. 1.)

§ 47F-3-111. Tort and contract liability.

(a)   Neither the association nor any lot owner except the declarant is liable for that declarant's torts in connection with any part of the planned community which that declarant has the responsibility to maintain.

(b)   An action alleging a wrong done by the association shall be brought against the association and not against a lot owner.

(c)   Any statute of limitation affecting the association's right of action under this section is tolled until the period of declarant control terminates. A lot owner is not precluded from bringing an action contemplated by this section because the person is a lot owner or a member of the association. (1998-199, s. 1.)

§ 47F-3-112. Conveyance or encumbrance of common elements.

(a)   Portions of the common elements may be conveyed or subjected to a security interest by the association if persons entitled to cast at least eighty percent (80%) of the votes In the association, or any larger percentage the declaration specifies, agree in writing to that action; provided that all the owners of lots to which any limited common element is allocated shall agree in order to convey that limited common element or subject it to a security interest. The declaration may specify a smaller percentage only if all the lots are restricted exclusively to nonresidential uses. Distribution of proceeds of the sale of a limited common element shall be as provided by agreement between the lot owners to which it is allocated and the association. Proceeds of the sale or financing of a common element (other than a limited common element) shall be an asset of the association.

(b)   The association, on behalf of the lot owners, may contract to convey common elements or subject them to a security interest, but the contract is not enforceable against the association until approved pursuant to subsection (a) of this section. Thereafter, the association has all powers necessary and appropriate to effect the conveyance or encumbrance, free and clear of any interest of any lot owner or the association in or to the common element conveyed or encumbered, including the power to execute deeds or other instruments.

(c)   Any purported conveyance, encumbrance, or other voluntary transfer of common elements, unless made pursuant to this section is void.

(d) No conveyance or encumbrance of common elements pursuant to this section may deprive any lot of its rights of access and support. (1998-199, s. 1.)

§ 47F-3-113. Insurance.

(a) Commencing not later than the time of the first conveyance of a lot to a person other than a declarant, the association shall maintain, to the extent reasonably available:

(1) Property insurance on the common elements insuring against all risks of direct physical loss commonly insured against including fire and extended coverage perils. The total amount of insurance after application of any deductibles shall be not less than eighty percent (80%) of the replacement cost of the insured property at the time the insurance is purchased and at each renewal date, exclusive of land, excavations, foundations, and other items normally excluded from property policies; and

(2) Liability insurance in reasonable amounts, covering all occurrences commonly insured against for death, bodily injury, and property damage arising out of or in connection with the use, ownership, or maintenance of the common elements.

(b) If the insurance described in subsection (a) of this section is not reasonably available, the association promptly shall cause notice of that fact to be hand-delivered or sent prepaid by United States mail to all lot owners. The declaration may require the association to carry any other insurance, and the association in any event may carry any other insurance it deems appropriate to protect the association or the lot owners.

(c) Insurance policies carried pursuant to subsection (a) of this section shall provide that:

(1) Each lot owner is an insured person under the policy to the extent of the lot owner's insurable interest;

(2) The insurer waives its right to subrogation under the policy against any lot owner or member of the lot owner's household;

(3) No act or omission by any lot owner, unless acting within the scope of the owner's authority on behalf of the association, will preclude recovery under the policy; and

(4) If, at the time of a loss under the policy, there is other insurance in the name of a lot owner covering the same risk covered by the policy, the association's policy provides primary insurance.

(d) Any loss covered by the property policy under subdivision (a)(1) of this section shall be adjusted with the association, but the insurance proceeds for that loss are payable to any insurance trustee designated for that purpose, or otherwise to the association, and not to any mortgagee or beneficiary under a deed of trust. The insurance trustee or the association shall hold any insurance proceeds in trust for lot owners and lienholders as their interests may appear. Subject to the provisions of subsection (h) of this section, the proceeds shall be disbursed first for the repair or restoration of the damaged property, and lot owners and lienholders are not entitled to receive payment of any portion of the proceeds unless there is a surplus of proceeds after the property has been completely repaired or restored, or the planned community is terminated.

(e) An insurance policy issued to the association does not prevent a lot owner from obtaining insurance for the lot owner's own benefit.

(f) An insurer that has issued an insurance policy under this section shall issue certificates or memoranda of insurance to the association and, upon written request, to any lot owner, mortgagee, or beneficiary under a deed of trust. The insurer issuing the policy may not cancel or refuse to renew it until 30 days after notice of the proposed cancellation or nonrenewal has been mailed to the association, each lot owner, and each mortgagee or beneficiary under a deed of trust to whom certificates or memoranda of insurance have been issued at their respective last known addresses.

(g) Any portion of the planned community for which insurance is required under subdivision (a)(1) of this section which is damaged or destroyed shall be repaired or replaced promptly by the association unless (i) the planned community is terminated, (ii) repair or replacement would be illegal under any State or local health or safety statute or ordinance, or (iii) the lot owners decide not to rebuild by an eighty percent (80%) vote, including one hundred percent (100%) approval of owners assigned to the limited common elements not to be rebuilt. The cost of repair or replacement in excess of insurance proceeds and reserves is a common expense. If any portion of the planned community is not repaired or replaced, (i) the insurance proceeds attributable to the damaged common elements shall be used to restore the damaged area to a condition compatible with the remainder of the planned community, (ii) the insurance proceeds attributable to limited common elements which are not rebuilt shall be distributed to the owners of the lots to which those limited common elements were allocated, or to lienholders, as their interests may appear, and (iii) the remainder of the proceeds shall be distributed to all the lot owners or lienholders, as their interests may appear, in proportion to the common expense liabilities of all the lots. Notwithstanding the provisions of this subsection, G.S. 47F-2-118 (termination of the planned community) governs the distribution of insurance proceeds if the planned community is terminated.

(h)   The provisions of this section may be varied or waived in the case of a planned community all of whose lots are restricted to nonresidential use. (1998-199, s. 1.)

§ 47F-3-114. Surplus funds.

Unless otherwise provided in the declaration, any surplus funds of the association remaining after payment of or provision for common expenses, the funding of a reasonable operating expense surplus, and any prepayment of reserves shall be paid to the lot owners in proportion to their common expense liabilities or credited to them to reduce their future common expense assessments. (1998-199, s. 1.)

§ 47F-3-115. Assessments for common expenses.

(a)   Except as otherwise provided in the declaration, until the association makes a common expense assessment, the declarant shall pay all common expenses. After any assessment has been made by the association, assessments thereafter shall be made at least annually.

(b)   Except for assessments under subsections (c), (d), and (e) of this section, all common expenses shall be assessed against all the lots in accordance with the allocations set forth in the declaration. Any past-due common expense assessment or installment thereof bears interest at the rate established by the association not exceeding eighteen percent (18%) per year.

For planned communities created prior to January 1, 1999, interest may be charged on any past-due common expense assessment or installment only if the declaration provides for interest charges, and where the declaration does not otherwise specify the interest rate, the rate may not exceed eighteen percent (18%) per year.

(c) To the extent required by the declaration:

(1) Any common expense associated with the maintenance, repair, or replacement of a limited common element shall be assessed against the lots to which that limited common element is assigned, equally, or in any other proportion that the declaration provides;

(2) Any common expense or portion thereof benefiting fewer than all of the lots shall be assessed exclusively against the lots benefitted; and

(3) The costs of insurance shall be assessed in proportion to risk and the costs of utilities shall be assessed in proportion to usage.

(d) Assessments to pay a judgment against the association may be made only against the lots in the planned community at the time the judgment was entered, in proportion to their common expense liabilities.

(e) If any common expense is caused by the negligence or misconduct of any lot owner or occupant, the association may assess that expense exclusively against that lot owner or occupant's lot.

(f) If common expense liabilities are reallocated, common expense assessments and any installment thereof not yet due shall be recalculated in accordance with the reallocated common expense liabilities. (1998-199, s. 1.)

§ 47F-3-116. Lien for sums due the association; enforcement.

(a) Any assessment attributable to a lot which remains unpaid for a period of 30 days or longer shall constitute a lien on that lot when a claim of lien is filed of record in the office of the clerk of superior court of the county in which the lot is located in the manner provided in this section. Once filed, a claim of lien secures all sums due the association through the date filed and any sums due to the association thereafter. Unless the declaration provides otherwise, fees, charges, late charges, and other charges imposed pursuant to G.S. 47F-3-102, 47F-3-107, 47F-3-107.1, and 47F-3-115 are subject to the claim of lien under this section as well as any other sums due and payable to the association under the declaration, the provisions of this Chapter, or as the result of an arbitration, mediation, or judicial decision.

(b)   The association must make reasonable and diligent efforts to ensure that its records contain the lot owner's current mailing address. No fewer than 15 days prior to filing the lien, the association shall mail a statement of the assessment amount due by first-class mail to the physical address of the lot and the lot owner's address of record with the association and, if different, to the address for the lot owner shown on the county tax records for the lot. If the lot owner is a corporation or limited liability company, the statement shall also be sent by first-class mail to the mailing address of the registered agent for the corporation or limited liability company. Notwithstanding anything to the contrary in this Chapter, the association is not required to mail a statement to an address known to be a vacant lot on which no dwelling has been constructed or to a lot for which there is no United States postal address.

(c)   A claim of lien shall set forth the name and address of the association, the name of the record owner of the lot at the time the claim of lien is filed, a description of the lot, and the amount of the lien claimed. A claim of lien may also appoint a trustee to conduct a foreclosure, as provided in subsection (f) of this section. The first page of the claim of lien shall contain the following statement in print that is in boldface, capital letters, and no smaller than the largest print used elsewhere in the document:

"THIS DOCUMENT CONSTITUTES A LIEN AGAINST YOUR PROPERTY, AND IF THE LIEN IS NOT PAID, THE HOMEOWNERS ASSOCIATION MAY PROCEED WITH FORECLOSURE AGAINST YOUR PROPERTY IN LIKE MANNER AS A MORTGAGE UNDER NORTH CAROLINA LAW."

The person signing the claim of lien on behalf of the association shall attach to and file with the claim of lien a certificate of service attesting to the attempt of service on the record owner, which service shall be attempted in accordance with G.S. 1A-1, Rule 4(j), for service of a copy of a summons and a complaint. If the actual service is not achieved, the person signing the claim of lien on behalf of the association shall be deemed to have met the requirements of this subsection if service has been attempted pursuant to both of the following: (i) G.S. 1A-1, Rule 4(j)(1)c, d, or e and (ii) by mailing a copy of the lien by regular, first-class mail, postage prepaid to the physical address of the lot and the lot owner's address of record with the association, and, if different, to the address for the lot owner shown on the county tax records and the county real property records for the lot. In the event that the owner of record is not a natural person, and actual service is not achieved, the person signing the claim of lien on behalf of the association shall be deemed to have met the requirements of this subsection if service has been attempted once pursuant to the applicable provisions of G.S. 1A-1, Rule 4(j)(3) through G.S. 1A-1, Rule 4(j)(9). Notwithstanding anything to the contrary in this Chapter, the association is not required to mail a claim of lien to an address which is known to be a vacant lot on which no dwelling has been constructed or to a lot for which there is no United States postal address. A lien for unpaid assessments is extinguished unless proceedings to enforce the lien are instituted within three years after the filing of the claim of lien in the office of the clerk of superior court.

(d)   A claim of lien filed under this section is prior to all liens and encumbrances on a lot except (i) liens and encumbrances, specifically including, but not limited to, a mortgage or deed of trust on the lot, recorded before the filing of the claim of lien in the office of the clerk of superior court and (ii) liens for real estate taxes and other governmental assessments and charges against the lot. This subsection does not affect the priority of mechanics' or materialmen's liens.

(e)   The association shall be entitled to recover the reasonable attorneys' fees and costs it incurs in connection with the collection of any sums due. A lot owner may not be required to pay attorneys' fees and court costs until the lot owner is notified in writing of the association's intent to seek payment of attorneys' fees, costs, and expenses. The notice must be sent by first-class mail to the physical address of the lot and the lot owner's address of record with the association and, if different, to the address for the lot owner shown on the county tax records for the lot. The association must make reasonable and diligent efforts to ensure that its records contain the lot owner's current mailing address. Notwithstanding anything to the contrary in this Chapter, there shall be no requirement that notice under this subsection be mailed to an address which is known to be a vacant lot on which no dwelling has been constructed or a lot for which there is no United States postal address. The notice shall set out the outstanding balance due as of the date of the notice and state that the lot owner has 15 days from the mailing of the notice by first-class mail to pay the outstanding balance without the attorneys' fees and court costs. If the lot owner pays the outstanding balance within this period, then the lot owner shall have no obligation to pay attorneys' fees, costs, or expenses. The notice shall also inform the lot owner of the opportunity to contact a representative of the association to discuss a payment schedule for the outstanding balance, as provided in subsection (i) of this section, and shall provide the name and telephone number of the representative.

(f) Except as provided in subsection (h) of this section, the association, acting through the executive board, may foreclose a claim of lien in like manner as a mortgage or deed of trust on real estate under power of sale, as provided in Article 2A of Chapter 45 of the General Statutes, if the assessment remains unpaid for 90 days or more. The association shall not foreclose the claim of lien unless the executive board votes to commence the proceeding against the specific lot.

The following provisions and procedures shall be applicable to and complied with in every nonjudicial power of sale foreclosure of a claim of lien, and these provisions and procedures shall control to the extent they are inconsistent or in conflict with the provisions of Article 2A of Chapter 45 of the General Statutes:

(1) The association shall be deemed to have a power of sale for purposes of enforcement of its claim of lien.

(2) The terms "mortgagee" and "holder" as used in Article 2A of Chapter 45 of the General Statutes shall mean the association, except as provided otherwise in this Chapter.

(3) The term "security instrument" as used in Article 2A of Chapter 45 of the General Statutes shall mean the claim of lien.

(4) The term "trustee" as used in Article 2A of Chapter 45 of the General Statutes shall mean the person or entity appointed by the association under subdivision (6) of this subsection.

(5) After the association has filed a claim of lien and prior to the commencement of a nonjudicial foreclosure, the association shall give to the lot owner notice of the association's intention to commence a nonjudicial foreclosure to enforce its claim of lien. The notice shall contain the information required in G.S. 45-21.16(c)(5a).

(6) The association shall appoint a trustee to conduct the nonjudicial foreclosure proceeding and sale. The appointment of the trustee shall be included in the claim of lien or in a separate instrument filed with the clerk of court in the county in which the planned community is located as an exhibit to

the notice of hearing. The association, at its option, may from time to time remove a trustee previously appointed and appoint a successor trustee by filing a Substitution of Trustee with the clerk of court in the foreclosure proceeding. Counsel for the association may be appointed by the association to serve as the trustee and may serve in that capacity as long as the lot owner does not contest the obligation to pay or the amount of any sums due the association, or the validity, enforcement, or foreclosure of the claim of lien, as provided in subdivision (12) of this subsection. Any trustee appointed pursuant to this subsection shall have the same fiduciary duties and obligations as a trustee in the foreclosure of a deed of trust.

(7) If a valid debt, default, and notice to those entitled to receive notice under G.S. 45-21.16(b) are found to exist, then the clerk of court shall authorize the sale of the property described in the claim of lien by the trustee.

(8) If, prior to the expiration of the upset bid period provided in G.S. 45-21.27, the lot owner satisfies the debt secured by the claim of lien and pays all expenses and costs incurred in filing and enforcing the association assessment lien, including, but not limited to, advertising costs, attorneys' fees, and the trustee's commission, then the trustee shall dismiss the foreclosure action and the association shall cancel the claim of lien of record in accordance with the provisions of G.S. 45-36.3. The lot owner shall have all rights granted under Article 4 of Chapter 45 of the General Statutes to ensure the association's satisfaction of the claim of lien.

(9) Any person, other than the trustee, may bid at the foreclosure sale. Unless prohibited in the declaration or bylaws, the association may bid on the lot at a foreclosure sale directly or through an agent. If the association or its agent is the high bidder at the sale, the trustee shall allow the association to pay the costs and expenses of the sale and apply a credit against the sums due by the lot owner to the association in lieu of paying the bid price in full.

(10) Upon the expiration of the upset bid period provided in G.S. 45-21.27, the trustee shall have full power and authority to execute a deed for the lot to the high bidder.

(11) The trustee shall be entitled to a commission for services rendered which shall include fees, costs, and expenses reasonably incurred by the trustee in connection with the foreclosure, whether or not a sale is held. Except as provided in subdivision (12) of this subsection, the trustee's commission shall

be paid without regard to any limitations on compensation otherwise provided by law, including, without limitation, the provisions of G.S. 45-21.15.

(12)   If the lot owner does not contest the obligation to pay the amount of any sums due the association or the validity, enforcement, or foreclosure of the claim of lien at any time after the expiration of the 15-day period following notice as required in subsection (b) of this section, then attorneys' fees and the trustee's commission collectively charged to the lot owner shall not exceed one thousand two hundred dollars ($1,200), not including costs or expenses incurred. The obligation to pay and the amount of any sums due the association and the validity, enforcement, or foreclosure of the claim of lien remain uncontested as long as the lot owner does not dispute, contest, or raise any objection, defense, offset, or counterclaim as to the amount or validity of any portion of the sums claimed due by the association or the validity, enforcement, or foreclosure of the claim of lien. Any judgment, decree, or order in any action brought under this section shall include costs and reasonable attorneys' fees for the prevailing party.

(13)   Lot owners shall be deemed to have the rights and remedies available to mortgagors under G.S. 45-21.34.

(g)   The provisions of subsection (f) of this section do not prohibit or prevent an association from pursuing judicial foreclosure of a claim of lien, from taking other actions to recover the sums due the association, or from accepting a deed in lieu of foreclosure. Any judgment, decree, or order in any judicial foreclosure or civil action relating to the collection of assessments shall include an award of costs and reasonable attorneys' fees for the prevailing party, which shall not be subject to the limitation provided in subdivision (f)(12) of this section.

(h)   A claim of lien securing a debt consisting solely of fines imposed by the association, interest on unpaid fines, or attorneys' fees incurred by the association solely associated with fines imposed by the association may only be enforced by judicial foreclosure, as provided in Article 29A of Chapter 1 of the General Statutes. In addition, an association shall not levy, charge, or attempt to collect a service, collection, consulting, or administration fee from any lot owner unless the fee is expressly allowed in the declaration, and any claim of lien securing a debt consisting solely of these fees may only be enforced by judicial foreclosure, as provided in Article 29A of Chapter 1 of the General Statutes.

(i)   The association, acting through its executive board and in the board's sole discretion, may agree to allow payment of an outstanding balance in installments. Neither the association nor the lot owner is obligated to offer or accept any proposed installment schedule. Reasonable administrative fees and costs for accepting and processing installments may be added to the outstanding balance and included in an installment payment schedule. Reasonable attorneys' fees may be added to the outstanding balance and included in an installment schedule after the lot owner has been given notice, as required in subsection (e) of this section. Attorneys' fees incurred in connection with any request that the association agrees to accept payment of all or any part of sums due in installments shall not be included or considered in the calculation of fees chargeable under subdivision (f)(12) of this section.

(j)   Where the holder of a first mortgage or first deed of trust of record or other purchaser of a lot obtains title to the lot as a result of foreclosure of a first mortgage or first deed of trust, the purchaser and its heirs, successors, and assigns shall not be liable for the assessments against the lot which became due prior to the acquisition of title to the lot by the purchaser. The unpaid assessments shall be deemed to be common expenses collectible from all the lot owners, including the purchaser, its heirs, successors, and assigns. For purposes of this subsection, the term "acquisition of title" means and refers to the recording of a deed conveying title or the time at which the rights of the parties are fixed following the foreclosure of a mortgage or deed of trust, whichever occurs first. (1998-199, s. 1; 2005-422, s. 6; 2009-515, s. 1; 2011-362, s. 1; 2013-202, s. 3.)

§ 47F-3-117. Reserved for future codification purposes.

§ 47F-3-118. Association records.

(a)   The association shall keep financial records sufficiently detailed to enable the association to comply with this Chapter. All financial and other records, including records of meetings of the association and executive board, shall be made reasonably available for examination by any lot owner and the lot owner's authorized agents as required in the bylaws and Chapter 55A of the General Statutes. If the bylaws do not specify particular records to be maintained, the association shall keep accurate records of all cash receipts and expenditures and all assets and liabilities. In addition to any specific information that is required by the bylaws to be assembled and reported to the lot owners at specified times, the association shall make an annual income and expense statement and balance sheet available to all lot owners at no charge and within 75 days after the close of the fiscal year to which the information relates. Notwithstanding the bylaws, a more extensive compilation, review, or audit of the association's books and records for the current or immediately preceding fiscal year may be required by a vote of the majority of the executive board or by the affirmative vote of a majority of the lot owners present and voting in person or by proxy at any annual meeting or any special meeting duly called for that purpose.

(b) The association, upon written request, shall furnish to a lot owner or the lot owner's authorized agents a statement setting forth the amount of unpaid assessments and other charges against a lot. The statement shall be furnished within 10 business days after receipt of the request and is binding on the association, the executive board, and every lot owner.

(c) In addition to the limitations of Article 8 of Chapter 55A of the General Statutes, no financial payments, including payments made in the form of goods and services, may be made to any officer or member of the association's executive board or to a business, business associate, or relative of an officer or member of the executive board, except as expressly provided for in the bylaws or in payments for services or expenses paid on behalf of the association which are approved in advance by the executive board. (1998-199, s. 1; 2005-422, s. 7.)

§ 47F-3-119. Association as trustee.

With respect to a third person dealing with the association in the association's capacity as a trustee under G.S. 47F-2-118 following termination or G.S. 47F-3-113 for insurance proceeds, the existence of trust powers and their proper exercise by the association may be assumed without inquiry. A third person is not bound to inquire whether the association has power to act as trustee or is properly exercising trust powers, and a third person, without actual knowledge that the association is exceeding or improperly exercising its powers, is fully protected in dealing with the association as if it possessed and properly exercised the powers it purports to exercise. A third person is not bound to assure the proper application of trust assets paid or delivered to the association in its capacity as trustee. (1998-199, s. 1.)

§ 47F-3-120. Declaration limits on attorneys' fees.

Except as provided in G.S. 47F-3-116, in an action to enforce provisions of the articles of incorporation, the declaration, bylaws, or duly adopted rules or regulations, the court may award reasonable attorneys' fees to the prevailing party if recovery of attorneys' fees is allowed in the declaration. (1998-199, s. 1.)

§ 47F-3-121. American and State flags and political sign displays.

Notwithstanding any provision in any declaration of covenants, no restriction on the use of land shall be construed to:

(1)   Regulate or prohibit the display of the flag of the United States or North Carolina, of a size no greater than four feet by six feet, which is displayed in accordance with or in a manner consistent with the patriotic customs set forth in 4 U.S.C. §§ 5-10, as amended, governing the display and use of the flag of the United States unless:

a.   For restrictions registered prior to October 1, 2005, the restriction specifically uses the following terms:

1.   Flag of the United States of America;

2.   American flag;

3.   United States flag; or

4.   North Carolina flag.

b.   For restrictions registered on or after October 1, 2005, the restriction shall be written on the first page of the instrument or conveyance in print that is in boldface type, capital letters, and no smaller than the largest print used elsewhere in the instrument or conveyance. The restriction shall be construed to regulate or prohibit the display of the United States or North Carolina flag only if the restriction specifically states: "THIS DOCUMENT REGULATES OR PROHIBITS THE DISPLAY OF THE FLAG OF THE UNITED STATES OF AMERICA OR STATE OF NORTH CAROLINA".

This subdivision shall apply to owners of property who display the flag of the United States or North Carolina on property owned exclusively by them and does not apply to common areas, easements, rights-of-way, or other areas owned by others.

(2) Regulate or prohibit the indoor or outdoor display of a political sign by an association member on property owned exclusively by the member, unless:

a. For restrictions registered prior to October 1, 2005, the restriction specifically uses the term "political signs".

b. For restrictions registered on or after October 1, 2005, the restriction shall be written on the first page of the instrument or conveyance in print that is in boldface type, capital letters, and no smaller than the largest print used elsewhere in the instrument or conveyance. The restriction shall be construed to regulate or prohibit the display of political signs only if the restriction specifically states: "THIS DOCUMENT REGULATES OR PROHIBITS THE DISPLAY OF POLITICAL SIGNS".

Even when display of a political sign is permitted under this subdivision, an association (i) may prohibit the display of political signs earlier than 45 days before the day of the election and later than seven days after an election day, and (ii) may regulate the size and number of political signs that may be placed on a member's property if the association's regulation is no more restrictive than any applicable city, town, or county ordinance that regulates the size and number of political signs on residential property. If the local government in which the property is located does not regulate the size and number of political signs on residential property, the association shall permit at least one political sign with the maximum dimensions of 24 inches by 24 inches on a member's property. For the purposes of this subdivision, "political sign" means a sign that attempts to influence the outcome of an election, including supporting or opposing an issue on the election ballot. This subdivision shall apply to owners of property who display political signs on property owned exclusively by them and does not apply to common areas, easements, rights-of-way, or other areas owned by others. (2005-422, s. 8; 2006-226, s. 15(b).)

§ 47F-3-122. Irrigation of landscaping.

Notwithstanding any provision in any declaration of covenants, no requirement to irrigate landscaping shall be construed to:

(1) Require the irrigation of landscaping, during any period in which the U.S. Drought Monitor, as defined in G.S. 143-350, or the Secretary of Environment and Natural Resources has designated an area in which the association is located as an area of severe, extreme, or exceptional drought and the Governor, a State agency, or unit of local government has imposed water conservation measures applicable to the area unless:

a. For declarations of covenants registered prior to October 1, 2008, the covenant specifically requires the irrigation of landscaping notwithstanding water conservation measures imposed by the Governor, a State agency, or unit of local government. The association may not fine or otherwise penalize an owner of land for violation of an irrigation requirement during a period of a drought as designated under this subdivision, unless the covenant specifically authorizes fines or other penalties.

b. For covenants registered on or after October 1, 2008, the covenant must specifically state that any requirement to irrigate landscaping is suspended to the extent the requirement would otherwise be prohibited during any period in which the Governor, a State agency, or unit of local government has imposed water conservation measures. The association may not fine or otherwise penalize an owner of land for violation of an irrigation requirement during a drought designated under this subdivision, unless the covenant authorizes the fines or other penalties. This authorization must be written on the first page of the covenant in print that is in boldface type, capital letters, and no smaller than the largest print used elsewhere in the declarations of covenants.

(2) For purposes of this section, the term "landscaping" includes lawns, trees, shrubbery, and other ornamental or decorative plants. (2008-143, s. 19(b).)

Chapter 47G.

Option to Purchase Contracts Executed With Lease Agreements.

§ 47G-1. Definitions.

The following definitions apply in this Chapter:

(1) Covered lease agreement or lease agreement. - A residential lease agreement that is combined with, or is executed concurrently with, an option contract.

(2) Cure the default. - To perform the obligations under the lease agreement and/or option contract that are described in the notice of default and intent to forfeit required by G.S. 47G-5 and that are necessary to reinstate the lease agreement and/or the option contract. This term is synonymous with the term "cure."

(3) Forfeiture. - The termination of an option purchaser's rights to exercise an option to purchase property that is the subject of the option contract, and those rights of persons or entities claiming by or through an option purchaser, to the extent permitted by this Chapter, because of a breach of one or more of the purchaser's obligations under the option contract and/or covered lease agreement.

(4) Option contract or contract. - An option contract for the purchase of property that includes or is combined with, or is executed in conjunction with, a covered lease agreement.

(5) Option fee. - Any payment, however denominated, made by the option purchaser to the option seller that constitutes the price the option purchaser pays for the right to buy the property at a specified price in the future.

(6) Option purchaser or purchaser. - An individual who purchases an interest in property under an option contract, or any legal successor in interest to that individual.

(7) Option seller or seller. - A person or entity that makes a sale of an option by means of an option contract, or the person's or entity's successor in interest. If an option contract is subsequently assigned or sold to a third party, the assignor shall be deemed to be an option seller or seller for purposes of this Chapter.

(8) Property. - Real property located in this State, upon which there is located or there is to be located a structure or structures designed principally for occupancy of from one to four families that is or will be occupied by the purchaser as the purchaser's principal dwelling. (2010-164, s. 3.)

§ 47G-2. Minimum contents of option contracts; recordation.

(a) Writing Required. - Every option contract, including any assignment of an option contract, shall be evidenced by a contract signed and acknowledged by all parties to it and containing all the terms to which they have agreed. The seller shall deliver to the purchaser an exact copy of the contract, containing all the disclosures required by subsection (b) of this section, at the time the purchaser signs the contract.

(b) Contents. - An option contract shall contain at least all of the following:

(1) The full names and addresses of all the parties to the contract.

(2) The date the contract is signed by each party.

(3) A legal description of the property to be conveyed subject to an option to purchase.

(4) The sales price of the property to be conveyed subject to an option to purchase.

(5) The option fee and any other fees or payments to be paid by each party to the contract.

(6) All of the obligations that if breached by the purchaser will result in forfeiture of the option.

(7) The time period during which the purchaser must exercise the option.

(8) A statement of the rights of the purchaser to cure a default, including that the purchaser has the right to cure a default once in any 12-month period during the period of the covered lease agreement.

(9) A conspicuous statement, in not less than 14-point boldface type, immediately above the purchaser's signature, that the purchaser has the right to cancel the contract at anytime until midnight of the third business day following execution of the option contract or delivery of the contract, whichever occurs last.

(c) Right to Cancel. - The purchaser may exercise the right to cancel the option contract until midnight of the third business day following execution of the option contract or delivery of a copy of the option contract, with the required minimum disclosures, whichever occurs last. If the purchaser cancels the option contract, the seller shall, not later than the tenth day after the date the seller receives the purchaser's notice of cancellation, return to the purchaser any and all property exchanged or payments made by the purchaser under the option contract minus an offset of an amount equal to the fair rental value of the use of the property during the duration of the purchaser's possession of the property plus an amount necessary to compensate the seller for any damages caused to the property by the purchaser beyond normal wear and tear.

(d) Recordation. - Within five business days after the option contract has been signed and acknowledged by both the seller and the purchaser, the seller shall cause a copy of the option contract or a memorandum of the option contract to be recorded in the office of the register of deeds in the county in which the property is located. If a memorandum of the contract is recorded, it shall be entitled "Memorandum of Option Contract" and shall contain, as a minimum, the names of the parties, the signatures of the parties, a description of the property, and applicable time periods as described in subdivisions (b)(7) and (8) of this section. A person other than a seller and purchaser may rely on the recorded materials in determining whether the requirements of this subsection have been met. The seller shall pay the fee to record the document unless the parties agree otherwise.

(e) Effect of Forfeiture. - Upon default and forfeiture after proper notice of default and intent to forfeit and failure of the purchaser to substantially cure the default, the purchaser's equitable right of redemption shall be extinguished by:

(1) A mutual termination executed by the parties and recorded in the office of the register of deeds of the county in which the property is located, or

(2) A final judgment or court order entered by a court of competent jurisdiction that terminates the purchaser's rights to the property and extinguishes the equity of redemption. A certified copy of the order shall be recorded in the office of the register of deeds of the county in which the property is located pursuant to G.S. 1-228.

(f) [Instrument Ineffective.] - No instrument purporting to extinguish the equity of redemption that is executed as a condition of the transaction or prior to a default will be effective. (2010-164, s. 3.)

§ 47G-3. Application of Landlord Tenant Law.

The provisions of Chapter 42 of the General Statutes apply to covered lease agreements. (2010-164, s. 3.)

§ 47G-4. Condition of forfeiture; right to cure.

A purchaser's right to exercise an option to purchase property under an option contract cannot be forfeited unless a breach has occurred in one or more of the purchaser's express obligations under the option contract and the option contract provides that as a result of such breach the seller is entitled to forfeit the contract. Notwithstanding any option contract or covered lease agreement provisions to the contrary, the purchaser's rights shall not be forfeited until the purchaser has been notified of the intent to forfeit in accordance with G.S. 47G-5 and been given a right to cure the default and has failed to do so within the time period allowed. The option purchaser is entitled to the right to cure a default once in every 12-month period during the period of the covered lease agreement. (2010-164, s. 3.)

§ 47G-5. Notice of default and intent to forfeit.

(a) A notice of default and intent to forfeit shall specify the nature of the default, the amount of the default if the default is in the payment terms, the date after which the contract will be forfeited if the purchaser does not cure the default, and the name and address of the seller or the attorney for the seller. The period specified in the notice after which the contract will be forfeited may not be less than 30 days after the notice of default and intent to forfeit is served, or before judgment is given in any action brought to recover the possession of the leased premises pursuant to Article 3 of Chapter 42 of the General Statutes, whichever is earlier.

(b) Any notice of default and intent to forfeit must be delivered to the option purchaser by hand delivery or by any manner authorized by G.S. 1A-1, Rule 4. (2010-164, s. 3.)

§ 47G-6. Effect of seller's default on loan secured by mortgage or lien on property.

If, at any time prior to the expiration of the time period in which the option purchaser has a right to exercise the option to purchase, a default occurs on a loan secured by a mortgage, security interest, or other lien on the property, the option purchaser may elect to exercise the option or cancel and rescind the contract and, in addition to any other remedies available at law or equity, seek the immediate return of all moneys paid by the option purchaser. If the purchaser elects to rescind the contract, the seller is entitled to an offset of an amount equal to the fair rental value of the use of the property during the duration of the purchaser's possession of the property plus an amount necessary to compensate the seller for any damages caused to the property by the purchaser beyond normal wear and tear. (2010-164, s. 3.)

§ 47G-7. Remedies.

A violation of any provision of this Chapter constitutes an unfair trade practice under G.S. 75-1.1. An option purchaser may bring an action for the recovery of damages, to void a transaction executed in violation of this Chapter, as well as for declaratory or equitable relief for a violation of this Chapter. The rights and remedies provided herein are cumulative to, and not a limitation of, any other rights and remedies provided by law or equity. Nothing in this Chapter shall be construed to subject an individual homeowner selling his or her primary residence directly to an option purchaser to liability under G.S. 75-1.1. (2010-164, s. 3.)

Chapter 47H.

Contracts for Deed.

§ 47H-1. Definitions.

The following definitions apply in this Chapter:

(1) Contract for deed or contract. - An agreement, whether denominated a "contract for deed," "installment land contract," "land contract," "bond for title," or any other title or description in which the seller agrees to sell an interest in property to the purchaser and the purchaser agrees to pay the purchase price in five or more payments exclusive of the down payment, if any, and the seller retains title to the property as security for the purchaser's obligation under the agreement.

(2) Cure the default. - To perform the obligations under the contract that are described in the notice of default and intent to forfeit required by G.S. 47H-4 and that are necessary to reinstate the contract. This term is synonymous with the term "cure."

(3) Down payment. - A payment made by the purchaser to the seller that constitutes part of the purchase price of property that is the subject of a contract for deed and that is made or agreed to in connection with the execution of that contract.

(4) Forfeiture. - The termination of all of a purchaser's rights, title, and interest, and those of persons or entities claiming by or through a purchaser, in property that is the subject of a contract for deed, to the extent permitted by this Chapter, because of a breach of one or more of the purchaser's obligations under the contract.

(5) Property. - Either (i) real estate located in this State, upon which there is located or there is to be located a structure or structures designed principally for occupancy of from one to four families that is or will be occupied by the purchaser as the purchaser's principal dwelling, or (ii) a manufactured home, as that term is defined in G.S. 143-149.9, that is located in this State and is or will be occupied by a purchaser as the purchaser's principal dwelling, if the purchase price is five thousand dollars ($5,000) or more.

(6) Purchaser. - An individual or entity that purchases an interest in property under a contract for deed, or any legal successor in interest to that individual.

(7) Seller. - A person or entity that makes a sale of property by means of a contract for deed, or the person's or entity's successor in interest. (2010-164, s. 4.)

§ 47H-2. Minimum contents for contracts for deed; recordation.

(a) Writing Required. - Every contract for deed shall be evidenced by a contract signed and acknowledged by all parties to it and containing all the terms to which they have agreed. The seller shall deliver to the purchaser an exact copy of the contract, containing all the disclosures required by subsection (b) of this section, at the time the purchaser signs the contract.

(b) Contents. - A contract for deed contract shall contain at least all of the following:

(1) The full names and addresses of all the parties to the contract.

(2) The date the contract is signed by each party.

(3) A legal description and the physical address of the property conveyed.

(4) The sales price of the property conveyed.

(5) Any charges or fees for services included in the contract separate from the sale price.

(6) The amount of the purchaser's down payment.

(7) The principal balance owed by the purchaser, which is the sum of the amounts stated in subdivisions (4) and (5) of this subsection, less the amount stated in subdivision (6) of this subsection.

(8) The amount and due date of each installment payment and the total number of installment payments.

(9) The interest rate on the unpaid balance, if any, and the method of determining the interest rate.

(10) A conspicuous statement of any pending order of any public agency or other matters of public record adversely affecting the property, provided the seller has actual knowledge of the pending order or matter.

(11) A statement of the rights of the purchaser to cure a default.

(12)   A statement setting forth the obligation of each party who is responsible for making repairs to the property, the payment of taxes, hazard insurance premiums, flood insurance premiums, homeowner association dues, and other charges against the property from the date of the contract.

(13)   A provision that the purchaser has the right to accelerate or prepay any installment payments without penalty; unless the property is encumbered by a deed of trust as permitted by G.S. 47H-6 and the loan secured by the property contains a prepayment penalty, in which case the contract may specify that the purchaser will compensate the seller for the prepayment penalty.

(14)   A description of conditions of the property that includes whether the property, including any structures thereon, has water, sewer, septic, and electricity service, whether the property is in a floodplain, whether anyone else has a legal interest in the property, and whether restrictive covenants prevent building or installing a dwelling. If restrictive covenants are in place that affect the property, a copy of the restrictive covenants shall be made available to the purchaser at or before the execution of the contract.

(15)   A statement indicating the current amount of any real estate taxes and/or homeowner association dues, or special assessments required to be paid on the property, and the amount of such taxes, dues, or assessments that are delinquent. To the extent these amounts are not known at the time the contract is executed, a reasonable estimate shall be given.

(16)   If the property being sold is encumbered by a deed of trust, mortgage, or other encumbrance evidencing or securing a monetary obligation which constitutes a lien on the property, and the seller is not a licensed general contractor within the meaning of Chapter 87 of the General Statutes, or a licensed manufactured home dealer within the meaning of Article 9A of Chapter 143 of the General Statutes, a statement of the amount of the lien, and the amount and due date, if any, of any periodic payments.

(17)   A conspicuous statement, in not less than 14-point boldface type, immediately above the purchaser's signature, that the purchaser has the right to cancel the contract at any time until midnight of the third business day following execution of the contract, or delivery of the contract, whichever occurs later.

(c)   Right to Cancel. - The purchaser may exercise the right to cancel the contract for deed until midnight of the third business day following execution of the contract for deed or delivery of a copy of the contract with the required minimum contents, whichever occurs later. If the purchaser cancels the contract, the seller shall, not later than the tenth day after the date the seller receives the purchaser's notice of cancellation, return to the purchaser any and all property exchanged or payments made by the purchaser under the contract minus an offset of an amount equal to the fair rental value of the use of the property during the duration of the purchaser's possession of the property plus an amount necessary to compensate the seller for any damages caused to the property by the purchaser beyond normal wear and tear.

(d) Recordation. - Within five business days after the contract has been signed and acknowledged by both the seller and the purchaser, the seller shall cause a copy of the contract or a memorandum of the contract to be recorded in the office of the register of deeds in the county in which the property is located. If a memorandum of the contract is recorded, it shall be entitled "Memorandum of a Contract for Deed" and shall contain, as a minimum, the names of the parties, the signatures of the parties, a description of the property, and applicable time periods as described in subdivisions (b)(8) and (11) of this section. A person, other than a seller and purchaser may rely on the recorded materials in determining whether the requirements of this subsection have been met. The seller shall pay the fee to record the document unless the parties agree otherwise.

(e) Effect of Forfeiture. - Upon default and forfeiture after proper notice of default and intent to forfeit and failure of the purchaser to substantially cure the default, the purchaser's equitable right of redemption shall be extinguished by:

(1) A mutual termination executed by the parties and recorded in the office of the register of deeds of the county in which the property is located, or

(2) A final judgment or court order entered by a court of competent jurisdiction that terminates the purchaser's rights to the property and extinguishes the equity of redemption. A certified copy of the order shall be recorded in the office of the register of deeds of the county in which the property is located pursuant to G.S. 1-228.

(f) [Instrument Ineffective.] - No instrument purporting to extinguish the equity of redemption that is executed as a condition of the transaction or prior to a default will be effective. (2010-164, s. 4.)

§ 47H-3. Conditions of forfeiture; right to cure.

A purchaser's rights under a contract for deed shall not be forfeited except as provided in this Chapter. A contract for deed cannot be forfeited unless a breach has occurred in one or more of the purchaser's express obligations under the contract and the contract provides that as a result of such breach the seller is entitled to forfeit the contract. Furthermore, the purchaser's rights shall not be forfeited until the purchaser has been notified of the intent to forfeit in accordance with G.S. 47H-4 and been given a right to cure the default and has failed to do so within the time period allowed. A timely tender of cure shall reinstate the contract for deed. (2010-164, s. 4.)

§ 47H-4. Notice of default and intent to forfeit.

(a) The notice of default and intent to forfeit shall contain all of the following:

(1) The name, address, and telephone number of the seller and the seller's agent or attorney giving the notice, if any.

(2) A description of the contract, including the names of the original parties to the contract for deed.

(3) The physical address of the property.

(4) A description of each default under the contract on which the notice is based.

(5) A statement that the contract will be forfeited if all defaults are not cured by a date stated in the notice which is not less than 30 days after the notice of default and intent to forfeit is served or any longer period specified in the contract or other agreement with the seller.

(6) An itemized statement of, or to the extent not known at the time the notice of default and intent to forfeit is given or recorded, a reasonable estimate of, all payments of money in default, and, for defaults not involving the failure to pay money, a statement of the action required to cure the default.

(7) Any additional information required by the contract for deed or other agreement with the seller.

(b) Any notice of default and intent to forfeit must be delivered to the purchaser by hand or by any manner authorized in G.S. 1A-1, Rule 4. (2010-164, s. 4.)

§ 47H-5. Periodic statements of account.

The seller shall provide the purchaser with a statement of account at least once every 12-month period for the term of a contract for deed. The statement must include at least the following information:

(1) The amount paid under the contract.

(2) The remaining amount owed under the contract.

(3) The number of payments remaining under the contract.

(4) The amounts paid to taxing authorities, if paid or collected by the seller or the purchaser.

(5) The amounts paid to insure the property on the purchaser's behalf, if collected by the seller.

(6) If the property has been damaged and the seller has received insurance proceeds, an accounting of the proceeds applied to the property.

(7) If the property is encumbered by a lien or mortgage pursuant to G.S. 47H-6, the outstanding balance of the loan that is secured by the property. (2010-164, s. 4.)

§ 47H-6. Title requirements.

(a) A seller may not execute a contract for deed with a purchaser if the seller does not hold title to the property. If the title is not held in fee simple, free from any deeds of trust, mortgages, or other encumbrances evidencing or securing a monetary obligation which constitutes a lien on the property, the seller may execute a contract for deed only if the mortgage or encumbrance is in the name of the seller and meets at least one of the following conditions:

(1)   It was agreed to by the purchaser, in writing, as a condition of a loan obtained to make improvements on the property.

(2)   It was placed on the property by the seller prior to the execution of the contract for deed if the seller is a licensed general contractor within the meaning of Chapter 87 of the General Statutes, a licensed manufactured home dealer within the meaning of Article 9A of Chapter 143 of the General Statutes, or a licensed real estate broker within the meaning of Chapter 93A of the General Statutes, provided that the general contractor, manufactured home dealer, or real estate broker continues to make timely payments on the outstanding mortgage or encumbrance.

(3)   It was placed on the property by the seller prior to the execution of the contract for deed, if the seller is not a licensed general contractor within the meaning of Chapter 87 of the General Statutes, a licensed manufactured home dealer within the meaning of Article 9A of Chapter 143 of the General Statutes, or a licensed real estate broker within the meaning of Chapter 93A of the General Statutes, if the lien is attached only to the property sold to the purchaser under the contract for deed, and the seller continues to make timely payments on the outstanding mortgage or encumbrance.

(b)   If the property being sold is encumbered by one or more deeds of trust, mortgages, or other encumbrances evidencing or securing a monetary obligation which constitutes a lien on the property, the seller must notify the purchaser in a separate written disclosure, provided at or before the execution of the contract, in 14-point type, boldface, capital letters, the following statement: THIS PROPERTY HAS EXISTING LIENS ON IT. IF THE SELLER FAILS TO MAKE TIMELY PAYMENTS TO THE LIEN HOLDER, THE LIEN HOLDER MAY FORECLOSE ON THE PROPERTY, EVEN IF YOU HAVE MADE ALL YOUR PAYMENTS.

(c)   In addition to any other remedies at law or equity, a seller's violation of this section entitles the purchaser to either a claim for damages or the right to rescind the contract and seek the return of all payments, deposits, and down payments that have been made under the contract. If the purchaser elects to rescind the contract, the seller is entitled to an offset of an amount equal to the fair market value of the use of the property during the duration of the purchaser's possession of the property plus an amount necessary to compensate the seller for any damages caused to the property by the purchaser beyond normal wear and tear. (2010-164, s. 4.)

§ 47H-7. Late fees.

No seller may charge a late payment charge under a contract for deed in excess of four percent (4%) of the amount of the payment past due. A late fee may only be charged on payments that are more than 15 days past due. (2010-164, s. 4.)

§ 47H-8. Remedies.

A violation of any provision of this Chapter constitutes an unfair trade practice under G.S. 75-1.1. A purchaser may bring an action for the recovery of damages, to rescind a transaction, as well as for declaratory or equitable relief, for a violation of this Chapter. The rights and remedies provided herein are cumulative to, and not a limitation of, any other rights and remedies provided by law or equity. Nothing in this Chapter shall be construed to subject an individual homeowner selling his or her primary residence directly to a buyer to liability under G.S. 75-1.1. (2010-164, s. 4.)

Chapter 49.

Children Born Out of Wedlock.

Article 1.

Support of Children Born Out of Wedlock.

§ 49-1. Title.

This Article shall be referred to as "An act concerning the support of children of parents not married to each other." (1933, c. 228, s. 11.)

§ 49-2. Nonsupport of child born out of wedlock by parents made misdemeanor.

Any parent who willfully neglects or who refuses to provide adequate support and maintain his or her child born out of wedlock shall be guilty of a Class 2 misdemeanor. A child within the meaning of this Article shall be any person less than 18 years of age and any person whom either parent might be required under the laws of North Carolina to support and maintain if the child were the legitimate child of the parent. (1933, c. 228, s. 1; 1937, c. 432, s. 1; 1939, c. 217, ss. 1, 2; 1951, c. 154, s. 1; 1977, c. 3, s. 1; 1993, c. 539, s. 414; 1994, Ex. Sess., c. 24, s. 14(c); 2013-198, s. 17.)

§ 49-3. Place of birth of child no consideration.

The provisions of this Article shall apply whether such child shall have been begotten or shall have been born within or without the State of North Carolina: Provided, that the child to be supported is a bona fide resident of this State at the time of the institution of any proceedings under this Article. (1933, c. 228, s. 2.)

§ 49-4. When prosecution may be commenced.

The prosecution of the reputed father of a child born out of wedlock may be instituted under this Chapter within any of the following periods, and not thereafter:

(1) Three years next after the birth of the child; or

(2) Where the paternity of the child has been judicially determined within three years next after its birth, at any time before the child attains the age of 18 years; or

(3) Where the reputed father has acknowledged paternity of the child by payments for the support thereof within three years next after the birth of the child, three years from the date of the last payment whether the last payment was made within three years of the birth of the child or thereafter: Provided, the action is instituted before the child attains the age of 18 years.

The prosecution of the mother of a child born out of wedlock may be instituted under this Chapter at any time before the child attains the age of 18 years. (1933, c. 228, s. 3; 1939, c. 217, s. 3; 1945, c. 1053; 1951, c. 154, s. 2; 2013-198, s. 18.)

§ 49-5. Prosecution; death of mother no bar; determination of fatherhood.

Proceedings under this Article may be brought by the mother or her personal representative or, if the child is likely to become a public charge, the director of social services or such person as by law performs the duties of such official in said county where the mother resides or the child is found. Proceedings under this Article may be brought in the county where the mother resides or is found, or in the county where the putative father resides or is found, or in the county where the child is found. The fact that the child was born outside of the State of North Carolina shall not be a bar to proceedings against the putative father in any county where he resides or is found, or in the county where the mother resides or the child is found. The death of the mother shall in no wise affect any proceedings under this Article. Preliminary proceedings under this Article to determine the paternity of the child may be instituted prior to the birth of the child but when the judge or court trying the issue of paternity deems it proper, he may continue the case until the woman is delivered of the child. When a continuance is granted, the courts shall recognize the person accused of being the father of the child with surety for his appearance, either at the next session of the court or at a time to be fixed by the judge or court granting a continuance, which shall be after the delivery of the child. (1933, c. 228, s. 4; 1961, c. 186; 1969, c. 982; 1971, c. 1185, s. 18; 1981, c. 599, s. 13.)

§ 49-6. Mother not excused on ground of self-incrimination; not subject to penalty.

No mother of a child born out of wedlock shall be excused, on the ground that it may tend to incriminate her or subject her to a penalty or a forfeiture, from attending and testifying, in obedience to a subpoena of any court, in any suit or proceeding based upon or growing out of the provisions of this Article, but no such mother shall be prosecuted or subjected to any penalty or forfeiture for or on account of any transaction, matter, or thing as to which, in obedience to a subpoena and under oath, she may so testify. (1933, c. 228, s. 5; 1939, c. 217, s. 5; 2013-198, s. 19.)

§ 49-7. Issues and orders.

The court before which the matter may be brought shall determine whether or not the defendant is a parent of the child on whose behalf the proceeding is instituted. After this matter has been determined in the affirmative, the court shall proceed to determine the issue as to whether or not the defendant has neglected or refused to provide adequate support and maintain the child who is the subject of the proceeding. After this matter has been determined in the affirmative, the court shall fix by order, subject to modification or increase from time to time, a specific sum of money necessary for the support and maintenance of the child, subject to the limitations of G.S. 50-13.10. The amount of child support shall be determined as provided in G.S. 50-13.4(c). The order fixing the sum shall require the defendant to pay it either as a lump sum or in periodic payments as the circumstances of the case may appear to the court. The social security number, if known, of the minor child's parents shall be placed in the record of the proceeding. Compliance by the defendant with any or all of the further provisions of this Article or the order or orders of the court requiring additional acts to be performed by the defendant shall not be construed to relieve the defendant of his or her responsibility to pay the sum fixed or any modification or increase thereof.

The court before whom the matter may be brought, on motion of the State or the defendant, shall order that the alleged-parent defendant, the known natural parent, and the child submit to any blood tests and comparisons which have been developed and adapted for purposes of establishing or disproving parentage and which are reasonably accessible to the alleged-parent defendant, the known natural parent, and the child. The results of those blood tests and comparisons, including the statistical likelihood of the alleged parent's parentage, if available, shall be admitted in evidence when offered by a duly qualified, licensed practicing physician, duly qualified immunologist, duly qualified geneticist or other duly qualified person. The evidentiary effect of those blood tests and comparisons and the manner in which the expenses therefor are to be taxed as costs shall be as prescribed in G.S. 8-50.1. In addition, if a jury tries the issue of parentage, they shall be instructed as set out in G.S. 8-50.1. From a finding on the issue of parentage against the alleged-parent defendant, the alleged-parent defendant has the same right of appeal as though he or she had been found guilty of the crime of willful failure to support a child born out of wedlock. (1933, c. 228, s. 6; 1937, c. 432, s. 2; 1939, c. 217, ss. 1, 4; 1944, c. 40; 1947, c. 1014; 1971, c. 1185, s. 19; 1975, c. 449, s. 3; 1977, c. 3, s. 2; 1979, c. 576, s. 2; 1987, c. 739, s. 1; 1989, c. 529, s. 6; 1997-433, s. 4.1; 1998-17, s. 1; 2013-198, s. 20.)

§ 49-8. Power of court to modify orders, suspend sentence, etc.

Upon the determination of the issues set out in G.S. 49-7 and for the purpose of enforcing the payment of the sum fixed, the court is hereby given discretion, having regard for the circumstances of the case and the financial ability and earning capacity of the defendant and his or her willingness to cooperate, to make an order or orders upon the defendant and to modify such order or orders from time to time as the circumstances of the case may in the judgment of the court require subject to the limitations of G.S. 50-13.10. The order or orders made in this regard may include any or all of the following alternatives:

(1)   Repealed By Session Laws 1994, Extra Session, c. 14, s. 35.

(2)   Suspend sentence and continue the case from term to term;

(3)   Release the defendant from custody on probation conditioned upon the defendant's compliance with the terms of the probation and the payment of the sum fixed for the support and maintenance of the child;

(4)   Order the defendant to pay to the mother of the said child the necessary expenses of birth of the child and suitable medical attention for her;

(5)   Require the defendant to sign a recognizance with good and sufficient security, for compliance with any order which the court may make in proceedings under this Article. (1933, c. 228, s. 7; 1939, c. 217, s. 6; 1987, c. 739, s. 2; 1994, Ex. Sess., c. 14, s. 35.)

§ 49-9. Bond for future appearance of defendant.

At the preliminary hearing of any case arising under this Article it shall be the duty of the court, if it finds reasonable cause for holding the accused for a further hearing, to require a bond in the sum of not less than one hundred dollars ($100.00), conditioned upon the reappearance of the accused at the further hearing under this Article. This bond and all other bonds provided for in this Article shall be justified before, and approved by, the court or the clerk thereof. (1933, c. 228, s. 8.)

Article 2.

Legitimation of Children Born Out of Wedlock.

§ 49-10. Legitimation.

The putative father of any child born out of wedlock, whether such father resides in North Carolina or not, may apply by a verified written petition, filed in a special proceeding in the superior court of the county in which the putative father resides or in the superior court of the county in which the child resides, praying that such child be declared legitimate. The mother, if living, and the child shall be necessary parties to the proceeding, and the full names of the father, mother and the child shall be set out in the petition. A certified copy of a certificate of birth of the child shall be attached to the petition. If it appears to the court that the petitioner is the father of the child, the court may thereupon declare and pronounce the child legitimated; and the full names of the father, mother and the child shall be set out in the court order decreeing legitimation of the child. The clerk of the court shall record the order in the record of orders and decrees and it shall be cross-indexed under the name of the father as plaintiff or petitioner on the plaintiff's side of the cross-index, and under the name of the mother, and the child as defendants or respondents on the defendants' side of the cross-index. (Code, s. 39; Rev., s. 263; C.S., s. 277; 1947, c. 663, s. 1; 1971, c. 154; 1977, c. 83, s. 1.)

§ 49-11. Effects of legitimation.

The effect of legitimation under G.S. 49-10 shall be to impose upon the father and mother all of the lawful parental privileges and rights, as well as all of the obligations which parents owe to their lawful issue, and to the same extent as if said child had been born in wedlock, and to entitle such child by succession, inheritance or distribution, to take real and personal property by, through, and from his or her father and mother as if such child had been born in lawful wedlock. In case of death and intestacy, the real and personal estate of such child shall descend and be distributed according to the Intestate Succession Act as if he had been born in lawful wedlock. (Code, s. 40; Rev., s. 264; C.S., s. 278; 1955, c. 540, s. 2; 1959, c. 879, s. 10; 1963, c. 1131.)

§ 49-12. Legitimation by subsequent marriage.

When the mother of any child born out of wedlock and the reputed father of such child shall intermarry or shall have intermarried at any time after the birth of such child, the child shall, in all respects after such intermarriage be deemed and held to be legitimate and the child shall be entitled, by succession, inheritance or distribution, to real and personal property by, through, and from his father and mother as if such child had been born in lawful wedlock. In case of death and intestacy, the real and personal estate of such child shall descend and be distributed according to the Intestate Succession Act as if he had been born in lawful wedlock. (1917, c. 219, s. 1; C.S., s. 279; 1947, c. 663, s. 2; 1955, c. 540, s. 3; 1959, c. 879, s. 11.)

§ 49-12.1. Legitimation when mother married.

(a)   The putative father of a child born to a mother who is married to another man may file a special proceeding to legitimate the child. The procedures shall be the same as those specified by G.S. 49-10, except that the spouse of the mother of the child shall be a necessary party to the proceeding and shall be properly served. A guardian ad litem shall be appointed to represent the child if the child is a minor.

(b)   The presumption of legitimacy can be overcome by clear and convincing evidence.

(c)   The parties may enter a consent order with the approval of the clerk of superior court. The order entered by the clerk shall find the facts and declare the proper person the father of the child and may change the surname of the child.

(d) The effect of legitimation under this section shall be the same as provided by G.S. 49-11.

(e) A certified copy of the order of legitimation under this section shall be sent by the clerk of superior court under his official seal to the State Registrar of Vital Statistics who shall make a new birth certificate bearing the full name of the father of the child and, if ordered by the clerk, changing the surname of the child. (1991, c. 667, s. 2; 1991 (Reg. Sess., 1992), c. 1030, s. 15; 1997-433, s. 4.9; 1998-17, s. 1.)

§ 49-13. New birth certificate on legitimation.

A certified copy of the order of legitimation when issued under the provisions of G.S. 49-10 shall be sent by the clerk of the superior court under his official seal to the State Registrar of Vital Statistics who shall then make the new birth certificate bearing the full name of the father, and change the surname of the child so that it will be the same as the surname of the father.

When a child is legitimated under the provisions of G.S. 49-12, the State Registrar of Vital Statistics shall make a new birth certificate bearing the full name of the father upon presentation of a certified copy of the certificate of marriage of the father and mother and change the surname of the child so that it will be the same as the surname of the father. (1947, c. 663, s. 3; 1955, c. 951, s. 2.)

§ 49-13.1: Repealed by Session Laws 2004-203, s. 3, effective August 17, 2004.

Article 3.

Civil Actions Regarding Children Born Out of Wedlock.

§ 49-14. Civil action to establish paternity; motion to set aside paternity.

(a) The paternity of a child born out of wedlock may be established by civil action at any time prior to such child's eighteenth birthday. A copy of a certificate of birth of the child shall be attached to the complaint. The establishment of paternity shall not have the effect of legitimation. The social security numbers, if known, of the minor child's parents shall be placed in the record of the proceeding.

(b) Proof of paternity pursuant to this section shall be by clear, cogent, and convincing evidence.

(c) No such action shall be commenced nor judgment entered after the death of the putative father, unless the action is commenced either:

(1) Prior to the death of the putative father;

(2) Within one year after the date of death of the putative father, if a proceeding for administration of the estate of the putative father has not been commenced within one year of his death; or

(3) Within the period specified in G.S. 28A-19-3(a) for presentation of claims against an estate, if a proceeding for administration of the estate of the putative father has been commenced within one year of his death.

Any judgment under this subsection establishing a decedent to be the father of a child shall be entered nunc pro tunc to the day preceding the date of death of the father.

(d) If the action to establish paternity is brought more than three years after birth of a child or is brought after the death of the putative father, paternity shall not be established in a contested case without evidence from a blood or genetic marker test.

(e) Either party to an action to establish paternity may request that the case be tried at the first session of the court after the case is docketed, but the presiding judge, in his discretion, may first try any pending case in which the rights of the parties or the public demand it.

(f) When a determination of paternity is pending in a IV-D case, the court shall enter a temporary order for child support upon motion and showing of clear, cogent, and convincing evidence of paternity. For purposes of this subsection, the results of blood or genetic tests shall constitute clear, cogent, and convincing evidence of paternity if the tests show that the probability of the alleged parent's parentage is ninety-seven percent (97%) or higher. If paternity is not thereafter established, then the putative father shall be reimbursed the full amount of temporary support paid under the order.

(g)   Invoices for services rendered for pregnancy, childbirth, and blood or genetic testing are admissible as evidence without requiring third party foundation testimony and shall constitute prima facie evidence of the amounts incurred for the services or for testing on behalf of the child.

(h)   Notwithstanding the time limitations of G.S. 1A-1, Rule 60 of the North Carolina Rules of Civil Procedure, or any other provision of law, an order of paternity may be set aside by a trial court if each of the following applies:

(1)   The paternity order was entered as the result of fraud, duress, mutual mistake, or excusable neglect.

(2)   Genetic tests establish the putative father is not the biological father of the child.

The burden of proof in any motion to set aside an order of paternity shall be on the moving party. Upon proper motion alleging fraud, duress, mutual mistake, or excusable neglect, the court shall order the child's mother, the child whose parentage is at issue, and the putative father to submit to genetic paternity testing pursuant to G.S. 8-50.1(b1). If the court determines, as a result of genetic testing, the putative father is not the biological father of the child and the order of paternity was entered as a result of fraud, duress, mutual mistake, or excusable neglect, the court may set aside the order of paternity. Nothing in this subsection shall be construed to affect the presumption of legitimacy where a child is born to a mother and the putative father during the course of a marriage. (1967, c. 993, s. 1; 1973, c. 1062, s. 3; 1977, c. 83, s. 2; 1981, c. 599, s. 14; 1985, c. 208, ss. 1, 2; 1993, c. 333, s. 3; 1995, c. 424, ss. 1, 2; 1997-154, s. 1; 1997-433, ss. 4.2, 4.10; 1998-17, s. 1; 2005-389, s. 3; 2011-328, s. 1.)

§ 49-15. Custody and support of children born out of wedlock when paternity established.

Upon and after the establishment of paternity pursuant to G.S. 49-14 of a child born out of wedlock, the rights, duties, and obligations of the mother and the father so established, with regard to support and custody of the child, shall be the same, and may be determined and enforced in the same manner, as if the child were the legitimate child of the father and mother. When paternity has been established, the father becomes responsible for medical expenses incident to the pregnancy and the birth of the child. (1967, c. 993, s. 1; 2013-198, s. 23.)

§ 49-16. Parties to proceeding.

Proceedings under this Article may be brought by:

(1) The mother, the father, the child, or the personal representative of the mother or the child.

(2) When the child, or the mother in case of medical expenses, is likely to become a public charge, the director of social services or such person as by law performs the duties of such official,

a. In the county where the mother resides or is found,

b. In the county where the putative father resides or is found, or

c. In the county where the child resides or is found. (1967, c. 993, s. 1; 1969, c. 982; 1975, c. 54, s. 2.)

§ 49-17. Jurisdiction over nonresident or nonpresent persons.

(a) The act of sexual intercourse within this State constitutes sufficient minimum contact with this forum for purposes of subjecting the person or persons participating therein to the jurisdiction of the courts of this State for actions brought under this Article for paternity and support of any child who may have been conceived as a result of such act.

(b) The jurisdictional basis in subsection (a) of this section shall be construed in addition to, and not in lieu of, any basis or bases for jurisdiction within G.S. 1-75.4. (1979, c. 542.)

Chapter 49A.

Rights of Children.

Article 1.

Children Conceived by Artificial Insemination.

§ 49A-1. Status of child born as a result of artificial insemination.

Any child or children born as the result of heterologous artificial insemination shall be considered at law in all respects the same as a naturally conceived legitimate child of the husband and wife requesting and consenting in writing to the use of such technique. (1971, c. 260.)

Vision Books Order Form

Fax Orders: 1-980-299-5965

Phone Orders: 1-704-898-0770

E-mail Orders: www.visionbooks.org

Mail Orders: Vision Books, LLC
P.O. Box 42406
Charlotte, NC 28215

Shipp To:
Name_____
Address_____
City_____State_____Zip_____
Phone_____Fax_____
Email_____@_____

Bill To: We can bill a third party on your behalf.
Name_____
Address_____
City_____State_____Zip_____
Phone____(_____)_____Fax_____
Email_____@_____

Pamphlet Number ($15.00 Each)	Qty	Total Cost
_____	_____	_____
_____	_____	_____
_____	_____	_____
_____	_____	_____
_____	_____	_____
_____	_____	_____
_____	_____	_____
_____	_____	_____
Full Volume Set 1-92	92 Pamphlets	1,380.00

Free Shipping Shipping & Handling on Full Volume Orders
Add $1.00 Shipping & Handling per pamphlet $_____

Total Cost $_____

Thank You for Your Support. Management!

DID YOU ENJOY THIS BOOK?

Vision Books, LLC would like to hear from you! If you or someone you know has been fasely imprisoned, we would like to hear your story. If the 'North Carolina Criminal Law and Procedure' has had an effect in your life or if you have suggestions, we would like to hear from you. Send your letters to:

Vision Books, LLC
Attn: Staff Writers
P.O. Box 42406
Charlotte, NC 28215
Email: staff@visionbooks.org

Order Additional Copies:

Fax Orders: 1-980-299-5965

Phone Orders: 1-704-898-0770

E-mail Orders: www.visionbooks.org

Mail Orders: Vision Books, LLC
                              P.O. Box 42406
                              Charlotte, NC 28215

www.ingramcontent.com/pod-product-compliance
Lightning Source LLC
Chambersburg PA
CBHW051630170526
45167CB00001B/133